Advance Praise for *Black Immigrants in North America*:

"In this timely collection, Awad Ibrahim achieves an impressive analysis of the existentialist intersections of race and Blackness, immigration and identity, all as tethered to Hip-Hop, pedagogy and being. In so doing, he excavates the fragmented habitat of naturalized Black liminality for new ways of 'repairing' warped subjectivities into liberated, even 'likable' personae. An impressive disquisition indeed, that should be read and shared widely."

—Ali A. Abdi, The University of British Columbia
Author of *Education and the Politics of Difference* (with Ratna Ghosh)

"*Black Immigrants in North America* is a rarity in researching and theorizing the unique lived experience of Black immigrants—both continental and diasporic Africans. Black immigrants, argues Dr. Ibrahim, complicate the very category of Blackness: moving it from a colonial and uni-dimensional category to a complicated and rhizomatic category that is forever becoming. Urgently needed, Black Immigrants in North America is a must read for those who are interested in the Black body, Black immigration, Black youth, and Black pedagogy."

—George J. Sefa Dei, OISE, The University of Toronto
Author of *Reframing Blackness and Black Solidarities through Anti-colonial and Decolonial Prisms*

"In this collection of compelling essays, Dr. Ibrahim offers critical insights into the complex and multi-layered aspects of identification and racialization pertaining to racialized students, and Black youth in particular, in relation to their schooling, education, and basically, life in Canada. Through his work, he disrupts existing conceptualizations, analyses and assumptions—or taken for granted truths—giving readers an enhanced understanding of the issues and additional avenues for theorization and action. For educators and others committed to social justice and equity, this work is a necessary read."

—Carl James, York University (Canada)
Jean Augustine Chair in Education, Community & Diaspora

BLACK IMMIGRANTS IN NORTH AMERICA

Copyright © 2020 | Myers Education Press, LLC

Published by Myers Education Press, LLC
P.O. Box 424
Gorham, ME 04038

All rights reserved. No part of this book may be reprinted or reproduced in any form or by any electronic, mechanical, or other means, now known or hereafter invented, including photocopying, recording, and information storage and retrieval, without permission in writing from the publisher.

> Myers Education Press is an academic publisher specializing in books, e-books, and digital content in the field of education. All of our books are subjected to a rigorous peer review process and produced in compliance with the standards of the Council on Library and Information Resources.

LIBRARY OF CONGRESS CATALOGING-IN-PUBLICATION DATA AVAILABLE FROM LIBRARY OF CONGRESS
13-digit ISBN 978-1-9755-0197-6 (paperback)
13-digit ISBN 978-1-9755-0196-9 (hard cover)
13-digit ISBN 978-1-9755-0198-3 (library networkable e-edition)
13-digit ISBN 978-1-9755-0199-0 (consumer e-edition)

Printed in the United States of America.

All first editions printed on acid-free paper that meets the American National Standards Institute Z39-48 standard.

Books published by Myers Education Press may be purchased at special quantity discount rates for groups, workshops, training organizations, and classroom usage. Please call our customer service department at 1-800-232-0223 for details.

Cover design by Sophie Appel.

Visit us on the web at www.myersedpress.com to browse our complete list of titles.

BLACK IMMIGRANTS IN NORTH AMERICA

Essays on Race, Immigration, Identity, Language, Hip-Hop, Pedagogy, and the Politics of Becoming Black

BY AWAD IBRAHIM

Myers Education Press

Gorham, Maine

I dedicate this book to my brother Hassan Hamadeen who taught me what an economy of unconditional hospitality might look like and what loving unconditionally might feel like. We will meet at the rendezvous of victory where we will hug and laugh as we always do. I miss your beautiful, loud, and genuine laughter. I hope you are resting.

Table of Contents

Immigrating While Black: An Introduction xi

1. ONE IS NOT BORN BLACK:
   BECOMING AND THE PHENOMENON(OLOGY) OF RACE 1

2. THE (UN)NATURALIZATION OF BLACKNESS:
   A RHIZOMATIC ANALYSIS OF BLACKNESS 13

3. BODY WITHOUT ORGANS: NOTES ON DELEUZE & GUATTARI,
   CRITICAL RACE THEORY AND THE SOCIUS OF ANTI-RACISM 25

4. THE QUESTION OF THE QUESTION IS THE FOREIGNER:
   TOWARDS AN ECONOMY OF HOSPITALITY 47

5. BECOMING BLACK: RAP AND HIP-HOP, RACE, GENDER,
   IDENTITY, AND THE POLITICS OF ESL LEARNING 65

6. INTERSECTING LANGUAGE, IMMIGRATION, AND THE POLITICS OF
   BECOMING BLACK: JOURNALING A BLACK IMMIGRANT DISPLACEMENT 89

7. THE NEW *FLÂNEUR*: SUBALTERN CULTURAL STUDIES, AFRICAN
   YOUTH IN CANADA, AND THE SEMIOLOGY OF IN-BETWEENNESS 103

8. DON'T CALL ME BLACK! RHIZOMATIC ANALYSIS OF BLACKNESS,
   IMMIGRATION, AND THE POLITICS OF RACE WITHOUT GUARANTEES 125

9. WHEN NEOLIBERALISM MEETS RACE, POST-COLONIAL DISPLACEMENT
   AND IMMIGRATION, IT CREATES *AMERICANAH*:
   A TEACHER EDUCATION COMPLICATED CONVERSATION 141

10. OPERATING UNDER ERASURE:
    ~~HIP-HOP~~ AND THE PEDAGOGY OF AFFECT 165

11. RESEARCH AS AN ACT OF LOVE: ETHICS, ÉMIGRÉS,
    AND THE PRAXIS OF BECOMING HUMAN. 191

12. WIDE-AWAKENESS: TOWARD A CRITICAL PEDAGOGY OF
    IMAGINATION, HUMANISM AND BECOMING. 211

Immigrating While Black (IWB): An Introduction

IT MUST BE extremely frustrating for students of immigration studies to hear Donald Trump talking about "immagrants" when most of the time he actually means "refugees." *Immigrants are not refugees.* The stark difference between the two does not need clarification, but given the confusion, this book has to start with a clarification and a distinction between the two categories. Donald Trump's father is an immigrant (Kranish & Fisher, 2016) whereas most of the students I interacted with in my three separate critical ethnographic research projects are refugees (see Ibrahim, 2014 for full discussion). Refugees are those who are fleeing violence, wars, and the brutality of famished lives (Bauman, 2016). Refugees have been knocking "on other people's doors since the beginning of time" (p. 1). In so doing, as I argue in Chapter 6, they do two things. First, they call human attention to their plight, which is momentous and consequential, and their poetic voice haunts us with its imagery. It tells us:

no one leaves home unless
home is the mouth of a shark
you only run for the border
when you see the whole city running as well
...
no one leaves home unless home chases you
fire under feet
hot blood in your belly
it's not something you ever thought of doing
until the blade burnt threats into
your neck
...

you have to understand,
that no one puts their children in a boat
unless the water is safer than the land
...

no one chooses refugee camps
or strip searches where your
body is left aching
or prison,
because prison is safer
than a city of fire.
   (Warsan Shire, 2015, as cited in Papa, 2017, pp. 51-52)

Second, the refugees who "make it" to safety through the deadly seas, those who show up unexpectedly and en masse to be called "aliens" or "strangers" tend to turn the familiar strange. "[U]nlike the people with whom we interact daily and from whom we believe we know what to expect," Bauman (2016) explains, refugees "tend to cause anxiety" (p. 8). That anxiety, for Bauman, is understandable—if not predictable—because the "familiar way of life" for the people whose doors are knocked upon is maimed, not to say being forever transformed (p. 8). To use Warsan Shire's ironic terms, in popular imagination, refugees are people who "smell strange," people who "messed up their country and now they want to mess ours up." When this popular imagining takes hold as we see now in Trumpistan's America (Rushdie, 2018), the understandable anxiety is turned into "'mixophobia," that is the "fear of the unmanageable volume of the unknown, untamable, off-putting and uncontrollable" (p. 9). In sum, refugees are people who are forced to move, people who put themselves in danger as they nomad their way from danger into safety. They are not futilitarian, quite the opposite, their psychic has a full grasp of what it means to be in danger. In Chapter Seven, I call them the "new *flâneurs*," these are the new nomads who walk the earth so that they are not killed or made to disappear, hence they become refugees precisely because their very soul is on the line.

Immigrants on the other hand are all-together different. First, they have no fear for their lives, tend to be highly educated, with a stable income, and migrate from their homeland to their new "home" voluntarily (Kymlicka, 2010). John Ogbu's framework, which is discussed in Ogbu & Simons (1998), identifies three typologies of minorities. These typologies fall under an umbrella theory: *cultural-ecological theory*, which seeks to understand "the broad societal and school factors [particularly school performance] as well as the dynamics within the minority communities" (p. 158). This theory, which is extremely relevant to the topic at hand deserves further attention. It begins with the very term, "minority," which it defines not in terms of numerical representation but on the basis of power relations. To use my terms: *no one is born a minority, one becomes a minority* precisely because, to use Ogbu's terms, one is occupying a subordinate power position in relation to another person within the same society.

Ogbu's three typologies of minority are autonomous, voluntary, and involuntary. *Autonomous minorities* "are people who belong to groups that are small in number [e.g., Amish, Jews, and Mormons in North America] ... Although these groups may suffer discrimination, they are not totally dominated and oppressed, and their school achievement is no different from the dominant group" (p. 164). There are no nonwhite autonomous minorities in North America and as such they are not affected by the issues that concern people of color, namely: a) the nature and the severity of exclusion and marginalization in becoming a minority and b) the reasons for their coming or how they are brought to North America. These two factors affect directly the two groups I will discuss next.

First, there are voluntary minorities, commonly known as immigrants. *Voluntary minorities* "are those who have more or less moved to [North America] because they expect better opportunities (better jobs, more political or religious freedom) than they had in their homelands or places of origin" (p. 164). Some examples of voluntary minorities in North America are immigrants from South Africa, Lebanon, China, Cuba, Japan, and India (among others). They may be different from the majority in race and ethnicity, religion, or language, but they have the knowledge that their presence in North America is not forced on them. They may experience difficulties in school, especially at the beginning, related to discrimination or language and cultural differences. "However," Ogbu and Simons explain, "immigrant minorities do not experience long-lasting school performance difficulty and long-lasting cultural and language problems" (p. 164). Indeed, according to Volante, Klinger, Bilgili, and Siegel (2017), in Canada, first and second-generation immigrants are doing as well as Canadian born students in Programme for International Student Assessment (PISA) tests, and by and large doing a bit better than Canadian born students. In the United States, immigrants are outperforming everyone, including Whites.

On the other hand, *involuntary minorities* are "[r]efugees who were forced to come to [North America] because of civil war or other crises in their places of origin are not immigrants or voluntary minorities" (p. 164). They are a category on/of their own. Interestingly enough, Ogbu and Simons clarify, when it comes to social progress and school achievement, a good percentage of refugees share some "attitudes and behaviors of immigrant minorities" (p. 165). For example, they both come to North America with a well-developed cultural, social, historical and linguistic framework. This framework eases the process of displacement, integration and even discrimination. It tells them, "It can't be worse than where you come from!" So, by and large, they tend to pick up the language and adapt to the new system without fear of losing their cultural and language identity. Even though this book only marginally deals with school performance, in my previous work (Ibrahim, 2014), I discuss many examples that show not only the school success of many African refugees in Canada but also their preparedness for the life and work in Canada in particular, and North America in general.

Second, there are involuntary minorities, which Ogbu and Simons call "nonimmigrant minorities." "Involuntary (nonimmigrant) minorities are people who have been conquered, colonized, or enslaved. Unlike immigrant minorities," Ogbu and Simons explain, "the nonimmigrants have been made to be a part of the [North American] society permanently *against their will*" (p. 165, original emphasis). They have the constant feeling that they did not choose to become a part of the United States or Canada and that they find themselves in a minority context even in their homeland (as is the case with Indigenous peoples in North America). Related to the psychic pain of conquest, colonization, and enslavement, involuntary minorities tend to be less economically successful, receive a high level of exclusion and discrimination, "usually experience greater and more persistent cultural and language difficulties, and do less well in school" (p. 166). Some examples of involuntary minorities in North America include Indigenous and First Nations, early Mexican American in the Southwest, and African Americans.[1]

---

1 In the United States., there are 41,393,491 African Americans, out of whom 4,135,442 are immigrants or "foreign born" (to use the U.S. census term) (for full details, see: https://factfinder.census.gov/faces/tableservices/jsf/pages/productview.xhtml?src=bkmk#). In Canada, the population of Black Canadians doubled between 1996 and 2016 moving from close to 1.8% to 3.5% of the total Canadian population. In 2016, the total population of Black Canadians is 1.2 million out of which 56.4% is first generation 'immigrants,' 35% is second generation (Canadian born), and 8.6% is third generation. Nova Scotia is an

The latter group is of particular interest to me as it shows a socio-psychic phenomenon that needs further investigation (see Chapter 10 in this book). For Ogbu and Simons, children of immigrant minorities are not only voluntary minorities but they embody and demonstrate the same features and social and school success as their forebears. Related to the arguments made in this book, however, there is an exception. The immigrant minorities (voluntary) that share affinity with nonimmigrant minorities (involuntary) tend to fall under the same umbrella of conquest, colonization, or slavery as the involuntary minorities. For example, Ogbu and Simon contend, because of residential and educational segregation and job and other forms of discrimination, Black immigrants to North America from Africa and the Caribbean are forced to reside and work alongside nonimmigrant, and eventually intermarry (see also Chapters One, Two, Three, and Four in this volume). Their descendants become part of the nonimmigrant community, tend to fully identify with them, and in the end "assume the same sense of peoplehood or collective identity" (Obgu & Simons, 1998, p. 166). Ogbu and Simons could have been describing what I am detailing in this book as the process of *becoming Black*, where for Black immigrants, *to become Canadian or American is to become Black* (see Chapters Five and Six). The process of becoming Black is rhizomatic in nature, as we shall see; that is, it is a convoluted, complex, non-linear, and ever shifting process (see Chapters Two and Eight).

***

Having made the distinction between immigrants and refugees and even though the book deals with refugees and immigrants, I will still hold on to the first part of the title of this book *Black Immigrants in North America*, for three reasons. First, I want to use a layperson's language but complicate it at the same time. Both in Canada and the United States, "immigrant" is a complicated umbrella term that is normally used to signify people of color, non-English (or French) speakers, guest and undocumented workers, refugees, as well as actual immigrants. Second, one of the major lessons we have learned from Foucault's (2002) work is not to abandon

---

interesting case where 71.8% is at least third generation. Interestingly enough, of the total Black migration, Black immigrants (both immigrants and refugees) coming from Africa jumped from 4.8% in 1981 to 65.1% in 2016 (for full discussion, see: https://www150.statcan.gc.ca/n1/pub/11-627-m/11-627-m2019006-eng.htm). Finally, in the United States as well as in Canada, in reference to Blackness, the term "immigrant" is convoluted, so the statistics breakdown by status (refugees vs. immigrants) is not commonly available and cannot be located.

problematic concepts (where immigrant is used to refer to both immigrants and refugees), instead we need to populate them, find cracks, and subvert them from within. We need to find ways of making use of them, be as loud as we can about those cracks (i.e., their possibilities), and explain them as frequently and plainly; hence the urgency of this book. Third and finally, within immigration studies in Canada and the United States, Black immigrants are a neglected category. Until my work (Ibrahim, 1999), there was little, if any, research on what it means to be Black and immigrant in North America. Unfortunately, this continues to be the case for the most part as I explain in Chapter Eight, which is why I chose to reprint my earlier work as chapters in this book, since I originally wrote and published them in venues that are not commonly and publicly accessible. However, mapping the landscape of education, sociology, cultural studies, and curriculum, one can see the need for such a book. It is an answer to large epistemological and ontological questions: What does it mean to be Black and an immigrant?; What are the socio-cultural processes that Black immigrants go through as they become Black?; What psychic events come with this process of becoming Black?; What is the outcome of this process, and why?; And, what are the research, curriculum, and pedagogical implications of the socio-psychic-and-cultural event of becoming Black?

In its totality, as we shall, *Black Immigrants in North America* deals with continental African immigrants' experience with both Blackness and immigration. So, appropriately, the first part of the title of this book should have been called *African Immigrants in North America*. But in invoking and reviewing the work by, among others, Coleman-King (2014) and Okpalaoka (2014)—see also Chapter Eight—one sees that going through the process of becoming Black is not different whether you are Black from Africa, Latin America, or the Caribbean.

***

Chapter One addresses the epistemological and ontological questions cited above by arguing that one is not born Black since Blackness (and race in general) is a performative category, it is something we do and perform daily in our hair, makeup, cloths, ways of talking, walking, etc. If one is not born Black, then one becomes Black. That is, if Blackness is a real social phenomenon that is both invented and constantly imposed on (Black) people – after all, someone will always remind you of your Blackness by the way they relate and talk to you, or by how they treat you, then the landscape of identity is limited by how one looks or is assumed to be. In sum, in North America, Blackness is so powerful as an invented yet socially real category that Black immigrants' sense of self and peoplehood is tied directly to nonimmigrant Blacks.

However, this tie is not linear. *Chapter 2* uses Deleuze and Guattari (1987) to conduct a rhizomatic analysis of Blackness. By rhizomatic analysis of Blackness I am referring to the complexity, multidirectional, and ever shifting nature of Blackness. Given the same nature and intensity of discrimination, exclusion, and anti-Black racism that both immigrant and nonimmigrant Blacks face, there is an implicit acceptance even within the Black communities that Black people are the same. Chapter Two is a cautionary note not to forget the rhizomatic nature of Blackness. I take similar arguments in *Chapter Three* and create a conversation between critical race theory and anti-racism while using Deleuze and Guattari's notion of "body without organs" (p. 150).

I have noted over the years that the two epistemologies have reached cul-de-sacs, so the notion of body without organs is both a way out for both frameworks and an organic intellectual concept both may benefit from.

Chapter Four introduces the notion of "economy of hospitality" as an episteme to conceive the "foreigner question." Using the Derridean notion of hospitality, the chapter begins with a distinction between conditional vs. unconditional hospitality and uses the latter pedagogically to put forth the idea that: the deeply human welcomes the foreigner unconditionally. That is to say, those who welcome the foreigner unconditionally humanize themselves as well as humanize the foreigner. This is how teachers should welcome their students in their classrooms, the chapter concludes, within an economy of unconditional hospitality. *Chapter Five* is a classic article that is situated squarely within applied linguistics. It shows how Black immigrants talk and the relevance of that talk to their identity formation process. Becoming Black meant learning Black English as a second language (thus introducing BESL) and learning BESL was an essential part of becoming Black. *Chapter Six* is a follow up and an update to the arguments made in Chapter Five. Chapter Six shows the direct link between (Black) immigration, language learning, and racial becoming. There is a substantial overlap between the two chapters but they also differ in their framing. Chapter Five was an introduction to the concept of 'becoming Black' whereas Chapter Six is a demonstration of the direct link between immigration, language and racial becoming.

Framed within cultural studies, *Chapter Seven* thinks through hybridity and in-betweenness and introduces the concept of 'new *flâneur*' as a way to understand how Black immigrants negotiate and keep their cultural heritage as they integrate themselves in the new socio-linguistic-and-cultural space. There is no either/or, instead we have the spectre of 'and' (e.g., being Black *and* female, *and* Muslim, *and* Senegalese, etc.) (Ibrahim, 2003). *Chapter Eight* is a review of the major studies I could locate that deal with Black immigrants. Unfortunately, beside mine, there are only two studies. *Chapter Nine* is situated within education and it is a critique of neoliberalism and is intended as a conversation within teacher education. I am arguing in this chapter that Black immigrants are neglected, especially their post-colonial, displacement and immigration histories. I discuss at length Adichie's novel *Americanah* and draw some pedagogical implications.

Turning to curriculum studies, *Chapter Ten* presents the educational and curriculum arguments for why we as educators need to pay very close attention to popular culture, especially Hip-Hop since, I am contending, the alternative to Hip-Hop is dead silence. Using Eisner's (1979) notion of curriculum, I offer Hip-Hop as a null curriculum, as a site of identity investment and language learning that is directly related to African youths' lives but not taught at the school. *Chapter Eleven* is a methodological framework that attempts to think about the challenges as well as the possibilities of conducting research in immigrant communities. The insider-outsider debate is addressed—where I argue that a new ethics is required, one where research is turned into an act of love—and the purpose of conducting research is turned away from data collection to humanizing. Originally, I had another chapter placed here (after Chapter Eleven), but I had to pay a good amount of money to reprint it (over $12,000). As a matter of principle, I refused to pay. Yet, I highly recommend that chapter for the interested (see Ibrahim, 2019). In it, I situate the Black immigrant question within curriculum studies as a way to conceptualize what I am calling "sensuous curriculum of investment." If Black immigrants are learning Black English as second language, then curriculum studies is confronted by a new and very interesting dilemma: what to teach, how, to whom, and why? Serving as the last chapter, *Chapter Twelve* is co-authored with a graduate student and is intended to think harder and deeper about how to answer these last difficult questions: what to teach, how, to whom, and why? We need to become wide-awake as we teach, we need a critical pedagogy of humanism, imagination, and becoming. Moving between the poetic, the pedagogical, and the deeply human, the ultimate yet unstated purpose of this chapter is to de-silence the Black immigrant question, introduce it and ground it in research, and create a space where the nuances of Blackness is addressed.

To conclude, each chapter is a story but there is no story that stands alone, so some chapters may feel similar. This is done purposefully for at least two reasons. First, all the chapters are looking at the same data but from different perspectives and angles and, second, the actual excerpts are used in a number of chapters. My gentle reader is requested to skim through those sections, but they are used to make a point. I have found in my own teaching that my audience understands a point better if I address it several times using similar examples. This is the idea behind the use of similar language and examples in this book. After all, immigrating while Black or IWB is a peculiar phenomenon, especially given the long suffering of Black people because of the Middle Passage, slavery, and colonization. It deserves not only extra attention, especially with the increasing murder of Black people (CBC, 2017), but repetition, reproduction, and republication with no apology.

Reference

Bauman, Z. 2016. *Strangers at our door*. London: Polity.
CBC. 2017. *14 high-profile police related deaths of U.S. blacks*. Retrieved from: https://www.cbc.ca/news/world/list-police-related-deaths-usa-1.4438618. Accessed 25 February, 2019.
Coleman-King, C. 2014. *The (re)making of a Black America: Tracing the racial and ethnic socialization of Caribbean American youth*. New York: Peter Lang.
Deleuze, G., and F. Guattari. 1987. *Thousand plateaus: Capitalism and schizophrenia*. London: Continuum.
Eisner, E. 1979. *The educational imagination on the design and evaluation of school programs*. New York: Macmillan.
Foucault, M. 2002. *The archaeology of knowledge*. New York: Routledge.
Ibrahim, A. 1999. Becoming Black: Rap and Hip-Hop, race, gender, identity, and the politics of ESL learning. *TESOL Quarterly, 33*(3), 349-369.
Ibrahim, A. 2003. The spectre of "and": Multiculturalism, antiracism, and the third continent. *Inquiry: Critical Thinking Across the Discipline, 21*(3), 5-16.
Ibrahim, A. 2014. *The rhizome of Blackness: A critical ethnography of Hip-Hop culture, language, identity, and the politics of becoming*. New York: Peter Lang.
Ibrahim, A. 2019. Intersecting race, language, and identity: Toward a sensuous curriculum of investment. In Gershon, W. (Ed.), *Sensuous curriculum: Politics and the senses in education* (pp. 115-134). Charlotte, NC: Information Age Publishing.
Kranish, M., & Fisher, M. 2016. *Trump revealed: The definitive biography of the 45th president*. New York: Scribner.

Kymlicka, W. 2010. *The current state of multiculturalism in Canada and research themes in Canadian multiculturalism 2008-2010*. Ottawa: Citizenship and Immigration Canada.

Ogbu, J. & Simons, H. 1998. Voluntary and involuntary minorities: A cultural-ecological theory of school performance with some implication for education. *Anthropology & Education Quarterly*, 29(2), 155-188.

Okpalaoka, C. 2014. *(Im)migrations, relations, and identities: Negotiating cultural memory, diaspora, and African (American) identities*. New York: Peter Lang.

Papa, R. 2017. *Finding her in history: Confronting the traditions of misogyny*. Cham, Switzerland: Springer.

Rushdie, S. 2018. Truth, lies, and literature. *The New Yorker*. Retrieved from https://www.newyorker.com/culture/cultural-comment/truth-lies-and-literature. Accessed 25 February, 2019.

Volante, L., Klinger, D., Bilgili, O., & Siegel, M. 2017. Making sense of the performance (dis)advantage for immigrant students across Canada. *Canadian Journal of Education/Revue Canadienne de e l'éducation* 40(3), 329-361.

CHAPTER ONE

One is Not Born Black: Becoming and the Phenomenon(ology) of Race

(REPRINTED WITH PERMISSION) Ibrahim, A. (2004). One is not born Black: Becoming and the phenomenon(ology) of race. *Philosophical Studies in Education, 35,* 89-97.

> [R]ace, exactly like sex, is taken as an "immediate given," a "sensible given," "physical features," belonging to a natural order. But what we believe to be a physical and direct perception is only a sophisticated and mythic construction, an "imaginary formation," which reinterprets physical features ... through the network of relationships in which they are perceived. (They are seen as black, therefore they are black; they are seen as women, therefore, they are women. But before being seen that way, they first had to be made that way).
>
> MONIQUE WITTIG, ONE IS NOT BORN A WOMAN

I BELIEVE THE luminous work of Monique Wittig deserves special attention, particularly her take on the network of relationships between perception and reality, the mental and the physical, matter and language, especially gender and race.[1] "They are seen as *black*," she writes, "therefore they are black; they are seen as *women*, therefore, they *are* women." First, I want to ask, "they are seen" by whom and second what is the translatability or conversion of "being seen" into "is"—that is, the psychic relation between visuality and reality? "But before being seen that way, they first had to be *made* that way." How does one make a woman woman or a Black person black? More importantly, what is the psychic and consequently ethnographic result of being made a woman or black? These are precisely the questions I would like to explore in this paper. I want to show that, much like gender, race is not a category we occupy or slot our selves into, but a performative category that we "do" every day. It is a role we play, a plot, a representational language that is beyond our control and since, as Wittig argues, "there is no nature in society," it is a historical and social product.[2]

Race, I contend, is a network of meanings against which we negotiate our psychic being; that is to say, who we are, what future we envision for ourselves and others, and where we invest and find our desires reflected. Being a network of meanings or a collection of stories we "tell" ourselves and others and henceforth live by, race is a symbolic capital that is either valued positively in schools and in the larger society—if your narrative is the "right" narrative—or negatively—if your telling does not have the "right" infrastructure of the symbolic market of exchange: namely, possessing an authorized language, being an authorized speaker, speaking with authority and hence command hearing.[3] In educational and curriculum studies, Pinar *et al.* have shown, race was the abject category that was always subsumed under "politics," the marginal and the outside of pedagogy, the unnecessary discourse that tells "us" little about the *politique réale*: the vulgar neo-Marxist bifurcation of economic structure, race and culture, thus reducing race to class.[4] Against these and other hegemonic discourses, Pinar et al. convincingly call for a pedagogical politics of "curriculum as racial text."

I shall begin, in what follows, by reintroducing the introduction, then theorize "becoming," and conclude on a discussion of an incident where I contend that, having arrived into North America as a refugee from Africa, I enter, so to speak, a *social imaginary*, a discursive space where I am already imagined, constructed, and thus treated as "Black" by hegemonic discourses and groups, respectively.

Elsewhere, I show how a group of immigrant and refugee continental African youth who are attending a French-language high school in southwestern Ontario, Canada, enter this social imaginary.[5] I also show its impact on their identity formation, who they identify with, and what they learn and how. First, I contended, these youth are not "Black" in Africa and that they become one once in North America. Becoming Black meant, I demonstrated, identifying with Black America which in turn influenced what and how they linguistically and culturally learnt. They learn "Black English as a second language" (BESL) which they access in and through Hip-Hop culture and Rap lyrical/linguistic styles.

Much like these youth, I am arguing, I was not considered "Black" in Africa, though I had other adjectives that patched together my identity, such as "tall," "Sudanese," "academic," "basketball player," and so on. In other words, except in South Africa, race is not "the" defining social identity in Africa. However, as we shall see, in direct response to the historical representation of Blackness and the social processes of racialization and racism where I am mapped against the hegemonic White state of mind: "Oh, they all look like Blacks to me!", these antecedent signifiers, adjectives become secondary to my Blackness, and I retranslate my being: I become Black. My main contention then is that, in North America, my Black body speaks a language of its own, it cheats me, it ritualizes me, where I become a condensed moment of historicity, an inscribed repetition of convention, a passerby who turns to the policeman to acquire an identity, "one purchased, as it were, with the price of guilt."⁶ Here, Judith Butler argues, the act of being recognized becomes an act of identity formation: the address animates me into an existence, constituting me within the possible circuit of recognition. To be recognized is to be interpellated, hailed within the terms of language and only there that my social existence becomes possible.⁷

Being Made I:
The African Body in North America, Against All Odds

Continental Africans recently have been crossing the Atlantic Ocean to North America in a considerable number. In a sense, as Molefi K. Asante has argued, this is a performative act of defiance to the history of colonialism, imperialism and the middle passage.⁸ They are joining the African diaspora by becoming part of it. But they have to first confront this history—the history of the present—where their bodies are already read as "Black." They have to translate, negotiate and answer two questions. What does being Black really mean in North America? and, if one is "becoming" Black, what does this call for, entail, and thus produce? At a personal level, I want to ask the following: as a continental African living in North America, am I a Black man? Conjugating the verb to be in the present tense is central and I am using Blackness as defined in North America. If the answer is negative, what does it mean *not to be* a Black man, while materially possessing the socially defined Black male body? That is, how does one translate and negotiate one's own sense of self vis-à-vis the already pronounced social order? On the other hand, if *I am* a Black man, when did I become one? Using personal narrative, I want to argue that my Blackness in Africa is at the shadow, the blind spot, the outside of the speech act of the dominant Other, refusing the latter's regulation, interpellation, subjection, normative gaze and even recognition. Simply, it was—a radical autonomy. But, as we shall see, by falling within the address of the Other, I was given a new spelling of my name: I was rendered and addressed as Black. The paper is thus a stare into the ethnography, the processes of *becoming black*. That is, the cultural, linguistic, and socio-psychic implications of what it means to possess the Black body in North America (and the Western world in general). I do believe that the narrative and the processes of becoming Black are not only applicable to continental Africans, but to most, if not all, émigrés and displaced refugees who move to North America and whose body is read or socially defined as Black.

This is what I want to term the "politics of ultra visibility." It is when the unmarked is marked and made visible.[9] This marking takes place in and through language and is felt on the surface of the body. If the "norm"–whiteness in North America, for example–is made obscure and invisible through technologies of normalisation and naturalisation, and if these technologies are embedded in language and work by hailing and pointing towards the Other and away from the Self, furthermore, if the hailer or the speaker possesses the authorized language and the authorised power to speak and be listened to, then the hailed Other–Blackness, in this case–can only be made ultra-visible.[10] This, I argue, is directly implicated in how I enter this politics of ultra-visibility, how people relate to my body, and hence how I experience the processes of becoming Black.

Being Made II:
Becoming as a Reiterative Position

There is a need, I presume by now, to distinguish between being and becoming. In his preface to Althea Prince's *Being Black*, Clifton Joseph poetically cites how he, among other West Indians, has entered this process of hailing, identification and ultimately becoming. He writes:

> We were a politicised grouping of student/activists, athletes, those looking for a place to hang/out, street-wise players & partiers, and people who were just dissatisfied with not seeing enough blackness in school and in the society, generally. We *weren't* "Black" where we came from in the West Indies, but in Toronto we had to confront the fact that we were seen as "Black," and had to check/out for ourselves what this blackness was.[11]

On his part, Hamlet once argued, "To be, or not to be–that is the question."[12] Or is it? *Being*, it has recently been argued, can never be (in full and in complete), since it is a *sujet-en-procès* or a work-in-progress, a continuous act of becoming.[13] In Clifton Joseph's quote, the negation and the past tense in "We werent 'Black'" assumes that we "are" now. I therefore distinguish between *being* and *becoming*. Being, as I already cited, is a continuous act of becoming. It is not a fixed entity; on the contrary, it is a production, a performative category that is never complete. Borrowing from Judith Butler, performativity is a concept that does not assume *idées fixes*, quite the opposite, it requires repetitive, parodic and continual acts of becoming.[14] For Butler, there is nothing fixed about, for example, gender or the category woman (and I would add race). So gender (or race) is for Butler the repeated stylisation of the body, a set of recurrent acts, words, gestures, or what Roland Barthes calls complex semiological languages.[15] These are signs that are open for signification and different readings since they cannot produce verbal utterances yet are ready to speak. For Butler, we produce and perform these complex languages on the surface of our bodies: in and through our modes of dress, walk, in our hair, *maquillage*, lip-gloss; also in architecture, photography, and so on. So we perform who we are, our identities, desires, and investments, at least in part, in and through these complex semiological languages: our dress, walk and talk. Following Simone de Beauvoir, Monique Wittig concludes that there is nothing inherent or guaranteed about being a woman. Indeed, one is not even born a woman, one becomes one.[16] If this be so, then one is not born Black either, one in fact becomes one, where Blackness is a set of norms, narratives, and everyday performative roles and acts.

Using the analogy of learning a language, *being* can be similar to a mother tongue while *becoming* is to learn a second language. Although no one can fully and completely master one's mother tongue, one is comfortable enough within it to know its nuances and to even know that which is beyond language: the excess. Whereas, in the case of a second language, one enters that language as an outsider; always with the hope that that which is outside will eventually belong to the self, a second will become a first language. In short, being is an accumulative memory, an understanding, a conception and an experience upon which individuals interact with the world around them, whereas becoming is the process of building this memory, experience.

May 16, 1999 was a culminating day in my understanding of what it means to be Black in North America, specifically in Canada. It was the day I was hailed, declared "Black," by an authorised speaker who possessed an authorised language. The following, published elsewhere, is an extract from my diary entitled *Being Under Surveillance: Who Controls My Black Body?*[7] It is cited here to demonstrate how my "Black" body was hailed, on the one hand, and the speech act, the address it produces in others, what it makes them "say," on the other. In *Teaching to Transgress*, bell hooks argues that, "experience can be a way to know and can inform how we know what we know" and that "personal testimony ... is such fertile ground for the production of liberatory [praxis] because it usually forms the base of our [knowledge and] theory making."[8] And so, I hope, is my narrative.

May 16, 1999: The Story of the "Dark Man"

Today was the last day of my trip to Toronto after a five-month absence in Ottawa. I had, to say the least, a wo(a)nderful time during my sojourn in Toronto: visited friends, had flavoury meals, and yes, saw *The Mummy*, too. It was 1:10 p.m. on a sunny and an unexpectedly hot Sunday. I was more in the mood for poetry than for prose; and bicycling on St. George Street had never been as light. However it is frightening how lightness can so easily whirl into an unbearable heaviness, and how heaviness can cause so much pain. It all began when I had just crossed the yellow light of Bloor Street West. I saw a white car curving into the bicycle lane and I heard hereafter a siren coming from it. Since I was bicycling, I was neither able to fully verify the car nor who was driving it nor why it was requesting me to stop. However, when it was fully halted before my bicycle, I realized it was a police car. From it came veering a rangy White man with full gear and a pair of sunglasses, along with a clean and handsome gun. My immediate thought was that it must be the bicycle helmet, since I was not wearing one; and seeing that there will always be a first time for our social experiences, I whispered to myself "oh God, this is my first ticket of my life." I was deadly mistaken.

He approached my bicycle and said "Have you ever been in trouble with the law before?" Shocked beyond any imaginable belief, I said "No." "Can I know why am I asked the question?" I added. "You fit the description of a man we are looking for, who just snatched a bag from Yorkville; and I just saw you around the Yorkville area," he said. Could I have avoided Yorkville, since to buy a muffler or a bandanna in Yorkville one needs at least few hundred and I had only forty-two dollars in my pocket? Coincidences have their own logic, which is beyond my humble understanding. At this point, he began a walkie-talkie conversation with a dispatcher; and I realized when he said "I am talking to him right now" that it was a continuation to a previous dialogue. The phrase "I am talking to him right now" was, however, traumatic. Involuntarily, it triggered and brought alive my unforgettable political prison memory in the early 1990s with the all-punishing dictatorial régime in Sudan. When memories are so deep, all they need is a match to find oneself burning and unwillingly shaking. The phrase was that match. It signified that I was already under surveillance; I was already "talked" about. Panopticism, somehow, keeps surfacing in my mind now. It was a situation where the marginalized and the invisible was becoming visible, if not the center of surveillance; where the "fictions" I was immersed into came alive into "reality." Looking sternly into his eyes, I repeated "Can I know why I was stopped?" In a panoptic régime, I now understand, like all totalitarian régime, the true opponent or enemy, if you like, is the person who asks questions. Squirmingly, his face turned red and he loudly regurgitated "I told YOU Sir that you fit the description of a man we are looking for."

Calmly but unaloofly, "And what is that description?" I wondered. "We are looking for a dark man with a dark bag," he said. First, I was curious about the "we." Who are "we"? I can hazard answers, but I am still not sure about the answer. Secondly I looked at my backpack which I was carrying, since I was leaving Toronto at 3:00 p.m., and it occurred to me that my bag was light-blue with one very small black (or as he said "dark") stripe at the edge. More with my eyes than with my voice, I repeated after him "A DARK man?" Selfconsciously, but pesteringly, he exclaimed "A Black man with a dark bag!" He insisted on my bag being "dark"; now I was significantly metamorphosed from "dark" into "black." Not that it matters either way, I reflected after, but it seems that some people can either not see or have "color problem." "Do you live around here, Sir?" he asked. "I don't" I responded. Up until now, I have no idea why his eyes steered out and his face changed when I said I did not live in Toronto. "Where do you live, Sir?" The appellation "Sir," at this point, was voiced with such an unease that I questioned the merit of its utterance. "Ottawa," I said. "What are you doing in Toronto?" What, indeed, are you doing in Toronto? I repeated to myself. Some questions, I guess, are meant to be repeated for their banality, if not stupefaction. I told him none of these; "I am visiting friends," I said. With an unconvinced face he murmured "Ohha!"

During this conversation, I saw another police car stopping behind the first; and from it came another White policeman. I was then asked for a piece of identification. I gave the first policeman my citizenship card. Before doing so, he asked me to lay down my (dark?) bag, which I did. With his order, I widely opened my bag for anyone in the street to see. Since it was a tourist area, with the well-attended Bata Shoe Museum, everyone was looking into my bag. Some, I observed, pitied my plight and one White woman was smiling. I was not only pitying my situation, which was abtrusely absurd, I was pitying also that Toni Morrison's *Paradise*, Margaret Atwood's *Alias Grace* and *Julia Kristeva's Reader* had to endure the same humiliation. These books were on top of my clothes. Not that these books mattered in and for themselves, because they didn't. Disrespectfulness for the authors was what pestered me. Anyway, it was getting closer to 2 p.m. and my ride for Ottawa was to leave at 3 p.m. At this point, I decided to use my University of Ottawa professor identification. I am still debating whether it was a favorable or unfavorable decision not to use it from the offset. After writing down my name and date of birth, he then announced to the dispatcher telling her "All is OK now."

With no apologies, I was ordered to collect my affairs and my bag and, as he uttered it, "You are free to go now." Given its inhumane nature, being under siege, believe me, is a feeling which should be avoided using all measures. Somehow, nonetheless, I pondered if the reasons for which I was stopped could or would be enough to stop any White man, should he be the suspect? Who among White men will be stopped? Most probably unsmartly dressed, with long bonny tail hair? Again, I kept wondering, what if I could not look at the policeman in the eyes and asked with a calm manner, which was not an evoked personae but a natural character, why I was stopped? What if I was just a shy man who is genuinely frightened by the police? As well, one might ask, did my Hip-Hop dress, my emerging dreadlocks and my youthfulness form part of the reasons why I was stopped? Given my panic, terror, and fright, what would have happened should I have run? The wrath I have seen in that man's eyes, I would be ready to say, and it would certainly not be a hazard guessing given the historical relationship between the police and the Black body, was not assuring.

L'étranger: A Bodily Speech Act of Love

The ... speech act performs its deed *at the moment* of the utterance, and yet to the extent that the moment is ritualized, it is never merely a single moment. The "moment" in ritual is a condensed historicity: it exceeds itself in past and future directions, an effect of prior and future invocations that constitute and escape the instance of utterance (*ES*, 3).

"Si je suis tranger, il n'y a pas d' trangers," I repeat after Julia Kristeva.[19] *L'étranger* or the stranger, the Other, the policeman needs to remember, is not outside the semiotic system of the Nation but within it; and language forms his imaginary which is in dire need of deconstruction. Blackness, he should also know, is a multicultural, multinational and multiethnic body of alterity and heterogeneity. The semiotic chora of the Black body, then, is not thetic, stable and fixed, but a sign that has no meaning in itself, in fact it receives meaning in its interdiscursive relation with other bodies. The story therefore should not be read as an expression of racism, but an aporetic metatranslation of this Black body that is caught up in a paradox, split; and of a man whose translation of himself is different than others of him. Henceforth, he finds himself at once subversive of and dependent on the signifying process of his own body.

He knows that, "a fully intentional speech is perpetually subverted by that in speech which subverts intentionality" (*ES*, 11). That is to say, our bodies cheat us all the time, what they "say" is almost always unknown since they "say" things that they do not intend. They say more, or say differently, than they mean to say; something is always in the excess. "In speaking," therefore Butler argues, "the act that the body is performing is never fully understood; the body is the blindspot of speech, that which acts in excess of what is said, but which also acts in and through what is said. That the speech act is a bodily act," Butler explains, "means that the act is redoubled in the moment of speech: there is what is said, and then there is a kind of saying that the bodily "instrument" of the utterance performs" (*ES*, 11). Moreover, Butler reminds us, the speech act itself has its own economy of exchange, where the Saying is not and should not be equated to what is being Said, since "to be addressed is not merely to be recognized for what one already is, but to have the very term conferred by which the recognition of existence becomes possible." That is to say, "One "exists" not only by virtue of being recognized, but, in prior sense, by being recognizable"

(*ES*, 5). To be recognizable, however, as we have seen, is to find oneself within a linguistic realm, a social rituality that works through exclusion and violence.

He also knows what Emmanuel Kant once argued, that *the thing in itself* is not the same as *the thing for me*. "Everything you see is part of the world around you," explained the protagonist Alberto in *Sophie's World*, "but how you see it is determined by the glasses you are wearing." So, Alberto continues, "you cannot say the world is red even though you conceived it as being so." As humans, Alberto concludes, "We are condemned to improvise. We are like actors dragged onto the stage without having learned our lines, with no script and no prompter to whisper stage directions to us. We must decide for ourselves how to live."[20] In a humanist mould, this actor posits himself (as) a Black subject and simultaneously questions the adequacy of that location, deconstructs t/his subjectivity as an always-already *work-in-progress* that can never "be" (in full). He is a *subject-in-process* that is always to become, and to become–for him–is to become human with the truth of love: "When I am in love, there is palpitating, passionate, unique meaning, but only right here and now, a meaning that may be absurd in another conjunction."[21] He loves deeply, and he knows, finally, that . . .

Love's procession is moving;
Beauty is waving her banner;
Youth is sounding the trumpet of joy;
Disturb not my contrition, my blamer.
Let me walk, for the path is rich
With roses and mint, and the air
Is scented with cleanliness.
Kahlil Gibran[22]

Notes

1 Monique Wittig, "One Is Not Born a Woman," in *Identities: Race, Class, Gender, and Nationality*, ed. L. Alcoff and M. Eduardo (Oxford: Blackwell, 2003), 159, original emphasis. I am grateful for reviewers' and editor's helpful comments and feedback.

2 Wittig, *One Is Not Born a Woman*, 159.

3 Pierre Bourdieu, *Language and Symbolic Power* (London: Polity Press, 1991).

4 William Pinar, William Reynolds, Patrick Slattery and Peter Taubman, *Understanding Curriculum* (New York: Peter Lang, 1995).

5 See for example Awad Ibrahim *'Hey, whassup homeboy?' Becoming Black: Race, Language, Culture, and the Politics of Identity. African Students in a Franco-Ontarian High School*. Unpublished doctoral dissertation (OISE: University of Toronto, 1998); "Becoming Black: Rap and Hip-Hop, Race, Gender, Identity, and the Politics of ESL Learning," *TESOL Quarterly 33*, no.3 (1999): 349-369; ""Hey, ain't I Black too?" The Politics of Becoming Black," in *Rude: Contemporary Black Canadian Cultural Criticism*, ed. R. Walcott (Toronto: Insomniac Press, 2000), 109-136; ""Whassup Homeboy?" Black/Popular Culture and the Politics of "Curriculum Studies": Devising an Antiracism Perspective," in *Power, Knowledge and Anti-racism Education: A Critical Reader*, ed. G. J. S. Dei and A. Calliste (Halifax: Feronwood, 2000), 57-72; "Operating Under Erasure: Hip-Hop and the Pedagogy of Affective," *Journal of Curriculum Theorizing 20*. no. 1 (2004): 113-133.

6 Judith Butler, *Excitable Speech: A Politics of the Performative* (New York & London: Routledge, 1997), 25. This book will be cited as ES in the text for all subsequent references.

7 See also Louis Althusser, *Lenin and Philosophy* (London: New Left Books, 1971); J. Austin, *How to Do Things With Words* (Cambridge, Mass: Harvard University Press, 1962); Butler, Excitable Speech.

8 See M. K. Asante, "Afrocentricity and Culture," in *African Culture: The Rhythms of Unity* ed. M. Asante & K. Asante (Trenton, NJ: Africa World, 1990), 3-12. Thanks, in part, to the discourse of Afrocentrism and diasporic/Africana studies departments, there is a new dialogue created between Africans and diasporic Africans (see also Paul Gilroy, *The Black Atlantic: Modernity and Double Consciousness* (London & New York: Routledge, 1993). And part of this dialogue is enhanced by, ironically, tourism and immigration, as well as involuntary displacement. In defiance of history, diasporic Africans in North America, for example, are making the journey back to Africa and continental Africans are making it to North America.

9 See also Stuart Hall ed., *Representation: Cultural Representations and Signifying Practices* (London: The Open University, 1997).

10 See Althusser, *Lenin and Philosophy*; Kathryn Woodward ed., *Identity and Difference* (London: The Open University, 1997); M. Fine, L. Powell, L. Weiss & L. M. Wong ed., *Off White: Readings on Race, Power and Society* (New York: Routledge, 1997); M. Foucault, *The Order of Things* (London: Tavistock, 1970); R. Frankenberg, *White Women, Race Matters: The Social Construction of Whiteness* (Minneapolis: University of Minnesota Press, 1993); Bourdieu, *Language and Symbolic Power*.

11 Althea Prince, *Being Black* (Toronto: Insomniac Press, 2001), 16-17, italics added.

12 William Shakespeare, *Hamlet Prince of Denmark* (London: Penguin, 1988).

13 Judith Butler, *Gender Trouble: Feminism and the Subversion of Identity* (New York: Routledge, 1999); Awad Ibrahim ""Hey, ain't I Black too?" The Politics of Becoming Black," in *Rude: Contemporary Black Canadian Cultural Criticism*, ed. R. Walcott (Toronto: Insomniac Press, 2000), 109-136; Julia Kristeva, *La révolution du langage poétique* (Paris: Lautréament et Mallarm, 1974); Jean-Paul Sartre, *Being and Nothingness: A Phenomenological Essay on Ontology* (New York: Pocket Books, 1980).

14 Butler, *Gender Trouble*.

15 Roland Barthes, *Elements of Semiology* (New York: Hill and Wang, 1983).

16 Butler, *Gender Trouble*.

17 Awad Ibrahim, "May 16, 1999: The Story of the "Dark Man"," *Inquiry: Critical Thinking Across the Disciplines* 22, no. 2 (2003): 21-25.

18 bell hooks, *Teaching to Transgress: Education as the Practice of Freedom* (London & New York: Routledge, 1994), 168.

19 Julia Kristeva, *Histoire d'amour* (Paris: Denoel, 1983), 3.

20 J. Gaarder, *Sophie's World: A Novel About the History of Philosophy* (New York: Berkley Books, 1996), 457.

21 Julia Kristeva, *Histoire d'amour* (Paris: Denoel, 1983), 259.

22 Kahlil Gibran, *The Prophet* (New York: Knopf, 1966), 120.

CHAPTER TWO

The (un)naturalization of Blackness: A rhizomatic analysis of Blackness

(REPRINTED WITH PERMISSION) Ibrahim, A. (in press). The (un)naturalization of Blackness: A rhizomatic analysis of Blackness. This chapter was originally written under a different title for The Nuances of Blackness Collective (Eds.), *Nuances of Blackness in the Canadian Academy*.

Take I: A Socius Analysis

BLACKNESS, IT SEEMS, is born into an existing 'socius.' This is a monstrous machine, a metaphor of and for society where attractors and opposites can and do co-exist. Their co-existence means a permanent presence of tension, a tug of war and on-going struggle. There are no simple resolutions within the socius, we are forever left with the curse of improvisation and living (with)in tension. But, we-humans-and-scholars are so immersed into the socius that we forget ourselves and the very structure of the socius itself. In fact, we even forget that we live in a socius, a very sophisticated machine that is *working on us* primarily subconsciously and through seduction, a machine that is "under way the moment the body has had enough of organs" (Deleuze and Guattari 1987, 150).

In this socius, Blackness is naturalized, so that the social fabrication is made into a biological entity *par excellence*. I see you Black, therefore you are Black! But one is not born Black yet, in the socius, one has to be made Black. Blackness is not a multiplicity in the socius, it is a singular that is signified not in itself but by what it is not: Whiteness. It is not an identity, it is an identity claim, a political space and a space we embody. We do not slot ourselves into it, it is a performative category, as I argued elsewhere (Ibrahim, 2014), which we perform on our bodies, in our hair, in our dress, in our talk, in our walk, in our desire and in how we feel about ourselves and others.

When it comes to Blackness, Deleuze and Guattari (D & G) (1987) make a distinction between two distinct processes. The first is linked to what they call *significance*. Here Whiteness, which they refer to as "white wall", equals significance equals face: White wall = significance = face. The second process is called *subjectification*. Here Blackness, which D & G call "black hole", equals subjectification equals behind-the-face: Black hole = subjectification = behind-the-face. In this sense, "The face constructs the wall that the signifier needs in order to bounce off of; it constitutes the wall of the signifier, the frame or screen. The face digs the hole that subjectification needs in order to break through; it constitutes the black hole of subjectivity as consciousness or passion, the camera, the third eye" (Deleuze and Guattari 1987, 168). It is significant to note, for D & G, "The face is not a universal. It is not even that of the white man; it is White Man himself, with his broad cheeks... The face is Christ. The face is the typical European..." (176).

Take II: The Theatre of the Absurd

D & G are not thinking about these descriptors in absolute terms because, if they do, one can only find the theatre of the absurd. Moving 'white man' into 'White Man' is a breakthrough into this theatre; a move from the terrain of the personal to the domain of concepts and ideas. It is only here we can understand the subjectification of Blackness. Of course, Black people do exist and they are loud about their existence. They certainly do not need Deleuze, Guattari, Lyotard, Foucault, Bourdieu, or whomever to arrogantly state whether they do exist or not. Not without some arrogance, what D & G are suggesting is how Blackness has been ontologically subjectified and epistemically colonized most of our modern history. This is especially true in the Western world, especially in Europe and North America. Whiteness beams (so much that it blinds itself and its otherness: Blackness); occupies and signifies; while Blackness is blinded by the beam, occupies holes in the wall of Whiteness and is therefore signified. Nugugi wa Thiango (1986) has called for Blackness to own its own signification, to name itself, to dim (if not block) the beaming light that is blinding it and decolonize the episteme that is used to define it.

In Canada, the present volume is building on a larger project where Blackness is naming itself. The work by Enid Lee (1985), Lawrence Hill (1996, 2007), Rinaldo Walcott (2000), Dionne Brand (2001), Afua Cooper (2006), George Dei (2009), Carl James et al. (2010), Joseph Mensah (2010) George Elliott Clarke (2014), Awad Ibrahim (2014) and Boulou Ebanda de B'béri et al. (2014), to name but very few, is the foundation of this larger political, social, historical and epistemic project. Here, Blackness speaks its own voice; its language is not without critique, but at least it is honest enough to create and assemble a cartography of and for its subjectivity; and along the way, links its word with its world. As it does so, however, there are three notions in Deleuze and Guattari's (1987) work that I think will be of direct benefit for this project: becoming-minoritarian, deterritorialization, and rhizome.

Take III: Becoming-Minoritarian

> It is important not to confuse "minoritarian," as a becoming or process, with a "minority", as an aggregate or a state ... One reterritorializes, or allows oneself to be reterritorialized. Even blacks, as the Black Panthers said, must become-black. Even women must become-women. Even Jews must become-Jewish ... [Here] man constitutes the majority, or rather the standard upon which the majority is based: white, male, adult, "rational," etc., in short, the average European, the subject of enunciation (Deleuze and Guattari 1987, 291-2).

If Blacks must become-Black and the White Man is the subject of enunciation, then the first notion we are dealing with is of two-fold: 'becoming' and 'minoritarian.' The term 'minority,' for D & G, is a question of number and aggregate, while 'minoritarian' is altogether different. Minoritarian is a never-ending process and state of becoming and de-re-territorialization. The majority territorializes, defines and frames, whereas minoritarian, as a process, re-and-deterritorializes, reshapes and redefines this frame. One is never a woman or Black. One is always becoming-woman or becoming-Black. Blackness in this sense is an every-day performative category that we deploy, make use of, refer to and hence in constant definition. It is not a simple category, but extremely complex and fluid 'assemblage,' that is to say an ensemble of conscious and sub-conscious processes the result of which is a sense of self, an identity. Blackness, moreover, becomes a political category we claim and declare as our own because, as D & G put it, "[b]coming-minoritarian is a political affair and necessitates a labor of power (*puissance*), an active micropolitics" (292).

Moreover, if Blackness is an every-day performative category, then Whiteness, as the majority, emerges as "a gigantic memory" (293) that is trying to crush Blackness, hence both end up in a constant tug of war and unresolved tension. But in this war machine, Blackness becomes "a line of becoming [that] has neither beginning nor end." This is "[a] line of becoming [that] has only a middle." For D & G, this middle "is not an average; it is fast motion, it is the absolute speed of movement." Put otherwise, "A becoming is neither one nor two, nor the relation of the two; it is the in-between, the border or line of flight or descent running perpendicular to both" (293). Blackness, in other words, is conceived as a decentralized and distributed category, which itself is a social and historical product. It is definitely more than skin color, hair texture and other phenotypes. Figure I B and C better describe the process of becoming-minoritarian/Black than the centralized and structured notion of Blackness as seen in Figure I A.

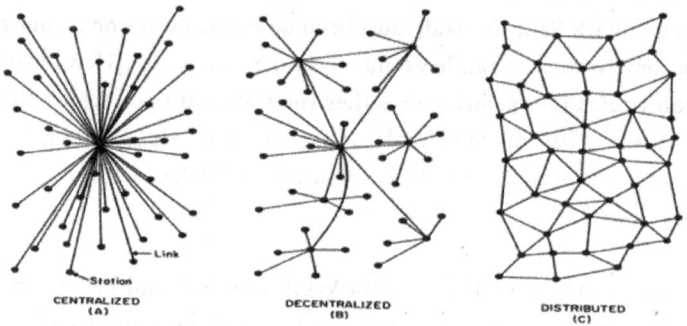

FIG. I — Centralized, Decentralized and Distributed Networks

Figure I: http://english113miw2014.pbworks.com/w/file/fetch/76616774/paul-baran-network.png

To liberate itself from the crushing of Whiteness, therefore, Blackness must realize that the liberation process is messy, it is not linear nor is it progressive where one moves from A to B to C, etc. To liberate itself, moreover, Blackness must go through what D & G call "striated" process. This is a non-linear process of struggle which is without guarantees; a harsh and sometimes extremely painful psychic agony which is emotionally taxing; and an epistemic orientation which is attempting to replace hopelessness with hopefulness through hard work.

Take IV: The Deterritorialization of Blackness

> Whenever a territorial assemblage is taken up by a movement that deterritorializes it (whether under so-called natural or artificial conditions), we say that machine is released (Deleuze and Guattari 1987, 333).

As a result one territorializes, that is to say one impregnates the space one occupies with one's uniqueness based on gender, class, ability, sexuality, language, culture, nationality, consciousness, etc. This is clearly shown in Figure I B and C. It is therefore both absolutely necessary but absolutely absurd to talk about 'Black people.' They do not exist. They are made. They are made through epistemic violence, colonization and Western arrogance, where they become its absolute Otherness: that which is objectified, studied and talked about. Blackness is not a 'natural' or even a biological category, it is a social and historical product. Blackness has to be conceived as an unfinished living entity; as a rhizome that is sitting in a middle ground receiving the sun, the snow and the rain without ever knowing how the final product of that planting will look like or how green eventually it will be; as an assemblage that is in constant move, and because of this, its edges are never fixed.

For precisely these reasons, I am introducing the notion of the rhizome, as a third idea from D & G, to the analysis of Blackness. To propose a 'rhizomatic analysis of Blackness' is to propose a political project that is both mindful of its necessity given the Western epistemic violence that is crushing Black people and their creativity, but simultaneously conscious of its nuances, multiplicities and ever-changing definition. For Deleuze and Guattari (1987), a rhizome is a crabgrass-like figuration which the authors contrast to the arborified tree-and-root system of power distribution as it functions on individuals and society at large (see Figure II). A rhizome is a web-like fabric which "must be produced, constructed, a map that is always detachable, connectable, reversible, modifiable, and has multiple entryways and exits and its own lines of flight" (21). Working against facile notions of 'roots' and 'origins,' a rhizome is always in "a middle (*milieu*) from which it grows and which it overspills" (21). As such, the rhizome resists verticality and chronological 'lines of flight,' where its growth is contained and conceived in a linear, arborescent and systematic line. Line of flight means a path, a line of possibilities. Used in the plural and the singular, in the end, line of flight is about pursuing and following paths where the end result is either unknown (rhizome) or assumed to be known, binary and totalizing (arborescent). As such, Deleuze and Guattari (1987)

> Every rhizome contains lines of segmentarity according to which it is stratified, territorialized, organized, signified, attributed, etc., as well as line of deterritorialization down which it constantly flees ... These lines always tie back to one another. That is why one can never posit a dualism or a dichotomy, even in the rudimentary form of the good and the bad (D & G 1987, 9).

argue, the rhizome is altogether different than the arborescent. It is more complex, complicated, fluid, multiple, multiplying and forever becoming. The rhizome is a constant flow or movement of deterritorialization. It is not a point we reach, and once and for all we say: We are finally there! Rather, it is a way of becoming which we are forever struggling to attain. Being open to the unknown, the rhizome is an uncontainable dimension "or rather directions in motion" (21) that are forever in "between things, interbeing, intermezzo" (7). This, for me, is how the analysis of Blackness should be approached: an extremely complex political project that is attempting to de-reterritorialize and name itself and its subjectivity, but as it does that, it needs to be conscious that its definition is never finished. Becoming-Black is an ontological as much as it is an epistemic project. Ontologically, the pain of the Middle Passage is real, racism is real and the killing of our people by the police, especially in the U.S., is real. How this pain is talked about epistemically, however, will find itself in a constant state of flow, deterritorialization and multiplicity. There is no simple reading and definitely no simple identity in which we slot ourselves; we are forever becoming. If we reach anything, as the chapters in this volume show, we reach what I am calling a *rhizomatic analysis of Blackness*.

Figure II: https://jennymackness.wordpress.com/rhizo14-research/

Take V: There is no Blackness without the Black Body

Thus, there is no rhizomatic analysis of Blackness without the Black body. The Black body is both real and invented semiotic space. The latter, which Deleuze and Guattari (1987) refer to as "institutional body" (158), is the idea of Blackness that was first invented by Linnaeus and fully developed by the Western episteme to enslave, colonize and subjugate so-called Black people (Sauer 1993). As such, it does not need the individual body; in fact, the individual body (the real) is subjugated to the idea. From a White Western perspective, I see your body as Black, therefore you are Black! That is to say, I will signify your individual so-called Black body according to what I already know about Blackness.

It is important to note that the knowledge and ideas that (White) people construct about Black people is not something that people simply carry in their heads; it has direct impact and repercussion and bodily felt by the subjugated Black body/person/subject. We thus move from the semiotic body (the idea, the institutional) to the anatomical body (the individual), but this move is bi-redirectional: there is no Black body without the idea of Blackness and there is no Blackness without the Black body. Each is dependent on the other. In the West, put otherwise, racism against the Black body can only flourish within a semiotic and a semantic framework where the idea of Blackness is already signified, drawn and assembled.

Take VI: The Story of the Assembled Body

> We were a politicized grouping of student/activists, athletes, those looking for a place to hang/out, street-wise players & partiers, and people who were just dissatisfied with not seeing enough blackness in school and in the society, generally. We *weren't* [italics added] "Black" where we came from in the West Indies, but in Toronto we had to confront the fact that we were seen as "Black," and had to check/out for ourselves what this blackness was (Clifton, cited in Prince 2000, 16-17).

Joseph Clifton is talking about and living the tension between the semiotic and anatomical Black body in Canada, where the Black body is assumed to belong somewhere else when the Black body has arrived in Canada as early as 1605 (Ibrahim and Abdi 2016). Over 54% of Black Canadians are born in this country. Except for Japanese Canadians, who have a higher Canadian-born rate (65%), more than half of Black Canadians are born in Canada, compared to 29% of South Asians and 25% of the Chinese (Milan and Tran 2004). Furthermore, more than 10% of Black Canadians are third-generation Canadians, and in certain parts of Canada where there is a longer history of Black settlement, more than 84% of Blacks are at least third-generation Canadians (James et al. 2010 35). Clearly, the Black body in Canada has a long history and ontological (i.e., physical) presence, but has very weak (if any) epistemic presence in Canadian history and in the psychic of the nation. In other words, despite its long history in Canada, it has but tenuous presence in Canadian history books.

This genealogy, however, has to be situated within a rhizomatic analysis where Blackness in Canada is ever-multinational, multilingual, multiethnic and multicultural. If studied or analyzed otherwise, it will fall into the trap of the striated and already framed Western analysis where Blackness becomes a phenotype and a biological category. Unfortunately, Blackness is here defined, framed and its meaning is already determined. My recent book, *The Rhizome of Blackness: A Critical Ethnography of Hip-Hop Culture, Language, Identity, and the Politics of Becoming*, tells the story and the odyssey of a group of continental Africans who find themselves in Canada. Some are immigrants, but primarily they are refugees. They are a group of French and English-speaking continental African youth living in southwestern and northeastern Ontario, Canada. Based on a series of critical ethnographic research projects (1996, 2007, 2011), I journal their odyssey into the process of *becoming Black*. This process is on the one hand marked by an *identification* with and a *desire* for North American Blackness; and it is on the other as much about gender and race as it is about language, displacement, identity and cultural performance. In the book, I delineate these youth desires for and identification with Blackness through language and I show how they are learning, not the so-called standard English as a Second Language (ESL), but Black English Black English as a Second Language or BESL, which they access in and through Black popular culture, namely Hip-Hop cultural identity, language practices, and ways of 'being.'

The main contention of the book is that once in North America, continental African youth enter, so to speak, or will be subject to a *social imaginary*: an assemblage of ideas, a discursive or a symbolic space in which they are already constructed, imagined, assembled, and positioned and thus treated by the hegemonic discourses and dominant groups, respectively, as Blacks. Here, I address the arborified and dominant White everyday communicative state of mind: "Oh, they all look like Blacks to me!" These youth, I contended, had no full understanding of the Black-White binaries in North America. As such, they were not Black in Africa, but they become Black in North America.

These youth form part of the political refugee and economic immigrant continental Africans who, especially since 1990s, have been crossing the Atlantic Ocean to North America in a considerable number (Ibrahim 2008; StatCan

2011). Once in North America, they join the African diaspora by becoming part of it. In a sense, one might argue, when continental Africans 'join' diasporic Africans (in North America or Europe) or when the latter 'go back' to Africa (mostly, interestingly, for tourism; otherwise in search for 'roots'), both are rubbing a symbolic act of defiance on the face of history of colonialism, imperialism and the Middle Passage. But, before joining diasporic Africans, continental Africans would have to confront this history—the history of the present (Foucault 1980)—where their bodies are *already assembled*: an *assemblage* that is set and in turn sets itself against a "striated" (Deleuze and Guttari 1987, 474) and "hegemonic" (Gramsci 1971) gaze which functions as a technology of semiotic control (Foucault 1980). This striated gaze, as I show in the book, turns their bodies into 'Black' bodies; thus making them Black. As they *become Black*, however, they would have to translate, negotiate and answer two questions. What does 'being Black' really mean in North America; that is, when Blackness is spoken, either through the body or otherwise, what kind of history and social order does it invoke and, second, if one is becoming-Black, what does this call for, entail, and hence produce? *The Rhizome of Blackness* was an answer to these questions, among others. What I have also shown in my book is the contiguous nature of identity: the cultures, histories, and languages that the youth brought with them from Africa, who came from ten different African countries from east to west and from north to south, was not seen in opposition to the 'new' cultures and languages they were learning. African traditions and languages were performed and uttered in the same sentence, at the same time, and on the same body; thus creating what I called a 'rhizomatic third space.' Clearly, there is no simple reading nor a simple process of identity formation. Blackness is complex and uniquely occupied by each of these youth.

Talking about the rhizome and the uniqueness of Blackness in the U.S., Chimamanda Ngozi Adichie (2014) addressed this episodically and with a sense of humor in her novel, *Americanah*. She locates her prose within the narratives of immigration and displacement and refers to 'Black' immigrants as non-American Blacks:

> Dear Non-American Black, when you make the choice to come to America, you become black. Stop arguing. Stop saying I'm Jamaican or I'm Ghanaian. America doesn't care. So, what if you weren't "black"

in your country? You're in America now. We all have our moments of
initiation into the Society of Former Negroes. Mine was in a class in
undergrad when I was asked to give the black perspective, only I have
no idea what that was (273).

Adichie's novel and my own studies are "working through" (Derrida,
2000) the nuances of Blackness, the complexity within, the rhizome, the multinational, multiethnic, multilingual and multicultural nature of Blackness.
We have to, therefore, broaden and decolonize Blackness from this striated
gaze, which locks it into unidimensionality. We need a rhizomatic analysis of
Blackness, where the violent Western epistemic is confronted head-on. The late
Edward Said (1994) declared it thus:

> Gone are the binary oppositions dear to the nationalist and imperialist enterprise. Instead we begin to sense that old authority
> cannot simply be replaced by new authority, but that new alignments made across borders, types, nations, and essences are rapidly
> coming into view, and it is those new alignments that now provoke
> and challenge the fundamentally static notion of *identity* that has
> been the core of cultural thought during the era of imperialism
> (xxiv, original emphasis).

And since we are not fully out this "era of imperialism" (see McLaren and
Farahampour 2005), we need to challenge this static notion of Blackness. The
present volume is a serious attempt to do this. Here, I am hoping my introduction to the *rhizomatic analysis of Blackness* is a rupture and a radical shift from
this era of colonialism and imperialism where Blackness is one-dimensionally
conceived and represented. As I show in my book, *The Rhizome of Blackness*,
identity, Blackness in this case, is not "as transparent or unproblematic" as
we previously thought, but "a "production," which is never complete, always
in process, and always constituted within, not outside, representation" (Hall
1990, 222). Without naming it as such, Stuart Hall has always called for a
rhizomatic analysis of Blackness, one where, in the case of African youth, *to
be* is *to become:* that is, to become a rhizomatic and an ambivalent product of
two, of both here *and* there, Africa *and* Canada, to become forever born in

two. This complex, fluid, multidimensional and ever-changing product is best conceived, dealt with, and analyzed within a rhizomatic analysis of Blackness. Here, there is a move between things and people, an establishment of the logic of AND, a foundation which is conscious of its own limits and its own agency and capacity for change and for liberation, an epistemic framework that is attempting to crush and demolish Western one-dimensionality, and a struggle for better conditions and a hopeful future which is working to bring into existence. Only then can we hope for an ontology, an epistemology, and a pedagogy of the oppressed (Freire 1993) that will not fall into the trap of turning us into oppressors once in positions of power.

Reference

Adichie, C. 2014. *Americanah*. Toronto: Vintage.

Brand, D. 2001. *A Map to the Door of No Return: Notes to Belonging*. Toronto: Random House

James, C., Este, D., Bernard, W., Benjamin, A., Lloyd, B., and Tuner, T. 2010. *Race & Well-being: The Lives, Hopes, and Activism in African Canadians*. Halifax: Fernwood.

Clarke, G. 2014. *Traverse*. Toronto: Exile Editions

Cooper, A. 2006. *The Hanging of Angélique: The Untold Story of Canadian Slavery and the Burning of Old Montreal*. Toronto: HarperCollins.

Dei, G. 2009. *Teaching Africa: Towards a Transgressive Pedagogy*. New York: Peter Lang

de B'béri, B., Reid-Maroney, N., and Wright, H. 2014. *The Promised Land: History and Historiography of the Black Experience in Chatham-Kent's Settlements and Beyond*. Toronto : University of Toronto Press.

Deleuze, G., and Guttari, F. 1987. *Thousand Plateaus: Capitalism and Schizophrenia*. London & New York: Continuum.

Derrida, J. 2000. *Of Hospitality*. Stanford, CA: Stanford University Press.

Foucault, M. 1980. *Power/Knowledge: Selected Interviews and Other Writings*. New York: Pantheon.

Freire, P. 1993. *Pedagogy of the Oppressed*. New York: Continuum.

Gramsci, A. 1971. *Selections from the Prison Notes*. New York: International Publishers.

Hall, S. 1990. "Cultural Identity and Diaspora." In *Identity, Community, Culture, Difference*, edited by J. Rutherford, 222-237. London: Lawrence & Wishart.

Hill, L. 2007. *The book of Negroes*. Toronto: HarperCollins.

Hill, L. 1996. *Trials and Triumphs: The Story of African-Canadians*. Toronto: Umbrella Press.

Ibrahim, A. 2008. "The New *Flâneur*: Subaltern Cultural Studies, African Youth in Canada, and the Semiology of In-betweenness." *Cultural Studies* 22(2): 234-253.

Ibrahim, A., and Abdi, A. 2016. *The Education of African Canadian Children: Critical Perspectives*. Montreal: McGill-Queen's University Press.

Ibrahim, A. 2014. *The Rhizome of Blackness: A Critical Ethnography of Hip-Hop Culture, Language, Identity, and the Politics of Becoming*. New York: Peter Lang.

Lee, E. 1985. *Letters to Marcia: A Teacher's Guide to Anti-Racist Education*. Toronto: CRRF.

McLaren, P., and Farahmandpur, R. 2005. *Teaching Against Global Capitalism and the New Imperialism: A Critical Pedagogy*. Lanham, Md.: Rowman & Littlefield.

Mensah, J. 2010. *Black Canadians: History, Experiences, Social Conditions*. Halifax: Fernwood.

Milan, A., and Tran, K. 2004. Blacks in Canada: A Long History. *Canadian Social Trends* 72: 2-7.

Prince, A. 2000. *Being Black*. Toronto: Insomniac Press.

Said, E. 1994. *Culture and Imperialism*. New York: Alfred A. Knopf.

StatCan. 2011. *Immigrant Languages in Canada*. Available: http://www12.statcan.gc.ca/census-recensement/2011/as-sa/98-314-x/98-314-x2011003_2-eng.cfm

Walcott, R. 2000. *Rude: Contemporary Black Canadian Cultural Criticism*. Toronto: Insomniac Press.

CHAPTER THREE

Body without Organs: Notes on Deleuze & Guattari, Critical Race Theory, and the Socius of Anti-racism

(REPRINTED WITH PERMISSION) Ibrahim, A. (2014). Body without organs: Notes on Deleuze & Guattari, critical race theory and the socius of anti-racism. *Journal of Multilingual and Multicultural Development* 35(3), 1-14.

> *My aim in this article is to epistemologically read Deleuze and Guattari (D & G) against critical race theory (CRT) and simultaneously delineate how D & G's notion of 'body without organs' can benefit from CRT. At first glance, especially for language instructors and researchers, these two epistemological frameworks not only compete against each other but in most cases also do not meet. For some, their utility might not even be as obvious given their philosophical and abstract nature. This article is conceptualised to show, in a modest way, their utility on the one hand and how, on the other hand, where and when they meet to create an 'anti-racism line of flight'. For those who are interested in race, language learning and institutional analysis, this is a line of flight that is full with infinite possibilities, twists and turns, and pleasant surprises, which I hope to epistemologically explore.*
>
> **Keywords:** *Deleuze & Guattari; body without organs; critical race theory; anti-racism; language learning*

A Prologue

The Body without Organs (BwO) is a limit, Deleuze and Guattari (1987) argue; specifically, it is the limit at which all the flows flow completely freely, each into the others, so that no distinctions exist among them any longer. Described as 'flows', all things in the world, Deleuze and Guattari (D & G) add, including humans, desire to flow unconstrained. In this sense, what marks a 'flow' from another 'flow' is not its distinction but its saturation. For example, as I intend to theorise in the paper using personal narrative (see also Kubota 2014, the introduction to this special issue), race is a flow but what makes it distinct from other social categories (other flows, that is) such as gender or social class is how it is experienced by different bodies. The intersection of these flows of race, gender, social class, etc. generally, but more specifically in Canada, is directly implicated in the language we learn and how we learn it (Ibrahim 2008; Kubota and Lin 2009). Building on notions of identity, investment, desire and identification, Ibrahim (2008) has shown that, in an Ontario context, a group of refugee and immigrant continental African youth invested not in 'standard' English as a second language (ESL) but Black English as a second language (BESL). Focusing on intonation, identity and citizenship, Morgan (1997), Norton (2000) and Haque (2012), respectively, have shown that the intersection between race, language learning, and institutional analysis is a 'line of flight' (a notion I will explain later) that, in Canada, is neither linear nor, unfortunately, without unpleasant surprises. In fact, Ibrahim (2008) has shown that this intersection was bodily experienced and has produced some of the most painful experiences with (individual and) institutional racism. So, instead of revisiting these contentions, my intent in this conceptual paper is to (1) build on D & G's notion of BwO, (2) introduce critical race theory (CRT) as an example of the BwO and (3) think through how this new 'rhizome' can feed into and further our understanding of anti-racism practices in general. My hope is that language instructors, researchers, and learners will find these practices useful. Here, an unstated contention in the paper is that D & G are too abstractly epistemological, rhizomatically theoretical and they might benefit from being introduced to CRT. However, CRT can also benefit from reading D & G. Stemming from this dialogic moment, this intersectionality and deterritorialisation is a new product I am calling anti-racism line of flight, which has major implications for language teachers.

There is no one but multiple: Body without Organs

> You never reach the Body without Organs, you can't reach it, you are forever attaining it, it is a limit. People ask, So what is this BwO?— But you're already on it, scurrying like a vermin, groping like a blind person, or running like a lunatic: desert traveler or nomad of the steppers. On it we sleep, live our waking lives, fight—fight and are

fought—seek our place, experience untold happiness and fabulous defeats; on it we penetrate and are penetrated; on it we love. (Deleuze and Guattari 1987, 150)

We-humans-and-scholars, it seems, are born into an existing 'socius'. This is a monstrous machine, which is experienced in and through language. It is a metaphor of and for society where attractors and opposites can and do coexist. Their coexistence means a permanent presence of tension, a tug-of-war and ongoing struggle. There are no simple resolutions within the socius, we are forever left with the curse of improvisation and living (with)in tension. But, we-humans-and-scholars are so immersed into the socius that we forget ourselves and the very structure of the socius itself. In fact, we even forget that we live in a socius, a very sophisticated machine that is working on us primarily subconsciously and through seduction, a machine that is 'under way the moment the body has had enough of organs' (Deleuze and Guattari 1987, 150). For language learners, the socius is a linguistic 'field' that is immersed into from the moment one is grasping the sound, the alphabets, the metaphors, and eventually the culture of the language and heretofore the language of the culture.

As scholars, we are 'trained' into this machine, this socius, be it through an initiation into a particular field of study, e.g. language, or a development of expertise into an area of research, e.g. linguistics. As humans, however, we are exposed, seduced (usually hegemonically) and thus left either to adapt or adopt a full range of pre-existing societal norms, values, behaviours, and ways of thinking and doing. This does not mean we become 'hypochondriac bodies', where 'organs are destroyed, the damage has already been done, nothing happens anymore' (Deleuze and Guattari 1987, 15). To the contrary, we still have subjectivity, agency, and individuality but an 'inhibited' one, in fact an 'artificial' one. We come into the world already classified and categorised based on, among others, genitals and race. We are thus given names: black/white and man/woman. But, for D & G, this categorization is neither haphazard nor without power relations, and for our discussion, it is directly implicated in the linguistic norm we learn and how we learn it (Norton 2000; Morgan 1997). Indeed, our very first initiation into language as infants teaches us how to classify, how to behave in diverse situations and especially how to behave towards differently classified and categorised 'bodies'.

Our absolute challenge here, however, is to experiment with how to humanise and liberate ourselves and our bodies from this socius, this hierarchical order of society where power is distributed vertically. When it comes to racism, some might refer to it as 'institutional racism' (see Varghese 2014). As such, those on top either imminently oppress or create a structure, a machine, and a (semiotic) language that helps continue their hierarchical position. Our experiment with becoming-human, D & G argue, begins with a name, by first conceptualising, understanding, and naming this machine: Body without Organs. Significant to note, to experience BwO is not the same as making oneself BwO (174), and the two (experiencing and making) should not be seen as separate procedures or events. After all, we are not always consciously making ourselves; sometimes we are too exhausted so we experience the socius as it comes, only to find ourselves cut in half by the machine.

But what is BwO? Carefully reading Deleuze and Guattari (1987), I see BwO in a metaphoric sense as an assemblage that does not have an end or a beginning, structure or restriction; as a state of becoming we are always at work to attain, we can never get there and once and for all say: we have reached the state of BwO. Having no beginning or an end, no structure or restriction, as we shall see below, should not obscure its reality and bodily effects. After all, some of us do experience the said 'institutional racism'. So, to grapple with this BwO, we must constantly ask not only what it is, but also (1) how is it fabricated, by what procedures and means (predetermining what will come to pass)? (2) what are its modes, what comes to pass and with what variants and what surprises, what is unexpected and what [is] expected?' (152). Put otherwise, BwO is an assemblage of ideas, structures, histories and becomings. It is a 'line of flight' or a constant state of possibilities, territorialisation, deterritorialisation and reterritorialisation. It is 'the full egg before the extension of the organism and the organisation of the organs, before the formation of the strata' (153). It is pure intensities.

> A BwO is made in such a way that it can be occupied, populated only by intensities. Only intensities pass and circulate. Still, the BwO is not a scene, a place, or even a support upon which something comes to pass. It has nothing to do with phantasy, there is nothing to interpret. The BwO causes intensities to pass; it produces and distributes them in a *spatium* that is itself intensive,

lacking extension. It is nonstratified, unformed, intense matter...
[where] there are no negative or opposite intensities. (Deleuze and
Guttari 1987, 153; emphasis in original)

If BwO is a 'nonstratified, unformed and intense matter' where 'there are no negative or opposite intensities', on the one hand, and that it is 'never yours or mine. It is a body. It is an involution but always a contemporary, creative involution' (Deleuze and Guattari 1987, 164), then we need to reconceptualise the idea of the 'body' itself. The notion of the body, for D & G, involves both the anatomical body that each one of us has (the individual body) and all social formations where people are relationally dependent on something or someone (the institutional body). The body is a structural 'whole' consistent of different 'parts' or 'organs' and these organs depend on each other and each functions individually for the benefit of the whole (the institution, if you like). The parts within this whole, also known as 'the entity' (158), are signified or become meaningful only within a 'field' or a 'plane'. By field and plane D & G are referring to a semiotic space, which has its own infrastructure, norms, values, expectations and ways of thinking and becoming. Thus, one may argue, there is no racism (the body) without a 'field' or a 'plane', where language is central, that allows it to flourish and creep in sometimes unexpectedly but mostly expectedly in the west (Stanley 2011).

Deleuze and Guattari (1987) refer to this organisation of the organs, this sophisticated and mostly subconscious process of becoming as 'organism'. To explain let us take the example of the far-right organisation, which advocates for white supremacy, white nationalism, and anti-immigration policies: The Ku Klux Klan (KKK). According to D & G's conceptualization, the body (KKK) is made up of parts (or organs, that is, actual people and ideas) with identifiable characteristics (ways of thinking, dressing, etc.) that predispose the whole to certain habitual patterns of behaviour and action. But this does not mean a loss of individuality, so what makes the KKK a 'body' or a 'flow' is precisely the similarity to itself across variations. That is to say, it is how the parts conflate and feed into each other that variations are subsumed under that which the parts have in common. So, the KKK-body is grasped solely from the point of view of its generality, i.e. the general idea or norm attached to it. For language learners, a 'table' is not a separate signifier, but it should be understood as part of and within a whole semiotic, syntactic, morphological and cultural system.

When it comes to us humans, we all, without exception and in any linguistic field or power relationship, function as 'organs of the organism'. Whether we like it or not, we are constantly named, categorised, and classified—be it at work or school (managers, workers, students, teachers, etc.), in the family (father, daughter, etc.), in politics (Member of Parliament, Prime Minister, voter, etc.), or in the media (audience, producers, etc.). We are continually stratified, and for Deleuze and Guattari (1987), there are three strata on the body: the organism, significance and subjectification. As 'the judgment of God, from which medical doctors benefit and on which they base their power' (159), 'the organism' functions as a body's whole articulation, that is to say as the complex ways in which a body presents itself in the given restrictions. The 'significance' functions as a space of semiotic accumulation and coagulation, which includes how the body gets interpreted and how it interprets others. As for 'subjectification' or 'subjection', it is the fenêtre or the window through which the body passes only to be looked at in exactly one way; and as a result of passing through that narrow labyrinth, it is forced to articulate itself in exactly that expected way and no other. Summarising these three strata, D & G put it thus:

> You will be organized, you will be an organism, you will articulate your body—otherwise you're just depraved. You will be signifier and signified, interpreter and interpreted—otherwise you're just a deviant. You will be a subject, nailed down as one, a subject of the enunciation recoiled into a subject of the statement—otherwise you're just a tramp. (159)

Two points to retain thus far: (1) as soon as we come into existence, through very complicated mechanisms including language, desire, belonging, and love, we absorb the values of society and in turn obey them as we are expected to, or else we are called 'depraved, deviant or tramp'. Therefore, unless she consciously takes herself out of the 'system', the child might end up absorbing institutional racism without ever knowing. That is why, (2) we must resist the organism, and our resistance will begin first and foremost by becoming conscious of the fact that we are supporting the organism and in turn our own suppression. Being trapped in this organism, Deleuze and Guattari (1987) explain, we find ourselves in a paradoxical, even paranoid if not schizophrenic, existence. We are taught using morality, ethics, religion, and education that we must strive to overcome, to transcend oppressive and discriminatory societal values but, we are squarely trapped in the organism, which makes it impossible to fulfil this desire. We are left exposed heretofore to infinite dissatisfaction. To reverse this with the aim of reaching a level of satisfaction we must make a radical shift from this oppressive, vertical hierarchy to a horizontal distribution of power. We must liberate ourselves and without a middle (wo)man we must talk to the liberated. We must talk to the liberated using our own voice and language, and that can happen only when we are conscious language learners. We must, finally, make ourselves Bodies without Organs. For D & G, when talking directly to each other as a liberatory linguistic event, there must not be any kind of medium between two liberated bodies. Only then can we commence to talk about the 'plane of consistency.'

To understand the plane of consistency, Deleuze and Guattari (1987) offer the idea of the 'rhizome'. Horizontally positioned, the rhizome is not a point we reach; it is a way of thinking and becoming. Tentatively, one may propose it as a radical way for language teaching and learning. Radically conceived, almost anarchist in nature, the goal of the rhizome is '[t]o reach, not the point where one no longer says I, but the point where it is no longer of any importance whether one says I' (3). The rhizome, then, is a metaphor that is invoked and provoked for three reasons: (1) to question the verticality of power relation as it is currently existing in the organism, (2) to remind us and indicate our rootedness into the organism, from which we need to liberate ourselves (including the traditional ways in which we learn language) and (3) to indicate the multiple possibilities that we need to envision, work towards and become aware of their existence. To envision these possibilities, we need a plane of consistency.

For Deleuze and Guattari (1987), consistency does not mean homogeneity, but a dynamic holding together of disparate elements, parts or organs. The plane of consistency is an existential place of consciousness where we practice constant 'experimentation' and 'nomadism'. It is a radical place where we 'destratify' ourselves, that is, totally de-skin ourselves and abolish the three strata of organism, significance, and subjectification. The plane of consistency requires us to get rid of most, if not all of our expectations and habits, including even language. To liberate ourselves we need to realise that the organism is not a judgement or fabrication of God but of people, a historical product that is kept there for a reason. So, how do we reach this plane of consistency? We cannot yet; not while we are existing in, conforming to and unquestionably absorbing the norms and values of the organism.

Nonetheless, Deleuze and Guattari (1987) offer us some possible ideas, or 'lines of flight' to think about as we attempt to work towards this plane of consistency. First, we need to 'conjugate the intensities produced' on and by each BwO, 'by producing a continuum of all intensive continuities' (158). In other words, we need to connect, help, and push each other to 'think through' (Derrida 1996) how to abolish the oppressive structure of the organism and, in turn, become BwO. Second, this connection should be conceived as an 'assemblage' of people and ideas: a 'whole diagram' (Deleuze and Guattari 1987, 161) as opposed to individual efforts. Through this assemblage we can create a committed coalition at least to begin dismantle the organism (e.g. institutional racism). But, third, caution is necessary; we need to be mindful of how far and how fast we dismantle the organism. After all, 'overdosage is a danger', and to dismantle 'has never meant killing yourself, but rather opening the body to connections that presuppose an entire assemblage, circuits, conjunctions, levels, and thresholds, passages and distributions of intensity, and territories and deterritorializations measured with the craft of a surveyor' (160). Moreover, D & G add, '[y]ou don't reach the BwO, and its plane of consistency, by wildly destratifying' because those who do would empty 'themselves of their organs instead of looking for the point at which they could patiently and momentarily dismantle the organisation of the organs we call the organism' (160–161). Put otherwise, consciousness—political, social or otherwise—does not happen overnight. If ever one has this feeling of an 'overnight consciousness', then one is in danger of harming not only her/himself but also most likely the people around her/him. Consciousness, after all, is not an event; it is an arduous and slow process.

Following the same line of thinking, Deleuze and Guattari (1987) remind us, fourth, not to 'throw the strata into demented or suicidal collapse, which brings them back down on us heavier than ever. This is how it should be done' (161). They write:

> Lodge yourself on a stratum, experiment with the opportunities it offers, find an advantageous place on it, find potential movement of deterritorialization, possible lines of flight, experience them, produce flow conjunctions here and there, try out continuums of intensities segment by segment, have a small plot of new land at all time. (161)

Fifth, if we 'are in a social formation', crucially important is the need to see how this social formation 'is stratified for us and in us and at the place where we are' (161). Then, finally:

> gently tip the assemblage, making it pass over to the side of the plane of consistency. It is only there that the BwO reveals itself for what it is: connection of desire, conjunction of flows, continuum of intensities. You have constructed your own little machine, ready when needed to be plugged into other collective machines. (161)

Body without Organs?: de/re/territorializing racism through CRT

Taking the preceding conceptualisation, I want to do two things in what follows. First, I will introduce the broad strokes and tenets of CRT, and second, think about race and its epiproduct, racism, as the organism that is emotionally taxing and painfully experienced by those at its receiving end (Kubota 2014). I will, in conclusion, offer this juxtaposition as an 'assemblage' that anti-racism workers and students might find useful in the Canadian and other contexts, especially for language learners, teachers, and researchers. Ultimately, I am arguing that Deleuze and Guattari's (1987) conceptualisation might be practiced in the most unexpected of places. That is, given the abstractly theoretical writing of D & G, I am proposing CRT as a helpful mechanism to concretely work through the notion of BwO. Introducing CRT, here is my way of grounding D & G and making them practically conceivable. CRT, on the other hand, can also benefit from deskinning by opening itself to some conceptual deterritorialisation, to new lines of flight. This new assemblage is what I am calling anti-racism line of flight.

According to Delgado and Stefancic (2001), CRT came into existence in the mid-1970s as a radical protest movement by scholars of colour within legal studies. Initiated by the African-American legal scholar and philosopher Derrick Bell, the movement was called Critical Legal Studies (CLS), and was set to question and expose the 'internal and external inconsistencies' of the legal doctrine and reveal the ways that 'legal ideology has helped create, support, and legitimate (North) America's present class structure' (Crenshaw 1988, 1350). 'Critical race theory is, thus, both an outgrowth of and a separate entity from ... critical legal studies (CLS)'

(Ladson-Billings 1998, 10). Central to both CLS and CRT is the saliency of race and its documented outcome: racism (Dei 1996; Ibrahim 2008; Kubota and Lin 2009).

Race is not seen here as competing with or conceived against gender, sexuality, class, ability and other social categories. CRT highlights race precisely because it is probably the only category that brings chill in the air once it is mentioned (Ibrahim 2004). People are uncomfortable talking about it and as CLS highlighted, race is legalistically, scholarly or societally either subsumed under 'ethnicity' or gets totally neglected (Collins and Solomos 2010). Yet, as an organism in North America, race is always-already present in every social configuring of people's lives, even in all white towns (Nelson 2010). Moreover, given the dominant nature of whiteness in North America, 'whites reach the conclusion that their whiteness is meaningful' (Roediger 1991, 3). This is why we need to open up and deterritorialise race in North America, especially whiteness. For Ladson-Billings (1998, 9):

> [i]t is because of the meaning and value imputed to whiteness that CRT becomes an important intellectual and social tool for deconstruction [deterritorializing], reconstruction [reterritorializing], and construction [territorializing]: deconstruction of oppressive structures and discourses, reconstruction of human agency, and construction of equitable and socially just relations of power.

Recapping CRT's contention and approach to race, Ladson-Billings (1998, 9) continues:

> Our notions of race (and its use) are so complex that even when it fails to 'make sense' we continue to employ and deploy it. I want to argue, then, that our conceptions of race, even in a postmodern and/or postcolonial world, are more embedded and fixed than in a previous age. However, this embeddedness or 'fixed-ness' has required new language and constructions of race so that denotations are submerged and hidden in ways that are offensive though without identification. Thus, we develop notions of 'conceptual whiteness' and 'conceptual blackness' (King 1992) that both do and do not map neatly on to bio-genetic or cultural allegiances.

One can already sense what Deleuze and Guattari (1987) were talking about: that the organism (race/racism) is too complex and complicated, it is rhizomatic, absorbed, and naturalised; so much so that, first, it requires 'new language' and, second, most people would have a 'whole diagram' (linguistic, semiotic and conceptual categories) tightly linked to whiteness (e.g. school success and achievement, beauty, middle classness, etc.) or blackness (gangs, basketball players, violence, etc.; see especially Leonardo 2009). As already indicated, this is by no means meant to create a modernist binary opposition between blackness and whiteness. Rather, following D & G, it is a testimony to 'how, in a racialised society where whiteness is positioned as normative, everyone is ranked and categorised in relation to these points of opposition' (Ladson-Billings 1998, 9). Not to your benefit, one could hear D & G repeating, 'You will be organized' (Deleuze and Guattari 1987, 159), numbered, and categorised. Therefore, if we want to become BwO, the new monster or the organism we need to struggle against is no longer solely the broad category of 'race' but more specifically 'whiteness': its language, norms, values, ways of thinking and becoming; the hierarchical strata it creates; the symbolic and material capital it generates to its own benefit; and its ultimate product: white supremacy (see also Stanley 2011). This critique is one of the five principles of CRT, to which I will turn now.

Grounding the rhizome: foundational principles of CRT

First, if it does not take it for granted, at minimum CRT begins with the notion that racism is an organism that is so much absorbed and naturalised that it is not aberrant any more, at least in North America. 'It is so enmeshed in the fabric of our social order', Ladson-Billings (1998) contends, 'it appears both normal and natural to people in this culture' (11) Clearly, there is nothing natural about social order and social phenomena. They are socially and historically specific and tend to work for the benefit of those who categorise, number and naturalise in the first place. Our strategy is to de-skin, destratify, unmask and expose the organism (racism) in its various forms, shapes, and permutations.

Second, CRT sees experiential knowledge and storytelling as two lines of flight for developing a CRT analytic standpoint. When CRT was initiated, the notion of storytelling as a legitimate mechanism for knowledge production was not a given idea. However, as Ladson-Billings (1998) has argued, deploying storytelling is a powerful tool to 'analyze the myths, presuppositions, and received wisdoms that make up the common culture about race and that invariably render blacks and other minorities one-down' (11). On the other hand, the shared history of abjection and otherness is experienced by so many that it creates an assemblage, a coalition of people where one story is recognised as many. Therefore, the experience of oppression (be it racism or sexism) can be a powerful starting point for the making of CRT. Experience, moreover, does not know exclusion. So, '[t]o the extent that Whites (or in the case of sexism, men) experience forms of racial oppression, they may develop such a standpoint' (11). For example, a white family who adopts transracially will, according to Ladson-Billings, no longer be white. They will become a racialised alterity or other. In sum, experiential knowledge and storytelling are deemed a crucial rhizome among CRT scholars precisely because they add necessary texture, 'contextual contours to the seeming "objectivity" of positivist perspectives' (11).

Third, CRT sees liberalism as a problem and mounts a fierce critique against it. To change the organism (racism), CRT argues, a monumental shift is required, but liberalism has neither the stamina nor the mechanism for such a change. In the USA, for example, it took close to 50 years to strike down the Jim Crow Law that segregated blacks and whites in the South (Bell 1992). Even though things do change in a liberal system, that change is so incremental and painstakingly slow that the Voting Rights Act, which restored and protected voting rights of African-Americans, was not passed until 1965 (Ward and Lott 2007). Liberals approach radical shifts with trepidation and agitation because they are comfortable and benefit from the current structure. They either do not understand the limits of current paradigms or find it hard to conceive that oppressed minorities can no longer sit-and-wait for change to happen. The urgency of the moment is a central line of flight for CRT; time will change nothing, people do.

Fourth, there are no guarantees in social, political, and justice struggle. Indeed, related to the previous point of the liberal perspective, it seems that the main beneficiaries of civil rights legislation in the USA, for example, which is proposed to close the gap with minority under-representation in income and the job place, are white women (Zamudio 2011). This is a significant piece of information to acknowledge as we look at how far we have come as a society of unequals striving for justice and better moral compass. Yet, as we name this discouraging fact, we-the-categorised-other need a coalition, an assemblage first among ourselves and then with the majoritarian-white people. We need to think about the common lines of flight, points of interest, and a rhizome under what Derrick Bell (2004) calls 'interest-convergence'. In Canada, we see this interest-convergence with our aboriginal residential schools. A large coalition of aboriginals, other minoritarian groups and whites came together under the rhizome of justice, thus forcing the Canadian federal government to acknowledge historical injustices and seek ways to rectify them (Donald 2010; Haig-Brown 2003). This assemblage, one may argue, is unified by three common interests: (1) to understand how a regime of white supremacy has been created historically and maintained in our present day structure and paradigm, (2) to decipher the complex and complicated ways in which this regime subordinates people of colour to the benefit of the organism and its different organs and (3) to challenge and change the unnatural bond between social orders, especially the law, and racial power.

Fifth, related to the point of storytelling, CRT scholars argue that the stories of 'ordinary people' are yet to be fully told (Zamudio 2011; Zinn 2010). This is because literary and research canons are in search for 'objective' and 'scientific' methodologies (Smith 2012). But the failure to make it to prominence in research and literature 'does not make the stories of ordinary people less important' (Ladson-Billings 1998, 13). Flipping the script (as we say in hip hop) by working upside down, CRT centralises the muted, silenced, and neglected stories of the marginalised. It focuses on the role and the power of 'voice' as a line of flight that brings untold stories to the forefront and additional power to the discourses of racial and social justice, especially in the law and education. Here, experience 'can be a way to know and can inform how we know what we know' and storytelling, voice, and personal testimony are 'such fertile ground for the production of liberatory (praxis) because (they) usually (form) the base of our (knowledge and) theory making' (Hooks 1994, 168). To fully understand the power of storytelling, voice, and testimony, I want to tell two stories. The first is by Gloria Ladson-Billings and the second is mine. Check the following:

> **Take I**
> It had been a good day. My talk as a part of the 'Distinguished Lecture' Series at a major research university had gone well. The audience was receptive; the questions were challenging, yet respectful. My colleagues were exceptional hosts. But it also had been a tiring day—all that smiling, listening with rapt interest to everyone's research, recalling minute details of my own, trying to be witty and

simultaneously serious had taken its toll. I could not wait to get back to the hotel to relax for a few hours before dinner.... My accommodation was on the hotel's VIP floor.... As I stepped off the elevator, I decided to go into the VIP lounge, read the newspaper, and have a drink. I arrived early, just before the happy hour, and no one else was in the lounge... Shortly after I sat down comfortably with my newspaper, a White man peeked his head into the lounge, looked at me sitting there in my best (and conservative) 'dress for success' outfit—high heels and all—and said with a pronounced Southern accent, 'What time are y'all gonna be servin'?' (Ladson-Billings 1998, 7–8)

Take II
Today was the last day of my trip to Toronto after a five-month absence in Ottawa. It was 1:10 pm on a sunny and an unexpectedly hot Sunday. It all began when I had just crossed the yellow light of Bloor Street West. I saw a white car curving into the bicycle lane and I heard hereafter a siren coming from it. When it was fully halted before my bicycle, I realised it was a police car. From it came veering a rangy White man with full gear, along with a clean and handsome gun. My immediate thought was that it must be the bicycle helmet since I was not wearing one; so I whispered to myself 'oh God, this is the first ticket of my life.' He approached my bicycle and said, 'Have you ever been in trouble with the law before?' I said 'No.' 'Can I know why am I asked the question?' I added. 'You fit the description of a man we are looking for, who just snatched a bag from Yorkville; and I just saw you around the Yorkville area', he said... Looking sternly into his eyes, I repeated 'Can I know why I was stopped?' 'I told YOU Sir that you fit the description of a man we are looking for.' 'And what is that description?' I wondered. 'We are looking for a dark man with a dark bag', he said. My bag was actually light-blue. More with my eyes than with my voice, I repeated after him 'A DARK man?' Self-consciously, he exclaimed 'A Black man with a dark bag!' Before giving him my ID, he ordered me to lay down my (dark?) bag, which I did. With his order, I widely opened my bag for anyone in the street to see. Since it was

a tourist area, with the well-attended Bata Shoe Museum, everyone was looking into my bag. Some, I observed, pitied my plight and one White woman was smiling. Anyway, it was getting closer to 2 pm and my ride for Ottawa was to leave at 3 pm. At this point, I decided to use my University of Ottawa professor identification. After writing down my name and date of birth, he then announced to the dispatcher telling her 'All is OK now.' With no apologies, I was ordered to collect my affairs and my bag and, as he uttered it, 'You are free to go now.' (Ibrahim 2004, 81–83)

It is frightening how lightness (bicycling joyfully, in my case, or enjoying a relaxing moment, in Ladson-Billings' case) can so easily whirl into an unbearable heaviness, and how heaviness can cause so much pain. It is worth knowing that both Ladson-Billings and myself are full professors and in the case of Ladson-Billings, she holds the Kellner Family Chair in Urban Education at the University of Wisconsin-Madison. But that would not save us from the organism: racism.

These stories are told not to gain sympathy, we need none, but to underscore and showcase why CRT insists on storytelling as a central tenet and an important point in its paradigm. The stories are told also to demonstrate how the organism works in the everyday, how despite 'the scientific refutation of race as a legitimate biological concept and attempts to marginalize race in much of the public (political) discourse, race continues to be a powerful social construct and signifier' (Ladson-Billings 1998, 8). It is these stories, finally, that will further our understanding of the everyday racism, human degradation, and general annihilation of minoritarian bodies. They are not different nor do they occupy different strata than the ones told by Kubota (2014).

We need to 'name our reality' as Delgado and Stefancic (2001, 18) argue. We need to historicize, contextualise and situate our social reality, only then will we be able to understand and talk either with or back to others' stories. Through telling of our own stories, counterstories, revisionist histories, and parables, moreover, we are able to preserve our psyche. Building on my own personal experiences, racism is haunting and emotionally draining. It demoralises marginalised groups to the extent of selfcondemnation. Indeed, it is a major factor in school achievement or the lack thereof (Ogbu 2003). Storytelling thus becomes a healing mechanism, a medicine that makes us wide-awake (Rautins and Ibrahim 2011) and wards off the assault of racial violence and oppression. Storytelling, finally, can serve to awaken the oppressor as well. If the work of Paulo Freire (2000) has taught us anything, it is that oppressors are too oblivious to oppression. Indeed, they do not see it as oppression. Once rationalised, oppression is not only naturalised but it will cause little self-examination by the oppressor. Here, stories by historically marginalised groups can serve as the necessary catalyst to jar what Joyce King (1992) calls 'dysconscious racism'. Only then do we start the process of becoming (i.e. making ourselves) Bodies without Organs: becoming fully conscious and wide-awake.

Anti-racism lines of flight: an epilogue

Juxtaposing the two rhizomes of BswO and CRT, I want to create a plane of consistency, drawing some anti-racism lines of flight and lessons learnt from this juxtaposition, especially for language teachers. To reiterate, lines of flight are possible new ways of thinking about something: anti-racism in my case. My approach is didactic and numerical, yet tentative and non-exhaustive:

- Categories of difference include not only race, class, gender, ability, and sexuality, but also language, religion, and culture, among others. These are all flows that flow freely but how they are bodily experienced saturate them making them distinct from other flows. Here, CRT scholars remind us as language teachers of the saliency of race, a saliency that stems from its social effects despite the concept's lack of scientific basis.

- Race is not superior or above other categories of difference, but it is one category that is consistently either neglected or marginalised. Even though it works rhizomatically as an interlocking system, that is, in concert with other social categories of difference, because of history and the law, race has a particular and peculiar history. It is this history that CRT attempts to highlight and trace the different ways in which it is still alive and present with us today. In language classrooms, this can be done by deconstructing the history behind the terms we use, e.g. 'white lies'.

- The assemblage, the coalition, and the struggle is not about simply defining race, but abolishing its by-product, the organism: racism. Having accurate and faithful conceptualisation of terms is the starting point in becoming BwO. However, we should not lose sight of the fact that the struggle is not purely linguistic and definitional but above all about how different bodies live these categories.

- Nonetheless, oppression is not hierarchical, hence there is no oppression that is more significant or privileged over others, and no form of oppression should be acceptable or tolerated. The racial discrimination cannot and should not be understood separately from other forms of discrimination; yet, given the history of the term in North America, CRT strategically essentialises race and racism for historical and political reasons and purposes.

- Becoming BwO is and can be a liberatory praxis. But to access it requires an exceptional level of consciousness, which can be reached only with an intensive level of what Nieto (2000) calls basic education. Beside reading, writing, and becoming literate (Masny and Cole 2012), basic education also involves accessing, making use, deploying, and constantly opening up, questioning, and deterritorialising language of power and the power of language. This is how we become and make ourselves BwO, create a coalition with other BwO and in the process dismantle the organism.

- Becoming BwO should not be a burden placed on a few, especially those of colour and the 'minoritarian'. We should do away with the idea that minoritarian groups should teach the majoritian about themselves. In language classroom, when studying a 'minority' text, the minority student should not be looked at as the expert who is supposed to teach everyone. Instead, it is the absolute responsibility of the majoritian to become conscious and teach itself. Indeed, since the majoritian becomes majoritarian without realising it, introducing BwO as anti-racism line of flight to the majoritarian may be more important than to the minoritarian.

- Teaching, writing, and talking about becoming BwO is a political act and choice in language classroom or elsewhere. Whether one calls it BwO or not, making our students conscious of their social environment and the choices they have is not a luxury. If one chooses not to address the process of how one can make herself BwO, that is a choice in itself.

- Minoritarians need to use their own voice and tell their own stories. Not only as a healing medicine, but as a way to deterritorialise and question the societal and historical mechanisms that delegitimate their lives, knowledge, and experience. Doing so should not be an act of pity, a simple gesture of sympathy or an add-on to the already existing organism. It should be done to establish agentive and liberatory rhizome, to multiply the assemblage of multiplicity, and to root the rooted consciousness.

- In a school or language classroom setting, becoming BwO is not a unit, a lesson plan or an event, but a plane of consistency that permeates all aspects of school and a revamping of everything educational. It is a radical praxis that shows how culturally programmed orientations may lead to different points of view and that our world views are linked to time, space, history, memory, identity, and language.

- There is no One but Multiple. That is, we are forever multiplying, developing 'the law of the One that becomes two, then of the two that becomes four.' (Deleuze and Guattari 1987, 5). If this is the case, then anti-racism line of flight should provide for a holistic understanding and appreciation of the human experience, comprising social, cultural, political, ecological, linguistic, and spiritual aspects: the link between mind, body, and soul. And the rhizome of education should attend to all these.

- We need to remind ourselves that, in educational contexts, especially in language classrooms, no one rhizome or curriculum can cover everything in the world. Otherwise, it becomes an exceedingly superficial and trivialised voyeurism. Ultimately, all should feed into the assemblage of becoming BwO and thus familiarise students to think horizontally and vertically. Our gift to our students here should be to excite them to pursue their own knowledge.

- Called a 'flow', identity for anti-racism line of flight is central to the schooling process, that is, to making oneself BwO. Anti-racism line of flight recognises that students, these complex assemblages, do not go to school as 'disembodied' generic youth. They are influenced by their linguistic disposition as much as by their gender, class, racial, dis/ability and sexual identities. These are flows that affect and are affected by the schooling processes and learning outcomes. When it comes to identity, it is a luxury to be without racial, class, gender, dis/ability, or sexual identity—a luxury very few can afford (Ibrahim 2011).

- Anti-racism line of flight sees diversity and difference as a wealth that is available for the benefit of all. To do so is to tap into the linguistic and cultural knowledge of parents, guardians, and community workers and link the school and the community. Here, an inclusive school(ing) for the purpose of becoming BwO should mean a sharing of power, an active recruitment, retention and promotion of minoritian staff and teachers, and an acknowledgement that different bodies bring different forms of knowledge.

- Finally, becoming BwO as anti-racism line of flight is a dynamic, ongoing process; one is always and forever in search for it, it can never be attained once and for all. No-one ever stops becoming BwO no matter how much progress one makes. This is because becoming BwO is relational, and to enable their students to become BwO, language teachers, for example, need to make themselves BwO. A centred (language) teacher—one who is radically conscious and wide-awake, one who is immersed in her/himself and her/his limits—is probably the best gift to her/his students, who, in turn, one would hope, are desiring to become BwO.

Defined as such, becoming BwO as anti-racism line of flight 'challenges the falsehood of Eurocentric history, brings out its complexity and plural narratives, and it also fosters social cohesion by enabling students to accept, enjoy, and cope with diversity', Parekh (2000, 230) contends. As an education in freedom, becoming BwO is a rhizome through which we empower ourselves as language teachers, and in the process our students (language learners), so that we are all able to locate ourselves in time and space and acknowledge our place in the socius, the machine and the organism—locally, nationally, and internationally—and at the same time critique the adequacy of that location. Only when we recognise and name our everyday realities—that which impercetibably make us act, feel, think, and speak—can we begin the flow of de-skining, deterritorializing, and destratifying the organism. Only then can we talk about becoming or making ourselves BwO; only then can we join our First Nations in their struggle for human dignity and claim a Canadianness that is conscious of its own limits.

References

Bell, D. (1992). *Faces at the Bottom of the Well*. New York: Basic Books.
Bell, D. (2004). *Silent Covenants: Brown v. Board of Education and the Unfulfilled Hopes for Racial Reform*. New York: Oxford University Press.
Collins, P. H., and J. Solomos. (2010). *The Sage Handbook of Race and Ethnic Studies*. London: Sage.
Crenshaw, K. W. (1988). "Race, Reform, and Retrenchment: Transformation and Legitimation in Antidiscrimination Law." *Harvard Law Review* 101 (7): 1331–1387. doi:10.2307/1341398.
Dei, G. (1996). *Anti-Racism Education in Theory and Practice*. Halifax: Fernwood.
Deleuze, G., and F. Guattari. (1987). *Thousand Plateaus: Capitalism and Schizophrenia*. London: Continuum.
Delgado, R., and J. Stefancic. (2001). *Critical Race Theory: An Introduction*. New York: New York University Press.
Derrida, J. (1996). *Monolingualism of the Other, or, The Prosthesis of Origin*. Stanford: Stanford University Press.
Donald, D. (2010). *On What Terms Can We Speak? Aboriginal-Canadian Relations as a Curricular and Pedagogical Imperative*. Invited Lecture, Faculty of Education Graduate Studies, University of Lethbridge, July 2–5.
Freire, P. (2000). *Pedagogy of the Oppressed*. New York: Continuum.

Haig-Brown, C. (2003). "Creating Spaces: Testimonio, Impossible Knowledge, and Academe." *International Journal of Qualitative Studies in Education* 16 (3): 415–433. doi:10.1080/0951839032000086763.

Haque, E. (2012). *Multiculturalism within a Bilingual Framework: Language, Race and Belonging in Canada*. Toronto: University of Toronto Press.

Hooks, B. (1994). *Teaching to Transgress: Education as a Practice of Freedom*. New York: Routledge.

Ibrahim, A. (2004). "One Is Not Born Black: Becoming and the Phenomenon(ology) of Race." *Philosophical Studies in Education* 35 (1): 77–87.

Ibrahim, A. (2008). "Operating under Erasure: Race/Language/Identity." *Canadian and International Education Journal* 37 (2): 56–76.

Ibrahim, A. (2011). "Will They Ever Speak with Authority? Race, Post-Coloniality and the Symbolic Violence of Language." *Educational Philosophy & Theory* 43 (6): 619–635. doi:10.1111/j.1469-5812.2010.00644.x.

King, J. E. (1992). "Diaspora Literacy and Consciousness in the Struggle against Miseducation in the Black Community." *The Journal of Negro Education* 61 (3): 317–340. doi:10.2307/2295251.

Kubota, R. (2014). "Introduction: Race and Language Learning in Multicultural Canada." *Journal of Multilingual and Multicultural Development*. doi:10.1080/01434632.2014.892496.

Kubota, R., and A. Lin, eds. (2009). *Race, Language and Identity: Exploring Critically Engaged Practice*. London: Routledge.

Ladson-Billings, G. (1998). "Just What Is Critical Race Theory and What's It Doing in a Nice Field like Education?" *International Journal of Qualitative Studies in Education* 11 (1): 7–24. doi:10.1080/095183998236863.

Leonardo, Z. (2009). *Race, Whiteness and Education*. New York: Routledge

Masny, D., and C. Cole. 2012. *Mapping Multiple Literacies: An Introduction to Deleuzian Literacy Studies*. New York: Continuum.

Morgan, B. (1997). "Identity and Intonation: Dynamic Processes in an ESL Classroom." *TESOL Quarterly* 31: 431–450. doi:10.2307/3587833.

Nelson, C., ed. (2010). *Ebony Roots, Northern Soil: Perspectives on Blackness in Canada*. Newcastle: Cambridge Scholars.

Nieto, S. (2000). *Affirming Diversity: The Sociopolitical Context of Multicultural Education*. 3rd ed. New York: Longman.

Norton, B. (2000). *Identity and Language Learning: Gender, Ethnicity and Educational Change*. New York: Longman

Ogbu, J. (2003). *Black American Students in an Affluent Suburb: A Study of Academic Disengagement*. Hoboken: Lawrence Erlbaum.

Parekh, B. (2000). *Rethinking Multiculturalism: Cultural Diversity and Political Theory*. Cambridge, MA: Harvard University Press.

Rautins, C., and A. Ibrahim. (2011). "Wide-Awakeness: Toward a Critical Pedagogy of Imagination, Humanism, and Becoming." *International Journal of Critical Pedagogy* 3 (2): 24–36.

Roediger, D. (1991). *The Wages of Whiteness: Race and the Making of the American Working Class.* London: Verso.

Smith, L. (2012). *Decolonizing Methodologies: Research and Indigenous Peoples.* London: Zed Books.

Stanley, T. (2011). *Contesting White Supremacy: School Segregation, Anti-Racism, and the Making of Chinese Canadians.* Vancouver, BC: UBC Press.

Ward, J., and T. Lott. (2007). *Philosophers on Race: Critical Essays.* Chichester: John Wiley & Sons.

Varghese, M. M. (2014). "Commentary." *Journal of Multilingual and Multicultural Development.* doi:10.1080/01434632.2014.892504.

Zamudio, M. (2011). *Critical Race Theory Matters: Education and Ideology.* New York: Routledge.

Zinn, H. (2010). *The Unraveling of the Bush Presidency.* New York: Seven Stories Press.

Note

1 For D & G, line of flight is a line of thinking, which refers to the infinite possibilities, the twists and turns and the pleasant surprises of making oneself a BwO, as we shall see later.

CHAPTER FOUR

The Question of the Question is the Foreigner: Towards an Economy of Hospitality

(REPRINTED WITH PERMISSION) Ibrahim, A. (2005). The question of the question is the foreigner: Towards an economy of hospitality. *Journal of Curriculum Theorizing, 21*(2), 149-162.

> Isn't the question of the foreigner [*étranger*] a foreigner's question? Coming the foreigner, from abroad [*étranger*]?
> —Jacques Derrida, *Of Hospitality*[1]

> The Law of World Citizenship Shall be Limited to Conditions of Universal Hospitality
> —Emmanuel Kant[2]

"IF SOMEONE ELSE could have written my stories," Elie Wiesel said: "I would not have written them. I have written them in order to testify." To testify, Shoshana Felman argues, is "to vow to tell, to promise and produce one's own speech as material evidence for truth." This is because "no one bears witness for the witness,"[3] and as a witness, this writer is under the ethics and the obligation to testify. Here, personal testimony, personal experience, as bell hooks put it, becomes "such a fertile ground for the production of liberatory [praxis] because it forms the base of our theory making."[4] It is, or can be, a way to know and can inform how we know what we know. The story I vow to tell in this article is a personal story. It dares to *think through* the reception of my body, my name, and my accent; that is, how I am gazed at, received, and hence treated. As a "foreigner" who is put in a different line every time I fly or go through the airport, as someone who is searched in person and who missed his flight because "they" had to check whether my name was in the terrorist list, and as someone who is always told "you speak different," with an accent, the repetition of this story "appoints"[5] me to think through its significance.

This is an immigrant Black body that is assumed to be Muslim in a post-9/11 United States. It was born and grew up in Sudan, studied in France, and holds the Canadian passport. For political reasons, it found itself as a political refugee in Canada, my second home, and for job reasons, it finds itself presently in a small college town in Northwest Ohio. Involuntarily, as we shall see, it finds itself in a "third space," torn between here-and-now and there-and-memory. Given this bodily experience, the question of the question is not a theoretical one, indeed, it is too personal to be otherwise. It summons and beseeches me as a witness, and raises a number of questions: First, "how can the hosts (*hôtes*) and guests of *cities of refuge* be helped to recreate, through work and creative activity, a living and durable network in new places and occasionally in a new language"?[6] Thinking specifically of the hosts, second, what reception do they extend to foreigners, those whose papers are not in order or those simply without papers (*CF*, 16)? Third, what is the nature of this ethic of reception, this economy of hospitality and how is it cultivated? Finally, do they receive foreigners as parricides, parasites or enemies with no right to asylum and who, in their minds, potentially commit acts of terrorism, or as beings at home with themselves (*l'être-soi chez soi*)?

Let us not anticipate simple responses to such questions, yet we already know certain things about foreigners. We know that they are coming, that they are already here, that they are staring us in the eye and reminding us that we have proper names and these names refer us somewhere else: to the old country. We walk up and ask them: "what is your name? tell me your name, what should I call you, I who am calling on you, I who want to call you by your name? What am I going to call you?" (*OH*, 27). Our question was not predicated on duty and obligation but on ethos and desire. We genuinely wanted to know, but the question seemed perturbing and confusing to them, hence they were not able to answer it. They did not understand the question. They did not speak "our" language. Language cheated us hosts and guests. It stood in the middle like a haunting Kafkaesquian figure. We didn't know in what language they could address us or in what language they could receive ours; we didn't know how to interrogate them; and above all, we didn't know their names. Questions such as "who are you? where do you come from? what do you want?" (*OH*, 131) became unnecessary, if not outright violent. Contrary to their original intentionality which was warm welcoming, these questions moved us from *hospitalité* to *pas d'hospitalité*, or from hospitality to hostility.[7]

This is the question of the foreigner. The foreigner is the other, the guest, the immigrant, the exile, the deported, the expelled, the rootless, the stateless, the lawless nomad, the displaced, those who come or go abroad, those who "turn up" at our front doors and "traumatize" (*OH*, 78). They traumatize, first, because we don't know what to do with them. Do we give them asylum, "home," and thus welcome them? If so, how? Or do we expel and return them to the place from which they were expelled? Second, they traumatize us through their stories. These tend to discomfort our comfortable selves and homes. This is well illustrated in the following example. I gave a public lecture on the genocide in DarFur, Sudan, to a group of highly educated senior citizens in Northwest Ohio. One of their central questions was why should they care. They worked all their lives, they said, they saved good money and they are living good and comfortable lives. Clearly, whenever the question of the foreigner is posed, it has to be inverted into ethics: How can we go on living after witnessing trauma? Being Sudanese myself and a refugee I wonder how much I traumatize their comfortable homes! I wonder how much empathy they will offer the next refugee who knocks on their door and say, "here I am!" (*OH*, 56) Despite their absolute best intention, they invited me to talk about DarFur after all, these senior citizens cannot talk about what they do not know. And this is what makes the question of the question so urgent, especially after 9/11.

Reading through Jacques Derrida's book, *Of Hospitality*, my intent in this article is to articulate an "economy of hospitality."[8] First and primarily, I want to ask: How do we welcome the foreigner; how conditional or unconditional this welcoming, this hospitality? Second, being the foreigner myself, when do I become the host, or will I always be the guest, the perpetual foreigner? Finally, in my classroom, where I am supposed to welcome students, be the host, what does this mean in relation to being a foreigner? The paper is guided by two hypotheses: 1) in North America, I shall always be the "foreigner" thanks to language, race, and my proper name, but 2) this foreignness becomes a resource, source, and capital from which to draw and thanks to which I can *be* a host in my classroom. I am using the term North America through out the paper to refer to Canada (where I lived) and the U.S. (where I am living). The reader is thus requested kindly to travel with me back and forth, North and South of the 49th Parallel.[9]

UN/CONDITIONAL HOSPITALITY

The law of hospitality is a law of tension. In fact, Derrida argued, the law of hospitality is plural, it contains two laws: conditional and unconditional. Unconditional or absolute hospitality is a law that breaks with the law of hospitality as right or duty. Instead, it "requires that I open up my home and that I give not only to the foreigner ... but to the absolute, unknown, anonymous other, and that I give place to them, that I let them come, that I let them arrive, and take place in the place I offer them, without asking of them either reciprocity (entering into a pact) or even their names" (*OH*, 25). It is an unquestioning welcome, where a double effacement takes place: an effacement of the question *and* the name. They both take a back seat, become unnecessary. However, Derrida asked, "Is it more just and more loving to question or not to question? to call by the name or without the name?" (*OH*, 29). His response is emphatic in that within the law of unconditional hospitality, "Let us say yes to who or what turns up, before any determination, before any anticipation, before any identification, whether or not it has to do with a foreigner, an immigrant, an invited guest, or an unexpected visitor, whether or not the new arrival is citizen of another country, a human ... or a divine creature ... male or female" (*OH*, 77).

To do so, unconditional hospitality calls for suspending language, holding back of the temptation to ask the other who s/he is, what her/his name is, where s/he comes from, etc. (135). Unconditional hospitality, in sum, is a gracious act, a gift that is not governed by duty (performed out of duty), and certainly not about paying a debt or participating in an economy of exchange: my gift should not make you feel that you owe me your life. It is a law without law (83), where the stranger turns into an awaited guest and someone to whom you say not only "come," but "enter": "enter without waiting, make a pause in our home without waiting, hurry up and come in, "come inside," "come without me," not only toward me, but within me: occupy me, take place in me" (123).

This gesture of unconditional gift, this act of love is impossible without sovereignty of oneself over one's home. The law of hospitality therefore, for Derrida, is the law of one's home. The alien, the stranger other is welcomed as non-enemy. Ironically, if not tragically, one can become xenophobic in order to protect one's sovereignty, one's own right to unconditional hospitality, the very home that makes the latter possible. (Think about the *Patriotic Act* passed by the U.S. Congress after the tragic events of 9/11, where conditional laws are imposed not only on foreigners, but on the very idea of democracy.)[10] Once this is the case, the guest becomes an undesirable foreigner and as host I risk becoming their hostage (55). Retaining the self as *self*, very significantly, I need to be master at home, affirm my being there, and retain authority over that place. I do so by "saying" (usually by passing laws): this place belongs to me, we are in my home, welcome and feel at home but on the condition that you obey the rules of hospitality. Henceforth, the foreigner is allowed to enter the host's home under conditions the host has determined.

Derrida refers to this unconditional hospitality as "*the* law,"[11] a universal, absolute and singular. For Derrida, unconditional hospitality is meaningless without its plural and dialectic other: "the laws." The laws of hospitality are an expression of earthly laws and duties that are always conditioned and conditional, hence creating conditional hospitality. *The* law is above the laws, however, as he succinctly put it, "even while keeping itself above the laws of hospitality, *the* unconditional law of hospitality needs the laws, it *requires* them" (79). This is because to become effective *the* law has to be concrete, tangible, determined, and near, otherwise it risks "being abstract, utopian, illusory, and so turning over its opposite." Conditional laws, Derrida adds, "would cease to be laws of hospitality if they were not guided, given inspiration, given aspiration, required, even, by the law of unconditional hospitality" (79).

If there are no laws governing items such as visas, border crossing, local, national and international traveling, arm sales, technological communication, or even the right to asylum, to name just a few, unconditional hospitality becomes an impossible possibility. This is due to the fact that, though we as individuals might desire living in the *ville refuge* (refuge city) or *ville franche* (open city) where migrants and the expelled may seek unconditional hospitality and sanctuary, these cities can not escape geography (where are they in the globe and how do people get there?), law (are they governed by the Geneva Convention and international laws?), language (what language do/will people speak once they get there?), etc. As a matter of fact, in the case of the State, it is illegal, not to say impossible, to welcome unconditionally, especially after 9/11 and especially in the United States. The "foreigners" in the U.S. with names like mine, Ibrahim, could recite by heart the book of "laws of conditional hospitality." Top of these laws is: Thou shall not piss off the U.S. government, represented in local police, FBI or CIA!

There can only be conditional hospitality there. Will Ibrahim always be a foreigner in North America? I will address this question later. The imaginary invoked by the name Ibrahim, significantly, recovers an *assumed* relationship between hospitality and the question, in other words of a conditional hospitality that begins with the name. The name invokes a place of birth and language. The foreigner is a foreigner by birth, born in a foreign land where people speak a different language than that of the host country. Inept at speaking the language, the foreigner "always risks being without defense before the law of the country that welcomes ... him; the foreigner is first of all foreign to the legal language in which the duty of hospitality is formulated, the right to asylum, its limits, norms, policing, etc. He has to ask for hospitality in a language which by definition is not his own" (15). A central question that Derrida poses in relation to this is: what if he was speaking the language of the host country, with all that that implies, would he still be a foreigner and how do we think about hospitality in regard to him? Thinking through my classroom, again, I will address this paradox later.

The exiles, the deported, the expelled, the rootless, the stateless, absolute foreigners, Derrida observes, share two sources of sighs, two nostalgias: *their dead ones and their language.* "On the one hand," he writes, "they would like to return, at least on a pilgrimage, to the place where their buried dead have their last resting place ... On the other hand, [they] often continue to recognize the language, what is called the mother tongue, as their ultimate homeland, and even their last resting place" (89). Clearly, we are dealing with a particular conception of language, a new name to an old phenomenon: language as a place, a homeland that never leaves us and we always come back to; a mother tongue that is a "sort of mobile habitat, a garment or a tent ... a second skin you wear on yourself" (89). Language as the last condition of belonging, the most mobile of personal bodies, my cellular phone that I carry "on me, with me, in me, as me ... a mouth, and ear, which make it possible to hear yourself-speaking" (91).

If language is so central to the experience of the foreigner, there is a second layer of language that concerns not only the foreigner but also the citizens of the host nation in general: the language of the law. In the U.S., the law (or more accurately laws) of conditional hospitality is the Law of the Father. The master of the house, the host, the authorities, the nation, the State, the boss, the spouse, the lord, the king, the president is the one who lays down the laws of hospitality. "He represents them and submits to them to submit the others to them," that is to say, he speaks with authority and through an authorized language (149). In so doing, he inflicts violence that most likely is recognized and recognizable only to and by those upon whom the laws are applied. Muslims and Middle-Easterns in the U.S. are currently experiencing what is recognized and recognizable to African Americans for a long time: the violence of being the absolute Other. Hospitality can only be conditional and to survive one is almost required to "have the gift of second sight" or, using Nietzschean terms, "the most subtle of ears" (20). That is to say, if we cannot *hear* the cry of the foreigner, and if we cannot *see* the foreigner crying—mostly because of lack experience ("For what one lacks access to from experience one will have no ear," Nietzsche argued (20)—that does not mean nothing is there, that the foreigner is not crying.

So, Derrida concludes, in the eyes of the law, the exiles, the deported, the expelled, the rootless, the stateless above all are foreigners. They should be warmly welcomed, given asylum, and have the right to hospitality, but they should fall under the law of the land, they have a reciprocal obligation. Hospitality must be extended to them, Derrida emphasized, "certainly, but remains, like the law, conditional, and thus conditioned in its dependence on the unconditionality that is the basis of the law" (73). In other words, a tension, a dialecticism must remain between *the* law and the laws of hospitality. The former is hyperbolic and unconditional and the latter is conditional and juridico-political. "We will," Derrida contends, " always be threatened by this dilemma between, on the one hand, unconditional hospitality that dispenses with law, duty, or even politics, and, on the other, hospitality circumscribed by law and duty" (135). The economy and the ethics of hospitality *must* straddle the two. The two are and should be inseparable. Ideally, they should meet in, at, and during that moment that Derrida calls "moment without moment," where they both imply *and* exclude each other, simultaneously, where they "incorporate one another at the moment of excluding one another," where they exhibit "themselves to each other, one to the others, the others to the other" (81).

PAS D'HOSPITALITÉ: BEING THE GHOST

To define who is the *xenos*, the foreigner, in a land of foreigners is virtually impossible. The very question, a critic might wonder, is unnecessary, feeds into xenophobia, and authorizes those who "speak an odd sort of language" (5) or with an "accent" be called "foreigners." My simple response is: not to speak about foreignness does not do away with the existential phenomenon of the "event" nor the violence incurred as a result of its presence. Not to talk about it is a luxury afforded to few, an ethical position that I as a displaced subject cannot afford to take. Quoting Eli Wiesel again: "If someone else could have written my stories, I would not have written them. I have written them in order to testify." And since testimony cannot be simply relayed, repeated or reported by another without thereby losing its function as a testimony,[12] there is a need for personal testimonies, as I already indicated. This debate is too significant to be put aside, but we must. We are confronted with questions of "being," not simply definitions, with the impossibility of this writer's being in North America. The questions were first raised in Canada and are continuing now in the United States. As I have shown elsewhere, most displaced subjects find themselves straddling between *here* and now and *there* and memory, between the "old" and the "new home."[13] Marked mostly by language, the question of hospitality poses itself in the everyday. It is not one that displaced subjects choose to answer but are required to answer. With regards to my "case," the question of the question is complicated by three factors: language, race, and my name. These have given me the "second sight," "the most subtle of ears" that Nietzsche talked about above, and I have every intention to use them.

Following a Hegelian philosophy, the foreigner is defined on the basis of the law which is laid down and determined by: the family, civil society, and the State (or the nation-state) (45). Within this law, the foreigner is the one who comes from abroad to a land or a country that is not his or her own by birth. They either seek permanent residency in their new "home" through immigration or for economic and/or political reasons, they seek asylum and political refugee status once in the host country. Increasingly, they could also come as students and then decide to stay. By and large, they tend to speak a different language (or languages) than the host country, but because of globalization, especially with the spread of the English language, more and more they speak the host country's language fluently but with an accent. They could even be native speakers of English, yet their "accent" will haunt and mark them forever as "foreigners." The work by Alistair Pennycook and Bonnie Norton is particularly informative in addressing this contention.[14]

In an interesting article, Sura P. Rath, an "American" of Indian descent, is asking us to "call him American." Living in the U.S. since August 31, 1975 first as a "non-resident alien" student and then as a trainee, as a permanent resident ("resident alien" or holder of the coveted "Green Card"), and finally as a "naturalized citizen"; and, on the other hand, armed with a passport that bears his name, a social security card that identifies him as a wage earner, a driver's license, a voter ID that recognizes him as a mentally sound person eligible to vote, etc. aren't these enough to "make" him "American"? His answer is:

> My self-description as an American is a spatial identity; constructed from the external territory, it has nothing to do with my *whatness*, my essence or *being* as a person, until the larger culture readjusts itself to accommodate my presence. For the time, it is a contractual arrangement: in exchange for my willingness to accept the subject-hood of the sovereign nation called the United States of America, I am 'subjectified,' branded with a territorial marker of citizenship ... Yet the territorial persona, as a mask of my identity, cannot fully represent the subject/object of my person, the material body and the psychic being.[15]

Therein lies my interest: "psychic being." The latter is not a question of law, as Hegel suggested, in fact we know the language of psychic and desire is beyond the law; lawless and can never be fully captured; something about it is always in the excess. For me, foreignness is a psychic event which is not defined solely by the foreigner but, and more importantly, by those who possess the authorized language to define, the sovereign subjects who lay out or lay down the laws of hospitality. Rath wants to "be American," but his language, culture and psychic cheat him. He will always be asked: "where are you from?" (not "who or what are you?") which is usually followed by: "no, I mean where are you *really* from?" These questions, my own experience tells me, sometimes signify a naïve curiosity but oftentimes are a resigned resentment or *ressentiment*, using a Nietzschean term.[16]

To repeat: I was born in Sudan, where I grew up and finished an undergraduate degree, the paper says, in *Études françaises*—French Studies—and Psychology. I also studied in France and spoke both French and English. Then as a political refugee, I found myself in Canada, my "home" away from "home", where I finished my graduate school in applied linguistics, curriculum and cultural studies. Given my background in linguistics, especially phonetics, I am what you might consider if not a native speaker at least a native-like speaker of English. Some words and expressions pronounce me a "foreigner" to North American English speakers, who have as many accents as there are regions. Ironically, and I have been accused of being too apt and gifted with languages, this is less so in French and the other languages I speak. More ironic is that, three years to date, I reside in Northwest Ohio as a Canadian teaching, among others, a graduate course titled, "Teaching Canada." I also teach an undergraduate course in social foundations (history, sociology, and philosophy of education) to preservice students and two graduate courses in cultural studies and philosophy of education.

Clearly, there are two sides and sites to the identity formation processes: the self and the other. My argument is that, in the larger Euro-American and Canadian societies, I shall always be asked where I come from, will I ever go back (I don't know where!), and do I like it "here." Contrary to the common saying, curiosity never kills the cat. What kills the cat is fact that it is never given a choice. Yes, I was born in a foreign land and yes, I am fully aware of the implications of this statement. By putting myself in a foreign land, one might ask, am I not feeding into, and giving ammunition to those who want to call me "foreigner"? As stated previously, I have no control over this. What I have control over is my desire, at some point, to claim – yes to tell myself that I "am" and should be treated as Canadian (and in Rath's case American).

Americanness and Canadianness are primarily narratives, stories we tell ourselves and others, a collective of ideas. The question we need to ask is whether this narrative is open to all to claim or whether it is exclusive. My contention is this, *in the imaginary and the eyes of "native speakers,"[47] if you have or speak with an accent, however slight or unpronounced it may be, and your name is Ibrahim, you will always be a foreigner.* In Canada, furthermore, if you are not White, even if you are born in Canada, foreignness will most likely be assumed. Adrienne Shadd brilliantly speaks to how psychologically taxing it can be to be "Black" and "Canadian":

> In my case, I am a fifth-generation Canadian whose ancestors came here [Canada] from the United States during the fugitive

slave era... Yet, routinely, I am asked, "Where are you from?"...
The scenario usually unfolds as follows:

"But where are you originally from?"

"Canada."

"Oh, you were born here. But where are your parents from?"

"Canada."

"But what about your grandparents?"

"They're Canadian."

As individuals delve further into my genealogy to find out where I'm "really" from, their frustration levels rise.

"No, uh (confused, bewildered) I mean ... your people. Where do your people come from?"

"The United States."

At this point, questioners are totally annoyed and/or frustrated. After all, Black people in Canada are supposed to come "the [Caribbean] islands," aren't they?[18]

As I already cited, my hospitality is conditioned by 1) language (having an accent), 2) my name (assumed to be Muslim and from the Middle East) and 3) race. Since I already addressed the language question, let me speak about the politics of race first and then my name. Before coming to North America, I argued elsewhere, I was not considered Black, as the term is defined in North America. Other terms served to patch together my identity, such as *tall*, *Sudanese*, and *basketball player*. In other words, my Blackness was not marked, it was outside the shadow of the other North American Whiteness. However, as a refugee in North America, my perception of self was altered in direct response to the social processes of racism and the historical representation of Blackness whereby the antecedent signifiers became secondary to my Blackness, and I retranslated my being: I became Black.[19]

There, I narrated a significant incident in my understanding of hospitality when one's skin color determines who/what one "is." It happened in May 16, 1999, the day I was officially declared "Black," with a White policeman who stopped me in Toronto, Canada, for no reason other than "We are looking for a dark man with a dark bag," as he uttered it. After questioning him about my "darkness," he said, "We are looking for a Black man with a dark bag." There is no need to mention that my bag is actually light-blue and now, however, I am metamorphosed from "dark" into "Black." Before asking for my ID, he asked me to lay down my (dark?) bag, which I did. With his order, I widely opened my bag for anyone in the street to see. Since it was a tourist area, everyone was looking into my bag. Some, I observed, were pitying my plight and one White woman was smiling. I first gave him my citizenship card and after 10 minutes, I decided to use my professor identification. After writing down my name and date of birth, he then announced to the dispatcher telling her "All is OK now." With no apologies, I was ordered to collect my affairs and my bag and, as he uttered it, "You are free to go now." For me, this was his way of saying: Welcome to your new "home"!

As for my name, in North America, it seems to invoke terrorism and Osama bin Laden, especially in the U.S. after 9/11, more than someone who is secular, not to say atheist. The idea that an Ibrahim can be atheist seems to surprise and trouble the imaginary of a number of people in North America. Three incidents will highlight my point. The first is a letter I received recently in February 2005 from an Islamic center in Greenville, South Carolina, to receive free copies of the Qur'an in different languages. The second is in Canada and also a letter from the Islamic Council of University Professors (ICUP) inviting me to attend a dinner hosted by the ICUP in October 2001 in Ottawa, Ontario. I did not know where my address and phone number were found, since the ICUP letter was followed by three phone calls. I wondered, subsequently, why I was invited to the ICUP dinner in the first place. I knew no one in the Council nor did I hear of it hitherto. My surprise came as no surprise, and it simply had to do with my name.

The third incident happened in Canada three days after the horror of September 11. While at home, a Pastor—who I worked with in a refugee organization—called. She explained that she was organizing a university-wide religious panel to offer condolences to and show solidarity with the victims of 9/11. Each, she added, would recite from his/her respective scripture. She would represent Christians, there was a "Jewish professor" and I would "represent Muslims," she explained. At this point, I did not know how or what "Muslims" would think of me *representing* them since to represent, for me, was to speak in their name and place. So I declined the invitation for I could not bear the responsibility of speaking in the name of "Muslims" while my very Islamic faith is doubtful.

These incidents, including the one with the police, invoke something larger than trivial letters, simple phone calls, and routine police search. Powerfully, they are telling me how my body and name are *already* "read," "marked," "positioned" and "imagined." They are imagined and read in ways that are beyond my control. Here, Ibrahim *is*, and *is* is already known. That is, given my name and my socially positioned "black" body, the Pastor, the police and the ICUP assumed their knowledge of me (almost with certainty). Thus, I become a tableau that people draw and read through however they want to. I become a ghost, a glassy figure to see through. These factors, henceforth, determine the nature of the laws (of hospitality) extended not to "me," if I can be *seen* and *heard*, but to what my accent, race, and name represent and invoke in the imaginary of the host, the "lawmaker."

IN CONCLUSION: BEING THE HOST

In my classroom, the situation is not as dramatic. In fact, not at all! It is, in two words, total opposite. I have one of the highest student evaluations at my school and university and have received a teaching award in 2001. The question I want to ask then is: what is happening to my foreignness in my classroom, and what am I doing in the classroom that students are able to *see* and *hear* me? I teach at a college of education and my undergraduate course, upon whom all my subsequent remarks are based, is a mandatory course. On average, I teach between 65-95 students each term; I have students lining up to take my course; and without any narcissism, I do receive some of the most heartwarming comments about my personality and teaching. The former would have to be put aside. It is worth noting that my students are primarily White, middle-class, females, from Northwest Ohio.

It seems that this foreigner is most at "home" in his classroom. I am able to occupy the position of the host, not in the larger North American society, but in my classroom. Once I close that door, it seems, my students and I are able to sail away in/to a "foreign" land, where *true* intellectual dialogue and human connection are possible. By virtue of culture, my students recognize—most likely, only—conditional hospitality, whereas I, as we shall see, recognize only unconditional hospitality in my cultural life. Tentatively, one might conclude, those who grow up in a culture where individuality and "my" room, "my" car, "my" house, "my" book, etc. are emphasized tend to have the cultural language of conditional hospitality. On the other hand, those who either grow up in a culture or have little material possessions tend to recognize and practice mostly unconditional hospitality.

There is a need in the following concluding paragraphs to name, sketch out my classroom philosophy, especially when it comes to the idea of teaching. Conscious of its significance in the learning process, the economy of hospitality in my classroom is best described as a Freireian praxis.[20] It does not side step the position of the foreigner, it works through it; it becomes a capital of exchange. Foreignness is not a deficit but a position to be occupied both by me and my students. It is seductive, incredibly stimulating, and a necessary imaginative space in imagining the Other. The Other is no longer outside, but inside; the Other is myself, within myself; and she is there not to be consumed but critically dialogued and engaged with.

I dare to teach—unconditionally—and "it" is not about making statements. Teaching, in my class, is an invitation, a form of seduction, a space of deskinning ourselves from ourselves and our comfortable subject positions and hence be able to meet at the rendezvous of true and absolute generosity. It is a space of open, inverted and unconditional hospitality; where unity does not mean sameness and working across difference is possible regardless of race, gender, class, ability and sexuality; where difference concerns the labor of love, freedom, and democracy as it does fear, poverty, and nihilism. It is where pedagogy of freedom becomes a second nature; the word and the world are connected; students and myself are not reduced to clients; and critical, transformative, and liberatory consciousness is our ultimate goal.

As a sovereign space, occupied by sovereign subjects, I tell my students to "enter," to "come." Once there, I am in no fear of using the power and the authority bestowed on me by credentials and institutional structures. Using does not mean abusing power, hence I lay down the classroom rules and hand to hand give the course outline as a contractual arrangement: we are hereby ready to begin a "true dialogue." It structures my power, on the one hand, and gives students responsibilities and obligations, on the other. Our rendezvous is usually in that "moment without moment," a moment of suspense, of working with and through even what we do not agree with.

This takes time and I am in no hurry. I take my time, I show my passion, I humanize and love the very act of teaching (without the grading!). I grew up within an economy of unconditional hospitality. In the African side of me, our home had little by way of material possessions, so we had to share. On the other hand, there was an unconditional gift of love, humor, security, patience, humility, and humanity. Coming to North America where individuality is the absolute signifier, my foreign consciousness manifests itself, wittingly or unwittingly, in my classroom and in my interaction with my students. I usually take my students to my "place," not the physical but the mental and the intellectual one. I invite them there, I ask them to come in, to enter that safe space. Apparently, they *see* that safety and most of the time they voluntarily come with me, within me, and I in turn within them. Once there, we laugh, we humanize and question each other. It is very beautiful there. Contrary to Anne Dufourmantelle who argued that, "Perhaps only the one who endures the experience of being deprived of a home can offer hospitality" (*OH*, 56), one doesn't have to endure the experience of being deprived of a home to be able to offer hospitality. At least, this is my hope with my students with their students. I hope, through empathy, being in my class and, like the senior citizens above, experiencing the foreigner, that the foreigner becomes them and they the foreigner. I want us to meet at the rendezvous of humanity. I want them to *see* and *hear* me, the foreigner, unconditionally. But above all, I want them to set me free, to be myself. I want to be and live in that *city of refuge*, where . . .

> *Love's procession is moving;*
> *Beauty is waving her banner;*
> *Youth is sounding the trumpet of joy;*
> *Disturb not my contrition, my blamer.*
> *Let me walk, for the path is rich*
> *With roses and mint, and the air*
> *Is scented with cleanliness.*
>   Kahlil Gibran[21]

Notes

1 Jacques Derrida, "Foreigner Question," in *Of Hospitality* (Stanford, CA: Stanford University Press, 2000), 1. This book will be cited as *OH* in the text for all subsequent references. For further, interesting, and insightful discussion on Derrida's notion of hospitality, see also Mireille Rosello, *Postcolonial Hospitality: The Immigrant as Guest* (Stanford, CA: Stanford University Press), 2001.

2 Cited in Meyda Yegenoglu, "Liberal Multiculturalism and the Ethics of Hospitality in the Age of Globalization," *Postmodern Culture* 13, 2 (2003), available: http://muse.jhu.edu/journals/postmodern_culture/v013/13.2yegenoglu.html.

3 See Shoshana Felman, "Education and Crisis, Or the Vicissitudes of Teaching," in *Testimony: Crisis of Witnessing in Literature, Psychoanalysis, and History*, eds. S. Felman & D. Laub (New York & London: Routledge, 1992), 3. Eli Wiesel is cited in Felman, 3, and "no one bears witness of the witness" is by Paul Celan and also cited in Felman, 3.

4 bell hooks, *Teaching to Transgress: Education as the Practice of Freedom* (London & New York: Routledge, 1994), 70.

5 Felman, "Education and Crisis," 1992.

6 Jacques Derrida. *On Cosmopolitanism and Forgiveness* (London & New York: Routledge, 2001), 12, emphasis added. This book will be cited as *CF* in the text for all subsequent references. For Derrida, "city of refuge" or "refuge city" (*ville refuge*) or "open city" (*ville franche*) is a new cosmopolitan (or cosmo-politics) city, a place, a concept that "has not yet arrived." It is where the foreigner in general, the immigrant, the exiled, the deported, the stateless or the displaced person may seek absolute and unconditional sanctuary from the pressures of persecution, intimidation, and exile.

7 Interestingly, if not ironically, the Latin etymology of the word "hospitality" is *hospitalitem* or *hospitalitas* meaning "friendliness to guests," which includes *hospes* or *hospitis* (meaning "guest") and *hostis* (meaning "enemy") (see http://www.etymonline.com). Therein lies the tension in the ethics of hospitality as we shall see. Do we welcome the *ghosti*, the "stranger" unconditionally as a guest or conditionally as an enemy?

8 I am using the term "economy" to think about and think through the law(s) of hospitality because the former has an implicit or assumed dynamic, on-going and organic creativity, whereas the latter has a heavy weight and top-down tone. Economy has a currency and capital of exchange. The law (or laws), on the other hand, assumes a sovereign being (the king, the president, the State, etc.) who *pronounces* it (or them) and this pronouncement (or pronouncements) in turn invokes and creates a haunting eye that is watching over us. Thinking of the visitor, this is how Derrida sees the law(s): "Above their heads, whether the visitors are sleeping, dreaming, or

making love, the laws keep watch. They watch over them, they oversee them from a place of impassivity, their glassy place, the tomb of this glass beneath which a past generation... must have laid them down, organized them, imposed them. A law is always laid down [*posée*], and even laid down against [*opposée à*] some nature; it is an instituted thesis" (*OH*, 85).

9 I recognize the sociohistorical difference between the U.S. and Canada. However, when it comes to race and the imaginary of the nation, Canada is more pronounced than the U.S. to be White (see Awad Ibrahim, ""Hey, ain't I Black too?" The Politics of Becoming Black," in *Rude: Contemporary Black Canadian Cultural Criticism*, ed. R. Walcott (Toronto: Insomniac Press, 2000), 109-136). See also the section, "Pas d'hospitalité: Being the Ghost."

10 See Noam Chomsky, *9/11* (New York: Seven Stories Press, 2001).

11 In *On Cosmopolitanism and Forgiveness*, Derrida refers to unconditional hospitality as "the Great Law of Hospitality" which he defines as "an unconditional Law, both singular and universal, which ordered that the borders be open to each and every one, to every other, to all who might come, without question or without their even having to identify who they are or whence they came. It would be necessary [therefore, he continues,] to study what was called *sanctuary*, which was provided by the churches so as to secure immunity or survival for refugees, and by virtue of which they risked becoming enclaves; and also *auctoritas*, which allowed kings or lords to shield their guests (*hôtes*) from all those in pursuit..." (*CF*, 18).

12 Felman, "Education and Crisis," 1992.

13 Awad Ibrahim, ""Hey, ain't I Black too?" The Politics of Becoming Black," in *Rude: Contemporary Black Canadian Cultural Criticism*, ed. R. Walcott (Toronto: Insomniac Press, 2000), 109-136; "Trans-re-framing Identity: Race, Language, Culture, and the Politics of Translation," *Trans/forms*, 5 (2000): 8-25.

14 Alastair Pennycook, "English in the World/the World in English," in *Analysing English in a Global context: A Reader*, eds. Anne Burns and Caroline Coffin (New York: Routledge, 2001), 78-92; *English and the Discourses of Colonialism* (New York & Londong: Routedge, 1998); Bonnie Norton, "Language, Identity, and the Ownership of English," *TESOL Quarterly*, 31 (1997): 409-429; "Toward a Pedagogy of possibility in the Teaching of English Internationally: People's English in South Africa," *TESOL Quarterly*, 23 (1989): 401-420.

15 Sura P. Rath, "Home(s) Abroad: Diasporic Identities in Third Spaces," *Jouvert*, 4, 3 (2000), available: http://social.chass.ncsu.edu/jouvert/v4i3/rath1.htm.

16 See Greg Dimitriadis and Cameron McCarthy, *Reading the Postcolonial: From Baldwin to Basquiat and Beyond* (New York & London: Teachers College Press, 2001).

17 Nuzhat Amin has shown that the Chomskyian "ideal native speaker" of English tends to be White, male, with an upper or middle-class background. See Amin, "Race and the Identity of the nonnative ESL teacher," *TESOL Quarterly*, 31 (1997): 580-583.

18 Adrienne Shadd, "Where are you really from? Notes of an "Immigrant" from North Buxton, Ontario," in *Talking about Difference,* eds. Carl E. James and Adrienne Shadd (Toronto: Between the Lines, 1994), 11.

19 See for example Awad Ibrahim *'Hey, Whassup Homeboy?' Becoming Black: Race, Language, Culture, and the Politics of Identity. African Students in a Franco-Ontarian High School*. Unpublished doctoral dissertation (OISE: University of Toronto, 1998); "Becoming Black: Rap and Hip-Hop, Race, Gender, Identity, and the Politics of ESL Learning," *TESOL Quarterly* 33, no.3 (1999): 349-369; ""Hey, ain't I Black too?" The Politics of Becoming Black," in *Rude: Contemporary Black Canadian Cultural Criticism,* ed. R. Walcott (Toronto: Insomniac Press, 2000), 109-136; "May 16, 1999: The Story of the "Dark Man"," *Inquiry: Critical Thinking Across the Discipline* 22, no. 2 (2003): 21-25.

20 See especially Antonia Darder, *Reinventing Paulo Freire: A Pedagogy of Love* (Cambridge, MA: Westview, 2002).

21 Kahlil Gibran, *The Prophet* (New York: Knopf, 1966), 120.

CHAPTER FIVE

Becoming Black: Rap and Hip-Hop, Race, Gender, Identity, and the Politics of ESL Learning

(Reprinted with permission) Ibrahim, A. (1999). Becoming Black: Rap and Hip-Hop, race, gender, identity, and the politics of ESL learning. *TESOL Quarterly* 33(3), 349-369.

> *This article is about the impact of becoming Black on ESL learning, that is, the interrelation between identity and learning. It contends that a group of French-speaking immigrant and refugee continental African youths who are attending an urban Franco-Ontarian high school in southwestern Ontario, Canada, enters a social imaginary—a discursive space in which they are already imagined, constructed, and thus treated as Blacks by hegemonic discourses and groups. This imaginary is directly implicated in whom the students identify with (Black America), which in turn influences what and how they linguistically and culturally learn. They learn Black stylized English, which they access in hip-hop culture and rap lyrical and linguistic styles. This critical ethnography, conducted within an interdisciplinary framework, shows that ESL is neither neutral nor without its politics and pedagogy of desire and investment.*

"The problem of the twentieth century is the problem of color-line," asserted Du Bois (1903, p. 13). If this is so, what are the implications of this prophetic statement for L2 learning and second language acquisition (SLA)? At the end of the 20th century, when identity formation is increasingly mediated by technological media, who learns what, and how is it learned? How do differently raced, gendered, sexualized, abled, and classed social identities enter the process of learning an L2? In a postcolonial era when postcolonial subjects constitute part of the metropolitan centers, what critical pedagogy is required in order not to repeat the colonial history embedded in the classroom relationship between White teachers and students of color? Finally, at a time when North American Blackness is governed by how it is negatively located in a race-conscious society, what does it mean for a Black ESL learner to acquire Black English as a second language (BESL)? In other words, what symbolic, cultural, pedagogical, and identity investments would learners have in locating themselves politically and racially at the margin of representation?

This article is an attempt to answer these questions. Conceptually, it is located at the borderline between two indistinguishable and perhaps never separable categories of critical discourses: race and gender. The article addresses the process of *becoming Black*, in which race is as vital as gender, and articulates a political and pedagogical research framework that puts at its center the social being as embodied subjectivities that are embedded in and performed through language, culture, history, and memory (Dei, 1996; Essed, 1991; Gilroy, 1987; Giroux & Simon, 1989; Ibrahim, 1998; Rampton, 1995). As an identity configuration, becoming Black is deployed to talk about the *subject-formation project* (i.e., the process and the space within which subjectivity is formed) that is produced in and simultaneously is produced by the process of language learning, namely, learning BESL. Put more concretely, becoming Black meant learning BESL, as I show in this article, yet the very process of BESL learning produced the epiphenomenon of becoming Black. I have argued elsewhere (Ibrahim, 1998) that to become is historical. Indeed, history and the way individuals experience it govern their identity, memory, ways of being, becoming, and learning (see also Foucault, 1979, pp. 170–184). To address questions of pedagogy in this context therefore requires attending to and being concerned with the linkages among the self, identity, desire, and the English(es) that students invest in.

BACKGROUND

This article is part of a larger ethnographic study (Ibrahim, 1998) that made use of the critical frames[1] just described and the newly developed methodological approach called *ethnography of performance*. The latter argues that social beings *perform* (Butler, 1990), at least in part, their subjectivities, identities, and desires in and through complex semiological languages, which include anything that cannot produce verbal utterances yet is ready to speak: the body, modes of dress, architecture, photography, and so on (see Barthes, 1967/1983; Halliday & Hasan, 1985). The research, which took place in an urban, French-language high

---

1 Although I do not directly cite them, my work is greatly influenced by other critical discourses, especially postcolonial (see Ashcroft, Griffiths, & Tiffin, 1995) and cultural studies (see Grossberg, Nelson, & Treichler, 1992). In fact, I see this article as a hopeful inauguration of a long dialogic journey between the encompassing field of cultural studies and the fields of ESL, applied linguistics, and SLA.

school in southwestern Ontario, Canada, looks at the lives of a group of continental Francophone African youths[2] and the formation of their social identity. Besides their youth and refugee status, their gendered and raced experience was vital in their *moments of identification*: that is, where and how they saw themselves reflected in the mirror of their society (see also Bhabha, 1994). Put otherwise, once in North America, I contend, these youths were faced with a *social imaginary* (Anderson, 1983) in which they were already Blacks. This social imaginary was directly implicated in how and with whom they identified, which in turn influenced what they linguistically and culturally learned as well as how they learned it. What they learned, I demonstrate, is *Black stylized English* (BSE), which they accessed in and through Black popular culture. They learned by taking up and repositioning the rap linguistic and musical genre and, in different ways, acquiring and rearticulating the hip-hop cultural identity.

BSE is Black English (BE) with style; it is a subcategory. BE is what Smitherman (1994) refers to as *Black talk*, which has its own grammar and syntax (see Labov, 1972). BSE, on the other hand, refers to ways of speaking that do not depend on a full mastery of the language. It banks more on *ritual expressions* (see Rampton, 1995, for the idea of rituality) such as *whassup* (what is happening), *whadap* (what is happening), *whassup my Nigger*, and *yo, yo homeboy* (very cool and close friend), which are performed habitually and recurrently in rap. The rituals are more an expression of politics, moments of identification, and desire than they are of language or of mastering the language per se. It is a way of saying, "I too am Black" or "I too desire and identify with Blackness."

By Black popular culture, on the other hand, I refer to films, newspapers, magazines, and more importantly music such as rap, reggae, pop, and rhythm and blues (R&B). The term *hip-hop* comprises everything from music (especially rap) to clothing choice, attitudes, language, and an approach to culture and cultural artifacts, positing and collaging them in an unsentimental fashion (Walcott, 1995, p. 5). More skeletally, I use hip-hop to describe a way of dressing, walking, and talking. The dress refers to the myriad shades and shapes of the latest *fly gear*: high-top sneakers, bicycle shorts, chunky jewelry, baggy pants, and polka-dotted tops (Rose, 1991, p. 277). The hairstyles, which include high-fade designs, dreadlocks, corkscrews,

---

2 By continental African, I mean Africans from the continent Africa, as opposed to diasporic African (the populace of African descent that does not live in Africa, e.g., African Americans). I use youths interchangeably with students, boys, girls, males, and females, given their arbitrary nature as a social construct.

and braids (p. 277) are also part of this fashion. *The walk* usually means moving the fingers simultaneously with the head and the rest of the body as one is walking. *The talk*, however, is BSE, defined above. Significantly, by patterning these behaviors African youths enter the realm of becoming Black. Hence, this article is about this process of becoming and how it is implicated in BSE learning.

In this process, the interlocking question of identification and desire is of particular interest. It asks the following: Who do we as social subjects living within a social space desire to be or to become? And whom do we identify with, and what repercussions does our identification have on how and what we learn? This question has already been dealt with in semiology (Barthes, 1967/1983; Eco, 1976; Gottdiener, 1995), psychoanalysis (Kristeva, 1974; Lacan, 1988), and cultural studies (Bhabha, 1994; Grossberg, Nelson, & Treichler, 1992; Hall, 1990; Mercer, 1994). I have not yet seen it raised, let alone incorporated seriously, in ESL and applied linguistics research. For instance, Goldstein (1987) focuses on the linguistic features of Black English as found in the speech of a group of Puerto Rican youths in New York City. However, she does not address the issue of what it means for Puerto Rican youths to learn Black English. What investment do they have in doing so? And what roles, if any, do race, desire, and identification have in the process of learning? Instead, Goldstein offers a very meticulous syntactico-morphological analysis. One approach does not rule out the other, but I strongly believe that it would be more fruitful for ESL pedagogy and that the nature of SLA would be better understood if both were located within a sociocultural context. Language, Bourdieu (1991) argues, has never been just an instrument of communication. It is also where power is formed and performed based on race, gender, sexuality, and social-class identity. My work differs from Goldstein's study in that it moves toward a cultural, political, and stylistic analysis.

In what follows, I discuss the research's guiding propositions, contentions, and questions and look at how I as the researcher am implicated in the research and the questions I ask. This is followed by a description of the methodology, site, and subject of my research. I then offer examples of African youths' speech in which BSE can be detected to demonstrate the interplay between subject formation, identification, and BESL learning. I also offer students' reflections and narratives on the impact of identification on becoming Black. Centralizing their everyday experience of identity, I conclude with some critical pedagogical (Corson, 1997; Peirce, 1989; Pennycook, 1994) and didactic propositions on the connections between investment, subjectivity, and ESL learning. Beginning with the premise that ESL learning is locality, I ask the following: If local identity is the site where we as teachers and researchers should start our praxis and research formulations (Morgan, 1997; Peirce, 1989; Rampton, 1995), then I would contend that any pedagogical input that does not link the political, the cultural, and the social with identity and, in turn, with the process of ESL learning is likely to fail.

My central working contention was that, once in North America, continental African youths enter a *social imaginary*: a discursive space or a representation in which they are already constructed, imagined, and positioned and thus are treated by the hegemonic discourses and dominant groups, respectively, as Blacks. Here I address the White (racist) everyday communicative state of mind: "Oh, they all look like Blacks to me!" This positionality, which is offered to continental African youths through netlike praxis[3] in exceedingly complex and mostly subconscious ways, does not acknowledge the differences in the students' ethnicities, languages, nationalities, and cultural identities. Fanon (1967) sums up this netlike praxis brilliantly in writing about himself as a Black *Antillais* coming to the metropolis of Paris: "I am given no chance, I am overdetermined from without.... And *already* [italics added] I am being dissected under White eyes, the only real eyes. I am *fixed* [italics added]. Having adjusted their microtomes, they objectively cut away slices of my reality" (p. 116).

In other words, continental African youths find themselves in a racially conscious society that, wittingly or unwittingly and through fused social mechanisms such as racisms and representations, asks them to racially fit somewhere. To fit somewhere signifies choosing or becoming aware of one's own being, which is partially reflected in one's language practice. Choosing is a question of agency; that is, by virtue of being a subject, one has room to maneuver one's own desires and choices. That is, although social subjects may count their desires and choices as their own, these choices are disciplined (Foucault, 1979) by the social conditions under which the subjects live. For example, to be Black in a racially conscious society, like the Euro-Canadian and U.S. societies, means that one is expected to be Black, act Black, and so be the marginalized Other (Hall, 1991; hooks, 1992). Under such disciplinary social conditions, as I will show, continental African youths express their moments of identification in relation to African

---

3   I understand *praxis* as a moment, a borderland of the intersection of discourse, action, and representations (Freire, 1970/1993, chap. 3). These representations and borderlands are mutually dependent and shoulder one another to create a web of meaning that can be deciphered only when all the strings are pulled together.

Americans and African American cultures and languages, thus becoming Black. That they take up rap and hip-hop and speak BSE is by no means a coincidence. On the contrary, these actions are articulations of the youths' desire to belong to a location, a politics, a memory, a history, and hence a representation.

Being is being distinguished here from *becoming*. The former is an accumulative memory, an experience, and a conception upon which individuals interact with the world around them, whereas the latter is the process of building this conception. For example, as a continental African, I was not considered Black in Africa; other terms served to patch together my identity, such as *tall, Sudanese, and basketball player*. However, as a refugee in North America, my perception of self was altered in direct response to the social processes of racism and the historical representation of Blackness whereby the antecedent signifiers became secondary to my Blackness, and I retranslated myself: I became Black.

METHOD

Site

Between January and June 1996, I conducted a critical ethnographic research project[4] at Marie-Victorin (MV),[5] a small Franco-Ontarian intermediate and high school (Grades 7–13). MV had a school population of approximately 389 students from various ethnic, racial, cultural, religious, and linguistic backgrounds. Although it is a French-language school, the language spoken by students in the school corridors and hallways was predominately English; Arabic, Somali, and Farsi were also spoken at other times. The school had 27 teachers, all of whom were White. The school archives show that until the beginning of the 1990s, students were also almost all White, except for a few students of African (read Black) and Middle Eastern descent.

For over six months, I attended classes at MV, talked to students, and observed curricular and extracurricular activities two or three times per week.

---

4   For Simon and Dippo (1986, p. 195), *critical ethnographic research* is a set of activities situated within a project that seeks and works its way towards social transformation. This project is political as well as pedagogical, and who the researcher is and what his or her racial, gender, and class embodiments are necessarily govern the research questions and findings. The project, then, according to Simon and Dippo, is "an activity determined both by real and present conditions, *and* certain conditions still to come which it is trying to bring into being" (p. 196). The assumption underpinning my project was based on the assertion that Canadian society is "inequitably structured and dominated by a hegemonic culture that suppresses a consideration and understanding of why things are the way they are and what must be done for things to be otherwise" (p. 196).
5   All names are pseudonyms.

Because of previous involvement in another project in the same school for almost two years, at the time of this research I was well acquainted with MV and its population, especially its African students, with whom I was able to develop a good relationship.

Being the only Black adult with the exception of one counselor and being a displaced subject, a refugee, and an African myself had given me a certain familiarity with the students' experiences. I was able to connect with different age and gender groups through a range of activities, initially "hanging out"[6] with the students and later playing sports with various groups. I was also approached by these students for both personal guidance and academic help. Because of my deep involvement in the student culture, at times my status as researcher was forgotten, and the line between the students and myself became blurred; clearly, we shared a safe space of comfort that allowed us to speak and engage freely. This research was as much about the youths themselves and their narration of their experiences as it was about my own; in most cases, the language itself was unnecessary to understand the plight of the youths and their daily encounters, both within MV and outside its walls.

Significantly, at the time of this research, students (or their parents) who were born outside Canada made up 70% of the entire school population at MV. Continental Africans constituted the majority within that figure and, indeed, within MV's population in general, although their numbers fluctuated slightly from year to year. However, with the exception of one temporary Black counselor, there was not one teacher or administrator of color at the school. Despite this fact, the school continued to emphasize the theme of unity within this multicultural and multiethnoracial population. The slogan that the school advertised, for instance, was *unité dans la diversité* (unity in diversity). This discourse of unity, however, remained at the level of abstraction and had little material bearing on the students' lives; it was the Frenchness of the school that seemed to be the capital of its promotion. That is, the French language, especially in Canada, represents a form of extremely important *symbolic capital*, which, according to Bourdieu (1991), can be the key for accessing *material capital*—jobs, business, and so on. Given their postcolonial educational history, most African youths in fact come to Franco-Ontarian schools already possessing a highly valued form of symbolic capital: *le français parisien* (Parisian French).

---

6 Staying somewhere to familiarize oneself with the place, its people, and their ways of being in that space. In the school, these sites are informal, such as hallways, the schoolyard, the school steps, the cafeteria, and the gymnasium, where the people in them are comfortable enough to speak their minds.

PARTICIPANTS AND PROCEDURE

My research subjects encompassed these youths and part of a growing French-speaking continental African population in Franco-Ontarian schools, which I refer to as *Black Franco-Ontarians*. Their numbers have grown exponentially since the beginning of the 1990s. The participants varied, first, in their length of stay in Canada (from 1–2 to 5–6 years); second, in their legal status (some were immigrants, but the majority were refugees); and, third, in their gender, class, age, linguistic, and national background. They came from places as diverse as Democratic Republic of Congo (formerly Zaire), Djibouti, Gabon, Senegal, Somalia, South Africa, and Togo. With no exception, all the African students in MV were at least trilingual, speaking English, French, and a mother tongue or L_1,[7] with various (postcolonial) histories of language learning and degrees of fluency in each language.

On my return to MV in January 1996 to conduct my research, I spent the first month talking to and spending time with male and female African youths of different age groups, with their permission as well as their parents' and the school administration's. I attended classes, played basketball, volleyball, and indoor soccer, and generally spent time with the students. After a month, I chose 10 boys and six girls (see Table 1) for extensive ethnographic observation inside and outside the classroom and inside and outside the school and interviewed all 16. Of the 10 boys, six were Somali speakers (from Somalia and Djibouti), one was Ethiopian, two were Senegalese, and one was from Togo. Their ages ranged from 16 to 20 years. The six girls were all Somali speakers (also from Somalia and Djibouti), aged 14–18 years.

I conducted individual interviews as well as two focus-group interviews, one with the boys and one with the girls. All interviews were conducted on the school grounds, with the exception of the boys' focus-group interview, which took place in one of the student residences. The students chose the language in which the interviews were conducted: Some chose English, but the majority chose French. I translated these interviews into English. The only Black counselor and the former Black teacher were also interviewed. The interviews were closely transcribed and analyzed. I consulted school documents and archives and occasionally videotaped cultural and sport activities; on two occasions, I gave tape recorders to students in order to capture their interactions among themselves (Rampton, 1995).

---

7 *Mother tongue* is the first-acquired language whereas L1 is the language of greatest mastery. One's mother tongue can be one's L1, but one can also have an L1 that is not one's mother tongue. This is quite common in postcolonial situations.

TABLE 1
Background of Participants Quoted in the Article

Name	Gender	Age	Grade	Country of origin	Other information
Amani	F	16	11	Somalia	Very active politically and culturally; organized Black History Month activities and wrote a theatrical play for the occasion; did not hesitate to speak her mind even before the highest official in the school's administration
Asma	F	16	11	Djibouti	Was considered one of the beauties of the school; was one of the school's most popular students; was proud of her mastery of French
Aziza	F	18	13	Somalia	Had a sister and two brothers at MV; came from a well-to-do, almost bourgeois family
Hassan	M	17	12	Djibouti	Although born in Ethiopia, presented himself as a Djiboutian as he grew up in Djibouti; was politically active; was considered by school administration and peers as an elder; received several social and academic awards
Jamal	M	18	12	Djibouti	Had dropped out of school for a period of time; at the time of the interview was holding a job while going to school part-time; was host of a local radio show airing rap in English and French
Juma	M	19	12	Senegal	Lived in the house where the focus-group interview with the boys was conducted; learned the Somali language by living with Somali students
Mukhi	M	19	12	Djibouti	Was quiet but held strong opinions; was one of the school's best basketball players
Najat	F	14	9	Djibouti	Came to Canada when she was 8 years old; lived with her single mother and her sister, who used to attend MV but transferred to an English-language school
Omer	M	18	12	Ethiopia	As an elder, spoke on behalf of African students before the school administration; was sought out for guidance by students
Sam	M	19	12	Djibouti	Had been at the school since Grade 7; was considered the "Michael Jordan" of the basketball team and "the rapper" of the school
Samira	F	16	11	Djibouti	Was popular; organized a fashion show
Shapir	M	17	12	Somalia	Had dropped out of school for one term; was taking advanced courses while enrolled in a co-op program

FINDINGS

Becoming Tri- or Multilingual: Sites and Sides of ESL Learning

Most Francophone African youths come to a Canadian English-speaking metropolis, such as Vancouver or Winnipeg, because their parents happen to have relatives in that city. I asked Hassan why his parents had considered moving to an English-speaking city as opposed to Quebec, a French-speaking province.

> First of all, we had relatives who were here. Yes, secondly, because there is French and English. It is more the relative question because you know when you go to a new country, there is a tendency to go towards the people you know. Because you don't want to adventure in the unknown; and you can't have, you also want to get help, all the help possible to succeed better. (individual interview, French)[8]

In this context, in which English is the medium of everyday interaction, African youths are compelled or expected to speak English in order to be understood and in order to perform simple daily functions like negotiating public transport and buying groceries. In the following excerpt, Aziza recounts her early days, when her competence in speaking English was limited:

> If I want to go to the boutique, I have to speak to the guy [she called him *monsieur*] in English because he doesn't speak French. If I go to the shop to buy clothes, I have to speak in English, you see. It is something that you have to do; you have to force yourself. In the early days, I used to go with my sister because my sister spoke English. So I always took her with me. Then I had to go by myself because she was not always going to be by my side. I had to speak, I had to learn to speak English so I can help myself, and I can you

---

8 Each extract is followed by the type of interview (individual or group) and the language in which it was conducted. The following transcription conventions are used:
   <u>underlined text</u> English spoken within French speech or French spoken within English speech
   [ ] Explanation or description of speaker's actions
   [...] Text omitted

> know, I can deal with anything, you see. So, in other words, you are obliged, it is something you can't escape from. Because the society is Anglophone, the country is Anglophone, the services are in English, you see, that's why. (individual interview, French)

For the youths, the inescapability of interacting in English translates into a will to learn English rapidly. Popular culture, especially television, friendship, and peer pressure, all hasten the speed of learning. The African students felt peer pressure especially in their early days in the school, when they were denigrated for not speaking English. Franco-Ontarian students, Heller (1992, 1994) explains, use English in their everyday interaction, especially outside class. If African students want to participate in schoolwide as well as in- and out-of-class activities, they have no option but to learn English. Once learned, English becomes as much a source of pride as it is a medium of communication, as Asma explained:

> If you don't speak English, like in my Grade 7, "Oh, she doesn't speak! Oh, we are sorry, you can explain to her, she doesn't understand English, *la petite*.[9] Can you?" They think that we are really stupid, that we are retarded, that we don't understand the language. Now I know English, I speak it all the time. I show them that I understand English [laughs], I show them that I do English. Oh, I got it, it gives me great pleasure.[10] (group interview, French)

Asma addresses, first, the teacher's condescending manner of speech on realizing that Asma did not speak English. Undoubtedly, this condescension leads to more pressure on Asma and African students in general to learn English. Secondly, her narrative addresses the threshold desire of a teenager who wants to fully participate in dominant markets and public spaces. Her inability to speak English, which would allow her to make friends, obstructs full participation. Yet making friends, and even learning English, is influenced by the popular

---

9   A disparaging expression commonly used to patronize and belittle
10 In another context, Asma argued that one reason for wanting to speak English is that I didn't want people talking behind my back. I wanted to so badly learn English to show them that I could do it [laughs]. And to speak English like they do. And I am really really <u>I'm happy I did that. I'm very proud of myself</u> (group interview, French).

imaginary, representation, and culture: television. I asked students in all of the interviews, "Où est-ce que vous avez appris votre anglais?" (Where did you learn English?). "Télévision," they all responded. However, within this *télévision* is a particular representation—Black popular culture—seems to *interpellate*[11] (Althusser, 1971) African youths' identity and identification. Because African youths have few African American friends and have limited daily contact with them, they access Black cultural identities and Black linguistic practice in and through Black popular culture, especially rap music videos, television programs, and Black films. Following is a response to my query about the last movies a student had seen:

> Najat: I don't know, I saw *Waiting to Exhale* and I saw what else I saw, I saw *Swimmer*, and I saw *Jumanji*; so wicked, all the movies. I went to *Waiting to Exhale* wid my boyfriend and I was like "men are rude" [laughs].
>
> Awad: Oh believe me I know I know.
>
> Najat: And den he [her boyfriend] was like, "no, women are rude." I was like we're like fighting you know and joking around. I was like, and de whole time like [laughs], and den when de woman burns the car, I was like, "go girl!" You know and all the women are like, "go girl!" you know? And den de men like khhh. I'm like, "I'm gonna go get me a popcorn" [laughs]. (individual interview, English)

Besides showing the influence of Black English in the use of *de, den, dat*, and *wicked* as opposed to, respectively, *the, then, that*, and *really really good*, Najat's answer shows that youths bring agency and social subjectivities to the reading of a text. These subjectivities, importantly, are embedded in history, culture, and memory. Two performed subjectivities that influenced Najat's reading of *Waiting to Exhale* were her race and gender identities. Najat identified with Blackness embodied in a female body; the Black/woman in burning her husband's car and clothes interpellates Najat.

---

11 The subconscious ways in which individuals, given their genealogical history and memory, identify with particular discursive spaces and representations and the way this identification participates hereafter in the social formation of the Subject (identity).

Another example in a different context demonstrates the impact of Black popular culture on African students' lives and identities. Just before the focus-group interview with the boys, *Electric Circus*, a local television music and dance program that plays mostly Black music (rap/ hip-hop, reggae, soul, and rhythm and blues) began. "Silence!" one boy requested in French. The boys started to listen attentively to the music and watch the fashions worn by the young people on the program. After the show, the boys code switched among French, English, and Somali as they exchanged observations on the best music, the best dance, and the cutest girl. Rap and hip-hop music and the corresponding dress were obviously at the top of the list.

The moments of identification in the above examples are significant in that they point to the process of identity formation that is implicated in turn in the linguistic norm to be learned. The Western hegemonic representations of Blackness, Hall (1990) shows, are negative and tend to work alongside historical and subconscious memories that facilitate their interpretations by members of the dominant groups. Once African youths encounter these negative representations, they look for Black cultural and representational forms as sites for positive identity formation and identification (Kelly, 1998). An important aspect of identification is that it works over a period of time and at the subconscious level. In the following excerpt, Omer addresses the myriad ways in which African youths are influenced by Black representations.

> Black Canadian youths are influenced by the Afro-Americans. You watch for hours, you listen to Black music, you watch Black comedy, Mr. T,[12] the Rap City, there you will see singers who dress in particular ways. You see, so. (individual interview, French)

Mukhi explored the contention of identification by arguing that

> We identify ourselves more with the Blacks of America. But, this is normal, this is genetic. We can't, since we live in Canada, we can't identify ourselves with Whites or country music, you know [laughs]. We are going to identify ourselves on the contrary with people of our color, who have our lifestyle, you know. (group interview, French)

---

12   Host of a local rap music television program called Rap City, which airs mostly U.S. rap lyrics.

Mukhi evokes biology and genetic connection as a way of relating to Black America, and his identification with it is clearly stated. For all the students I spoke to, this identification was certainly connected to their inability to relate to dominant groups, the public spaces they occupied, and their cultural forms and norms. Black popular culture emerged as an alternative site not only for identification but also for language learning.

"A'ait, Q7 in the House!"[13]

For the students I interviewed, rap was an influential site for language learning. The fact that rap linguistic performance was more prevalent in the boys' narratives than in the girls' raises the question of the role of gender in the process of identification and learning.

On many occasions, the boys performed typical gangster rap language and style, using language as well as movement, including name calling. What follows are just two of the many occasions on which students articulated their identification with Black America through the recitation of rap linguistic styles.

> Sam: One two, one two, mic check. A'ait [aayet], a'ait, a'ait.
>
> Juma: This is the rapper, you know wha 'm meaning? You know wha 'm saying?
>
> Sam: Mic mic mic; mic check. A'ait you wonna test it? Ah, I've the microphone you know; a'ait.
>
> Sam: [laughs] I don't rap man, c'mon give me a break. [laughs] Yo! A'ait a'ait you know, we just about to finish de tape and all dat. Respect to my main man [pointing to me]. So, you know, you know wha 'm mean, 'm just represen'in Q7. One love to Q7 you know wha 'm mean and all my friends back to Q7 ... Stop the tapin' boy!
>
> Jamal: Kim Juma, live! Put the lights on. Wardap. [students talking in Somali] Peace out, wardap, where de book. Jamal 'am outa here.
>
> Shapir: Yo, this is Shapir. I am trying to say peace to all my Niggers, all my bitches from a background that everybody in the house. So, yo, chill out and this is how we gonna kick it. Bye and with that pie. All right, peace yo.

---

13 *A'ait* = all right; Q7 = the clique to which the students belong; *in the house* = present.

> Sam: A'ait, this is Sam represen'in AQA [...] where it's born, represen'in you know wha 'm mean? I wonna say whassup to all my Niggers, you know, peace and one love. You know wha 'm mean, Q7 represen'in for ever. Peace! [rap music]
>
> Jamal: [as a DJ] Crank it man, coming up. [rap music] (group interview, English)

Of interest in these excerpts is the use of BSE, particularly the language of rap: "respect to my main man," "represen'in Q7," "peace out, wardap," "'am outa here," "I am trying to say peace to all my Niggers, all my bitches," "so, yo, chill out and this is how we gonna kick it," "I wonna say whassup to all my Niggers," "peace and one love." On the other hand, when Shapir offers "peace to all" his "Niggers," all his "bitches," he is first reappropriating the word *Nigger* as an appellation that is common in rap/hip-hop culture. That is, friends, especially young people, commonly call a Black friend *Nigger* without its traditional racist connotation. Second, however, Shapir is using the sexist language that might exist in rap (Rose, 1991). These forms of sexism have been challenged by female rappers like Queen Latifa and Salt-N-Pepa and were critiqued by female and male students. For example, Samira expressed her dismay at the sexist language found in some rap circles:

> OK, hip-hop, yes I know that everyone likes hip-hop. They dress in a certain way, no? The songs go well. But, they are really really, they have expressions like fuck, bitches, etc. Sorry, but there is representation. (group interview, French)

Here, Samira addresses the impact that these expressions might have on the way society at large perceives the Black female body, which in turn influences how it is represented both inside and outside, rap/hip-hop culture. Hassan as well expressed his disapproval of this abusive language: "Occasionally, rap has an inappropriate language for the life in which we live, a world of violence and all that" (individual interview, French).

In rap style, one starts a performance by "checking the mic": "One two, one two, mic check." Then the rapper either recites an already composed lyric or otherwise "kicks a freestyle," displaying the spontaneity that characterizes rap. The rapper begins the public performance by introducing herself or himself with a true or made-up name ("Yo, this is Shapir") and thanking her or his "main man," or best friend, who often introduces the rapper to the public. Specific to gangster rap, one represents not only oneself but a web of geophysical and metaphorical spaces and collectivities that are demarcated by people and territorial spaces: "represen'in Q7," "a'ait, this is Sam represen'in AQA." At the end of the performance, when the recitation or freestyle is completed, again one thanks the "main man" and "gives peace out" or "shad out" (shouts out) to the people.

The boys were clearly influenced by rap lyrics, syntax, and morphology (in their broader semiological sense), especially by gangster rap. In learning ESL in general and BSE in particular through music, Jamal used significant strategies, including listening, reading, and repeating: He was listening to the tunes and lyrics while reading and following the written text. Acting as a DJ, he then repeated not only the performer's words and expressions but also his accent.

Depending on their age, the girls, on the other hand, had an ambivalent relationship with rap, although they used the same strategies as Jamal in learning English through music. For example, during a picnic organized by a group of males and females, the females listened to music while following the written text and reciting it (complete with accents) along with the singer. The girls' choice of music (including songs performed by Whitney Houston and Toni Braxton) differed in that it was softer than that chosen by the boys and contained mostly romantic themes.

For the most part, the older females (16–18 years old) tended to be more eclectic than the younger ones in how they related to hip-hop and rap. Their eclecticism was evident in how they dressed and in what language they learned. Their dress was either elegant middle class, partially hip-hop, or traditional, and their learned language was what Philip (1991) calls *plain Canadian English*. The younger females (12–14 years old), on the other hand, like the boys, dressed in hip-hop style and performed BSE.

In spite of their ambivalent relationship to rap and hip-hop, I detected the following three features of BE in both the older and the younger girls' speech:

1. the absence of the auxiliary be (19 occasions, e.g., "they so cool" and "I just laughing" as opposed to *they are so cool* and *I am just laughing*);

2. BE negative concord (4 occasions; e.g., "all he [the teacher] cares about is his daughter you know. If somebody just dies or if I decide to shoot somebody you know, he is *not* doing *nothing* [italics added]"; the expression would be considered incorrect in standard English because of the double negative); and
3. the distributive *be* (4 occasions, e.g., "I be saying dis dat you know?" or "He be like 'Oh, *elle va être bien*' [she's going to be fine]").

These BE markers are both expressions of the influence of Black talk on the girls' speech and performances of the girls' identity location and desire, which they apparently ally with Blackness. (For a description of BE features, see Goldstein, 1987; Labov, 1972.)

Performing Acts of Desire

I have identified rap and hip-hop as influential sites in African students' processes of becoming Black, which in turn affected what and how the students learned. Their narratives also show that the youths were quite cognizant of their identification with Blackness and the impact of race on their choices. In the following conversation, Mukhi reflected on the impact of rap (as just one among many other Black popular cultural forms) on his life and the lives of those around him:

Awad: But do you listen to rap, for example? I noticed that there are a number of students who listen to rap eh? Is . . .

Sam: It is not just us who listen to rap, everybody listens to rap. It is new.

Awad: But do you think that that influences how you speak, how . . .

Mukhi: *How we dress, how we speak, how we behave* [italics added].
(group Interview, English)

The linguistic patterns and dress codes that Mukhi addresses are accessed and learned by African youths through Black popular culture. As I have noted, these patterns and codes do not require mastery and fluency. Indeed, they are performative acts of desire and identification. As Amani contended,

> We have to wonder why we try to really follow the model of the Americans who are Blacks. Because *when you search for yourself, search for identification, you search for someone who reflects you, with whom you have something in common* [italics added]. (group interview, French)

Hassan supported Amani as follows:

> Hassan: Yes yes, African students are influenced by rap and hip-hop because they want to, yes, they are influenced probably a bit more because it is the desire to belong maybe.
>
> Awad: Belong to what?
>
> Hassan: To a group, belong to a society, to have a model/fashion [he used the term *un modèle*]; you know, the desire to mark oneself, the desire to make, how do I say it? To be part of a rap society, you see. It is like getting into rock and roll or heavy metal. (individual interview, French)

Hence, *one invests where one sees oneself mirrored*. Such an investment includes linguistic as well as cultural behavioral patterns. In an individual interview, Hassan told me it would be unrealistic to expect to see Blackness allied with rock and roll or heavy metal, as they are socially constructed as White music. On the other hand, he argued emphatically that African youths had every reason to invest in basketball—which is constructed as a Black sport—but not hockey, for example.

CONCLUSION: IDENTITY, DISCIPLINE, AND PEDAGOGY

Analogously, the desire on the part of African youths, particularly the boys, to invest (Peirce, 1997) in basketball is no different from their desire to learn BESL. Learning is hence neither aimless nor neutral, nor is it free of the politics of identity. As I have shown, an L2 learner can have a marginalized linguistic norm as a target. But why would these youths choose the margin as a target? What is their investment and politics in doing so? And what role, if any, do race, gender (sexuality), and differences in social class play in their choices? In other words, if youths come to the classrooms as embodied subjectivities that are embedded in history and memory (Dei, 1996), should we as teachers not couple their word with their world (Freire, 1970/1993)?

Clearly, my perspective is an interdisciplinary one that may have raised more questions than it has satisfactorily answered. However, my intention has been to ask new questions that link identity, pedagogy, politics, investment, desire, and the process of ESL learning by borrowing from cultural studies. I have discussed how a group of continental African youths were becoming Black, which meant learning BESL. Becoming Black, I have argued, was an identity signifier produced by and producing the very process of BESL. To become Black is to become an ethnographer who translates and looks around in an effort to understand what it means to be Black in Canada, for example. In becoming Black, the African youths were interpellated by Black popular cultural forms, rap and hip-hop, as sites of identification. Gender, however, was as important as race in what was being chosen and translated, and by whom and how it was chosen and translated.

Choosing the margin, I emphasize, is simultaneously an act of investment, an expression of desire, and a deliberate counterhegemonic undertaking. The choice of rap especially must be read as an act of resistance. Historically, rap has been formed as a voice for voicelessness and performed as a prophetic language that addresses silence, the silenced, and the state of being silenced. It explores the hopes and the human, political, historical, and cultural experience of the Black Atlantic (Gilroy, 1993). As Jamal argued,

> Black Americans created rap to express themselves; how do I say it? Their ideas, their problems, [and] if we could integrate ourselves into it, it is because rappers speak about or they have the same problems we have. (individual interview, French)

Such problems may include human degradation, police brutality, and everyday racism (Anthias & Yuval-Davis, 1992; Essed, 1991).

If learning is an engagement of one's identity, a fulfillment of personal needs and desires (of being), and an investment in what is yet to come, any proposed ESL pedagogy, research, or praxis that fails to culminate in these will quite obviously not draw in the youths described in this article and is therefore bound to be unsuccessful, if not plainly damaging. Identity, as re- and preconfigured here, governs what ESL learners acquire and how they acquire it. What is learned linguistically is not and should not be dissociable from the political, the social, and the cultural. Hence, to learn is to invest in something (e.g., BESL) that has a personal or a particular significance to who one is or what one has become. Because language is never neutral, learning it cannot and should not be either. Thus we as teachers must, first, identify the different sites in which our students invest their identities and desires and, second, develop materials that engage our students' raced, classed, gendered, sexualized, and abled identities.

I therefore identify and propose rap and hip-hop (and Black popular culture in general) as curriculum sites where learning takes place and where identities are invested. In the language of antiracism education (Dei, 1996; hooks, 1994), this proposition is, on the one hand, a call to centralize and engage marginalized subjects, their voices, and their ways of being and learning and, on the other, a revisit to this question: In the case of African youths, whose language and identity are we as TESOL professionals teaching and assuming in the classroom if we do not engage rap and hip-hop? That is, whose knowledge is being valorized and legitimated and thus assumed to be worthy of study, and whose knowledge and identity are left in the corridors of our schools? To identify rap and hip-hop as curriculum sites in this context is to legitimize otherwise illegitimate forms of knowledge. As Bourdieu (1991) shows, wittingly or unwittingly, schools sanction certain identities and accept their linguistic norm by doing nothing more than assuming them to be the norm; we as teachers should remember that these identities are raced, classed, sexualized, and gendered.

However, because rap and hip-hop are also historical and social productions, they are as much sites of critique as they are sites of hope. As noted, rap and hip-hop are not immune to, for example, sexism (and homophobia; see also Rose, 1991). Therefore, they should not be readily consumed but should be critically framed, studied, and engaged with. To be able to do so, however, teachers need first to be in tune with popular culture, for television, music, newspapers, and other media—not the classroom—are increasingly the sources from which students learn English. Second, teachers who are unfamiliar with popular culture should engage the Freireian notion of dialecticism, in which their students can become their teachers. In practical terms, this might mean planning activities in which students explain to the teacher and to the rest of the class what rap and hip-hop are and what they represent to the students.

Rap and hip-hop are also sites of hope and possibility: the hope that all learners (from dominant groups or others) can be introduced to and be able to see multiple ways of speaking, being, and learning. In the case of African students, in particular, rap and hip-hop are sites of identification and investment. To introduce them in the classroom, to paraphrase Freire (1970/1993), is to hope to link their world, identities, and desires with their word. To put it more broadly, maybe the time has come to close the split between minority students' identities and the school curriculum and between those identities and classroom pedagogies, subjects, and materials.

Acknowledgments

I thank Loreli Buenaventura, Alastair Pennycook, and the anonymous reviewers for their comments and feedback.

The Author

Awad El Karim M. Ibrahim teaches at the Faculty of Education, University of Ottawa. His areas of interest are antiracism, cultural studies, the sociology of race and ethnicity, and the sociology of language.

References

Althusser, L. (1971). *Lenin and philosophy and other essays*. London: New Left Books.
Anderson, B. (1983). *Imagined communities: Reflections on the origin and spread of nationalism*. London: Verso.
Anthias, F., & Yuval-Davis, N. (1992). *Racialized boundaries*. London: Routledge.
Ashcroft, B., Griffiths, G., & Tiffin, H. (Eds.). (1995). *The postcolonial studies reader*. New York: Routledge.
Barthes, R. (1983). *Elements of semiology*. New York: Hill & Wang. (Original work published 1967)
Bhabha, H. (1994). *The location of culture*. London: Routledge.
Bourdieu, P. (1991). *Language and symbolic power* (G. Raymond & M. Adamson, Trans.). Cambridge: Polity Press.
Butler, J. (1990). *Gender trouble: Feminism and the subversion of identity*. New York: Routledge.
Corson, D. (1997). Critical realism: An emancipatory philosophy of applied linguistics? *Applied Linguistics*, 18, 166–188.

Dei, G. J. S. (1996). *Anti-racism education: Theory and practice.* Halifax, Canada: Fernwood.
Du Bois, W. E. B. (1903). *The souls of black folk.* New York: Penguin Books.
Eco, U. (1976). *A theory of semiotics.* Bloomington: Indiana University Press.
Essed, P. (1991). *Understanding everyday racism.* Newbury Park, CA: Sage.
Fanon, F. (1967). *Black skin, white masks.* New York: Grove Weidenfeld.
Foucault, M. (1979). *Discipline and punish: The birth of the prison* (A. Sheridan, Trans.). New York: Vintage Books.
Freire, P. (1993). *Pedagogy of the oppressed.* New York: Continuum. (Original work published 1970)
Gilroy, P. (1987). *There ain't no black in the Union Jack: The cultural politics of race and nation.* London: Hutchinson.
Gilroy, P. (1993). *The Black Atlantic: Modernity and double consciousness.* London: Routledge.
Giroux, H. A., & Simon, R. (1989). Popular culture as a pedagogy of pleasure and meaning. In H. A. Giroux & R. Simon (Eds.), *Popular culture, schooling, and everyday life* (pp. 1–29). Boston: Bergin & Garvey.
Goldstein, L. (1987). Standard English: The only target for nonnative speakers of English? *TESOL Quarterly, 21,* 417–438.
Gottdiener, M. (1995). *Postmodern semiotics.* Oxford: Blackwell.
Grossberg, L., Nelson, C., & Treichler, P. (Eds.). (1992). *Cultural studies.* New York: Routledge.
Hall, S. (1990). Cultural identity and diaspora. In J. Rutherford (Ed.), *Identity, community, culture, difference* (pp. 222–237). London: Lawrence & Wishart.
Hall, S. (1991). Ethnicity: Identity and difference. *Radical America, 13*(4), 9–20.
Halliday, M. A. K., & Hasan, R. (1985). *Language, context, and text: Aspects of language in a social-semiotic perspective.* Oxford: Oxford University Press.
Heller, M. (1992). The politics of codeswitching and language choice. *Journal of Multilingual and Multicultural Development, 13,* 123–142.
Heller, M. (1994). *Crosswords: Language, education and ethnicity in French Ontario.* Berlin: Mouton de Gruyter.
hooks, b. (1992). *Black looks.* Boston: South End Press.
hooks, b. (1994). *Teaching to transgress: Education as the practice of freedom.* London: Routledge.
Ibrahim, A. (1998). *"Hey, whassup homeboy?" Becoming black: Race, language, culture, and the politics of identity. African students in a Franco-Ontarian high school.* Unpublished doctoral dissertation, Ontario Institute for Studies in Education of the University of Toronto, Canada.
Kelly, J. (1998). *Under the gaze: Learning to be Black in White society.* Halifax, Canada: Fernwood.
Kristeva, J. (1974). *La révolution du langage poétique* [Revolution in poetic language]. Paris: Lautréament et Mallarmé.

Labov, W. (1972). *Language in the inner city: Studies in the Black English vernacular.* Philadelphia: University of Pennsylvania Press.
Lacan, J. (1988). *The seminars of Jacques Lacan.* New York: Norton.
Mercer, K. (1994). *Welcome to the jungle: New politics in Black cultural studies.* New York: Routledge.
Morgan, B. (1997). Identity and intonation: Dynamic processes in an ESL classroom. *TESOL Quarterly,* 31, 431–450.
Peirce, B. N. (1997). Language, identity, and the ownership of English. *TESOL Quarterly,* 31, 409–429.
Peirce, B. N. (1989). Toward a pedagogy of possibility in the teaching of English internationally: People's English in South Africa. *TESOL Quarterly,* 23, 401–420.
Pennycook, A. (1994). *The cultural politics of English as an international language.* London: Longman.
Philip, M. N. (1991). *Harriet's daughter.* Toronto, Canada: Women's Press.
Rampton, B. (1995). *Crossing: Language and ethnicity among adolescents.* London: Longman.
Rose, T. (1991). "Fear of a Black planet": Rap music and Black cultural politics in the 1990s. *Journal of Negro Education,* 60, 276–290.
Simon, R. I., & Dippo, D. (1986). On critical ethnography work. *Anthropology and Education Quarterly,* 17, 195–202.
Smitherman, G. (1994). *Black talk: Words and phrases from the hood to the amen corner.* Boston: Houghton Mifflin.
Walcott, R. (1995). *Performing the postmodern: Black Atlantic rap and identity in North America.* Unpublished doctoral dissertation, Ontario Institute for Studies in Education of the University of Toronto, Canada.

CHAPTER SIX
===

Intersecting Language, Immigration, and the Politics of Becoming Black: Journaling a Black Immigrant Displacement

(REPRINTED WITH PERMISSION) Ibrahim, A. (original, not published). Intersecting language, immigration and the politics of becoming Black: Journaling a Black immigrant displacement

DEAR BLACK IMMIGRANTS, it seems, unbeknownst to you, when you come to North America, you have decided to "become Black." This is the case whether you come to North America voluntarily (immigrant) or involuntarily (refugees), and whether you find yourself in Canada or in the United States. As the chapters in this book show, when the Black body encounters the syntax of (im)migration and displacement, a "complicated conversation" seems to come into existence (Pinar, 2011; Ng-A-Fook, Ibrahim, & Reis, 2016). This is because, within immigration studies, Black (im)migrants not only complicate the process of displacement but also offer an identity experience that is yet to be fully understood. Adichie's (2014) novel *Americanah* offers a window into that experience. Situated squarely in the United States and using episodic style, *Americanah* offers some of the most complex conversations and perceptive prose on what it means to be Black *and* immigrant in the United States. Adichie makes her reader bear witness as her characters walk through, so to speak, what it means to become Black (Ibrahim, 2014). A tour de force, *Americanah* is narrated by a Nigerian female blogger, Ifemelu, who blogs primarily about race and immigration, namely what it means to "become (Black) American." Part of becoming American, Ifemelu concludes in one of her blogs, is the realization that "in America, you are black, baby" (p. 273). "America doesn't care" if you are Ghanaian, Jamaican, or from Jamaica, New York, Ifemelu explains, because in the case of Black immigrants, becoming American means "becoming Black." "Stop arguing. Stop saying I'm Jamaican or I'm Ghanaian. America doesn't care," Ifemelu concludes, "So, what if you weren't "black" in your country?" (p. 273).

Writing the preface of Althea Prince's book, *Being Black*, Clifton Joseph (2001) *thinks through* his experience as a Black West Indian who is encountering the *process of becoming Black* for the first time in Canada: "We weren't 'Black' where we came from in the West Indies, but in Toronto we had to confront the fact that we were seen as 'Black,' and had to check/out for ourselves what this blackness was" (pp. 16-17). The tension between Clifton Joseph's negation and the past tense in "We weren't 'Black'" in the West Indies, on the one hand, and that "in Toronto we had to confront the fact that we were seen as 'Black'," on the other, marks a radical identity shift. At both epistemological and ontological level, some have argued *to be* can never *be* (in full and in complete), since it is a work-in-progress, a continuous act of becoming (Butler, 1999; Ibrahim, 2000; Kristeva, 1974; Sartre, 1980). As such, it is a performative category that is never complete. To explain, let us take race as an example. As Chapter One in this book argues, race is not a fixed category but the repeated stylization of the body, a set of recurrent acts, words, and gestures that are performed on the surface of our bodies: in and through our modes of dress, walk, in our hair, maquillage, lip-gloss, etc. If this is the case, then race/Blackness is an ever-changing category; a set of norms, narratives, and everyday performative roles and acts; something we do every day in how we dress, walk, and talk. Conceived as such, Blackness then becomes a language we speak but it is also a language that speaks us. Given its negative history, however, it says things that are beyond our control: that Black people are violent, criminals, underachievers, etc.

One of the main objectives of this book is to rethink race, particularly Blackness, as it rubs shoulders with the experiential experience of displacement and identity. So, when this new conceptualization of race/Blackness is juxtaposed against the psychic and complicated process of immigration, it produces at least three phenomena. First, given their unfamiliarity with what it means *to be Black* in North America, Black immigrants turn into some of the best ethnographers: they observe, look around, take thorough notes, and reach some conclusions. However, given their limited interaction and friendship with actual Black bodies, especially early in their arrival in North America, Black immigrants' ethnographic notes are influenced by the representations of Blackness in the media (Ibrahim, 2014). As a result, second, Black popular culture emerges not only as a site of accessing narratives and stories of Blackness, but also as a site of language learning, as we saw in Chapter Five. Third, and finally, as they observe, take note, and make sense of the plight of Blackness in North American, a subconscious process of negotiation takes place, where Black immigrants, like all other immigrants and displaced subjects, decide on what to keep as cultural norms that they bring with them from their "homeland" and what not to keep. On the other hand, from the new socio-cultural-and-linguistic space, they take up and integrate what they like and fend off what they do not like. This is where the line between ethnicity (defined in cultural and linguistic terms) and race (defined in phenotypical basis) is so thin that it does not exist.

This space of in-betweenness where immigrants find themselves in between two or more cultures, languages, norms, or values (see Chapter Seven). If this is the case with all immigrants, Black immigration in/to North America occupies a particular and interesting place. This is because, on the one hand, Blackness has a long and complicated history in North America that goes back to the Middle Passage and slavery. On the other, when Black immigrants arrive in North America, they are immediately folded under this long history of Blackness in North America. This history, this "social imaginary" (see Chapter Five) does not allow for the multicultural, multilingual, and multinational nature of Blackness to come through. This social imaginary closes Blackness to a unidirectional painting, thus fencing it off its rhizomatic nature.

As I show in Chapter Two, the process of becoming Black and the general politics of identity and identification are and should be approached rhizomatically. There is no simple reading and definitely no simple identity into which we slot ourselves, especially when it comes to that ever-complicated intersection of immigration and Blackness. Here, we are forever becoming. If we reach anything, as this book demonstrates, we reach what I have termed elsewhere *rhizomatic identity*: a rhizomatic "assemblage" that is welcoming sociality, with everything that it brings (the good and the ugly), but with no guarantees as to what it might finally look like or what maze it has to go through to get there (Ibrahim, 2014). The rhizomatic identity of becoming Black is a tree that is welcoming the sun, the rain, the snow, and so on, whose branches and leaves are growing horizontally. There are no certainties about what shape or form they will take, or how green they will turn out to be. This rhizomatic identity of becoming Black thus finds itself in a constant state of flow, deterritorialization, and multiplicity. In this sense, to use Michael Eric Dyson's (2012) language, "Blackness is not limiting but freeing; not closed but open; not rigid but fluid" (p. xiii).

Becoming Black I: Intersecting Blackness and Language

Stuart Hall (2002) has argued that "[r]ace works like a language, and signifiers ... gain their meaning not because of what they contain in their essence, but in the shifting relations of difference which they establish with other concepts and ideas in a signifying field" (n.p.). This is why, he continues, "there is ... always something about race left unsaid" (n.p.). If race (Blackness in my case) works like a language, this presupposes that race/Blackness has grammar, syntax, and ways of speaking. I am interested in what might be called the communicative system of Blackness: how we "speak" it, what we "say" through our bodies, and what our bodies "say" to others. Clearly, how others read our Black bodies is beyond our control since their reading is historically, contextually, and socially situated. This is why I have argued: we speak Blackness as much as it speaks us. Thus, as Fanon (1967) put, the Black body, especially in Western world in general and North America in particular, no longer represents only itself, but becomes responsible for a whole race and ancestors.

Dyson (2012) argued that President Obama was "unavoidably representative of [all of] Blackness" in the United States as well as globally (p. xii). His speech, Dyson explains, became an index of his Blackness, a container where Blackness was both formed and performed. To fully grabble with and understand Dyson's argument, the very category of "language" has to be opened up. It has to be approached not in its classic linguistics sense but in a semiotic sense, where language is more than what people say (Barthes, 1983). Indeed, Barthes explains, most of what we communicate is nonverbal: through our bodies, clothes, hair, makeup, etc. He calls these "signifiers," which in turn constitute "texts" that are open for different interpretations depending on the context, the message, the sender, and the receiver (p. 13). In a semiotic sense, language does not work in mimesis; that is to say, like a mirror, where the faithful correspondence is one-to-one between language and the so-called real world (Minh-ha, 2011; Rose, 2000; Woodward, 1997). This is because meaning does not lie in the object, person, or event. "Things don't *mean*," Stuart Hall (2013) argues, "we *construct* meaning, using representational systems" (p. 25, original emphasis).

If this is the case, then the intersection between Blackness and language is complicated by at least four factors. First, if the meaning does not lie in the object, then Blackness is an empty signifier, it has no inherent meaning unless it is perceived, acknowledged, and situated within a historical, social, political, symbolic, and signifying system. This system is performed in the grammar of the every day, and its meaning is both unconsciously internalized and fixed through an exercise of power. Outside this grammar, Blackness is stripped of any market value. This is precisely the reason why, second, in my research (see for example, Ibrahim, 2017), I emphasize not race per se, but racialization—the processes of becoming Black. Third, according to Beneviste (2000), meaning is produced at the borderline between two interdependent yet dialectic entities: language system (or any other representational system) and social actors (those who create, use, and make meaning of that system). In the case of Blackness in North America, White social actors govern (Foucault, 1980) and in so many ways completely close the meaning of Blackness; thus, turning it from a subject position into an objecthood that is already known. Fourth, and finally, my own research is attempting to untangle Blackness, to free it from this infernal cyclical position. Intersecting Blackness and language is an attempt to bring humanity back into Blackness by giving language its normal functioning position. In the latter position, language is where subjectivity is constructed (formed) and represented (performed). Language allows us to re/present ourselves, and while doing so, we come to form ourselves. Put otherwise, our subjectivities are constructed and formed in and through language, and it is only in language, broadly or semiotically conceived, that we are able to talk about and/or "speak" them or be legible. In sum, read as language, Blackness is a complex syntactic, morphological, phonological, and semantic system that is forever dual: conscious and unconscious, forming and performing, constructing and representing.

Becoming Black II: Intersecting Blackness, Language, and Immigration

In what follows, we get to see the conclusions that Black immigrants reached in their understanding of what it means to be Black in North America, especially how to speak Black(ness). Except for a few studies (e.g., Coleman-King, 2014; Ibrahim, 2014; Okpalaoka, 2014), there is a lack of empirical studies that study Black immigrants systematically (see also Cooper & Ibrahim, in press). To systematically document the Black immigrant experience, I conducted three critical ethnographic studies (1998, 2007, 2011) in Ontario, Canada, where the focus was on groups of continental African youths. These youths came from across the continent and spoke at least two languages (their mother tongues and a colonial language: English and/or French). The three studies took place in three separate high schools in three regions of Ontario and asked the following questions: 1) First, what are the roads taken by African youths in their journey of integration in Canadian society, the journey of becoming Black?; 2) What is the role of race and racism in their identity formation?; 3) How are continental African youths positioned and constructed in and out of school?; 4) What are the implications of this construction in youths' social identity formation?; and 5) What are the outcomes of this journey?

Methodologically, I developed what I called elsewhere (Ibrahim, 2011) "ethnography of performance" to understand how the youths "speak" their identities, desires, and investments (p. 232). In all three studies, I was well acquainted with the schools and their populations at the time of the research. I began visiting these schools and hung out¹ with African students at least once a week, and in most cases, two or three times a week for almost six months as part of each study. I took the role of a participant-observer, keeping regular field notes. Having determined what they could offer to my research, I chose my research participants with the idea of purposeful sampling in all three studies for extensive observation in and out of school. I also interviewed them, individually or in groups at the school or at their residences. Interviews were either in English or French. I also videotaped and on two occasions handed over the tape recorders to students to capture interactions among themselves when I was not present. I attended soirées, plays, basketball games, and graduations, and I was delighted to be invited to their residences.

The sites of the research included one French-language high school in southwestern Ontario with approximately 400 diverse students from across the Francophone world, and two English-language high schools with 700 and 900 students, respectively, in northeastern Ontario. All three schools had a high concentration of continental African youths, with the continental African youth constituting close to 70% of the French-language high school. The research participants varied in their length of stay in Canada (some had arrived six months prior to the time of the research and others had been in Canada for over five years), their legal status (some were immigrants, but the majority were refugees), gender, class, age, and their linguistic and national backgrounds. They came from places as diverse as the Democratic Republic of Congo (formerly Zaïre), Djibouti,

Gabon, Nigeria, Senegal, Somalia, South Africa, Sudan, South Sudan, Togo, and Zimbabwe (among others). With no exception, all of the African students were at least bilingual, and the majority were trilingual, speaking English, French, and their mother tongues, with various postcolonial histories of language learning and degrees of fluency in each language. Despite this language history, most of them were classified as English-language learners.

All three studies were guided by the contention that African youths were not too familiar with the politics of Blackness in North America; that is, the everyday sustained and emotional subjection of what it means to be Black in North America. Once in North America, I contended, these youths were faced with a *social imaginary* in which they were already racialized as Blacks. This social imaginary was directly implicated in how and with whom they identified, which, in turn, influenced what they learned, linguistically and culturally. What they did learn was what I called Black Stylized English (BSE), which they accessed in and through Black popular culture (see Ibrahim, 2011). They learned by taking up and repositing the Rap linguistic and musical genre and, in different ways, acquiring and rearticulating Hip-Hop cultural identities.

It is worth noting that BSE is a subcategory of Black English, but it does not require a full mastery of the language (see Chapter Five). It banks on ritual expressions, which are not about language per se; they are more an expression of politics and moments of identification. It is the youths' way of saying: "We too are Black!." All three studies supported three conclusions. First, it was clear that continental African youth were taking up, performing, and "speaking" Blackness through their dress (including the myriad shades and shapes of the latest fly gear: high-top sneakers, bicycle shorts, chunky jewelry, baggy pants, and polka-dotted tops), walk (moving the fingers simultaneously with the head and the rest of the body while walking), and talk (BSE). In patterning these behaviors, African youth enter the realm of *becoming Black*. Second, as Chapter 5 shows, becoming Black meant learning Black English as a Second Language (BESL). This is a cyclical process where becoming Black means learning BESL; yet the very process of BESL learning produces the contiguous or co-phenomenon of becoming Black. Third, and finally, in a racially conscious society like the North American society, continental African youths find themselves in a difficult context where, wittingly or unwittingly and through fused social mechanisms such as racist representations, they are asked to racially fit somewhere. Fully grasping what it means to be Black in North America, these youths express their moments of identification in relation to African American and African Canadian cultures and languages, thus becoming Black. Both learning BSE/BESL and taking up Hip-Hop identity are these youths' way of "speaking" about their desire to belong to a location, a politics, a memory, and a history.

Chapter Five in this book shows that Black popular culture emerged as a site of identity and identification as well as a site of language learning. When I asked Najat (14, F, Djibouti) about the most recent movies she had seen, she responded:

> Najat: I don't know, I saw *Waiting to Exhale* and I saw, what else I saw? I saw *Swimmer*, and I saw *Jumanji*; so wicked, all the movies. I went to *Waiting to Exhale* wid my boyfriend and I was like "men are rude" [laughs].
>
> Awad: Oh believe me I know, I know.
>
> Najat: And den he [her boyfriend] was like "no women are rude." I was like we're like fighting you know and joking around. I was like, and de whole time like [laughs], and den when de woman burns the car, I was like "go girl!" You know and all the women are like "go girl!" you know? And den de men like khhh [expression of disgust]. I'm like "I'm gonna go get me a popcorn" [laughs]. (individual interview, English)

Also discussed elsewhere in this book, Najat's response is of particular interest for two reasons. First, it shows the influence of Black English in how the fricative [θ] (in the, then, and that) moves from dental (where the tongue is near the top of the teeth) to labiodental (where the lower lip is near the top teeth). Thus, the, then, and that become de, den, dat. Secondly, Najat's response shows that youths' social subjectivities, embedded in history, culture, and memory influence what they read and how they interpret it. For example, Najat's reading of *Waiting to Exhale* was influenced by her race and gender identities that were becoming and which, in turn, influenced her identification and language investments.

The following is another example (a videotaped moment), which was also discussed elsewhere in this book, demonstrating the impact of Black popular culture on African students' lives and identities. Just before a focus group interview

I conducted with the boys, *Electric Circus*, a now defunct local television music and dance program that plays mostly, if not exclusively, Black music (Hip Hop, reggae, soul and R&B) began. The boys started to listen attentively to the music and to pay attention to the different fashions of the young people on the program. After the show, the boys code-switched between French, English, and Somali as they exchanged observations on the best music, the best dance, and the cutest girl. Rap and Hip-Hop music and the corresponding dress were the spaces they named, desired, and identified with.

Clearly, there is a conclusion to be reached here: what we identify with impacts our identity formation which, in turn, impacts what we learn and how we learn it. But, it is worth noting, the work of identification is not a conscious act; indeed, most of it happens subconsciously and over a period of time. As Omer (18, M, Ethiopia) put it in the following excerpt, African youths are influenced by their identification with Black representations:

> Black Canadian youths are influenced by the Afro-Americans. You watch for hours, you listen to Black music, you watch Black comedy, Mr. T. [a Hip-Hop program anchor], the Rap City. There you will see singers who dress in particular ways. You see, so (individual interview, French)

Another student, Mukhi (19, M, Djibouti) explored the work of identification by arguing:

> We identify ourselves more with the Blacks of America. But, this is normal; this is genetic. We can't, since we live in Canada, we can't identify ourselves with Whites or country music, you know [laughs]. We are going to identify ourselves, on the contrary, with people of our color, who have our life style, you know. (group interview, French)

Here, Mukhi's invocation of "genes" is an anomaly since he was the only one in all three studies who invoked genes as connecter between him as a continental African and "Blacks of America." On the other hand, if identity is a claim (as Stuart Hall, 1996, has argued), then Mukhi and other students are claiming Blackness as a space of identification. Throughout the three studies, the youths claimed the identity they performed and performed the identity they claimed. This claim, it is worth noting, is a clear indictment of their exclusion from dominant public spaces, especially in Canada: "[W]e can't identify ourselves with Whites or country music." For Mukhi and all the students I spoke to, their inability to relate to dominant groups and their cultural practices, made Black popular culture a logical alternative site of identification and eventually language learning.

In all three studies, Hip-Hop emerged not only as a site of entertainment but as a space for language learning (see Chapter Five). However, we see this trend more dominant with the boys than the girls, which raises the gender question. Clearly, the boys throughout their ages invest in this economy of Hip-Hop and its cultural and linguistic styles. The girls, on the other hand, invest in this economy until the age of 15, then they mix styles, oscillating between African, Western, and Hip-Hop style. One explanation for this style shift in the girls is that the social, religious (quite number of my research participants are of Muslim background), and cultural norms are applied more strictly on the girls more than on the boys (see also Chapter Seven in this book).

In Chapter Five, I offer two lengthy excerpts, among so many others, in which students perform their investment in Black North America through the re/citation of Hip-Hop linguistic styles. They use this Hip-Hop linguistic style though an invocation of certain ritual expressions that are common in Hip-Hop: "peace out," "wardap," "whassup," "shad out," etc. As all social products, however, Hip-Hop is not without its critics given the sexism and the homophobia it embodies. As Samira (16, F., Djibouti) put it: "OK, Hip Hop, yes I know that everyone likes Hip Hop. They dress in a certain way, no? The songs go well. But, they are really really, they have expressions like fuck, bitches etc. Sorry, but there is representation" (group interview, French).

Samira's contention on representation needs further exploration. Samira is addressing the impact that Hip-Hop expressions might have on the way society at large relates to, consumes, and perceives the Black female body, which in turn influences how it is represented both inside and outside Hip-Hop culture. One may even argue that these narratives, which express a psychic representation and mentality, are in part responsible for Samira's precarious relation with Hip-Hop. Some boys also cited similar language of critique: "Occasionally, rap has an inappropriate language for the life in which we live, a world of violence and all that" (Hassan – 17, M, Djibouti—individual interview, French).

In sum, Hip Hop was obviously an influential site of identification and language learning. Both the boys and the girls used the same three strategies in learning ESL in general, and BSE in particular, through music: listening, reading, and reciting. Jamal, for instance (see Chapter 5), was listening to the tunes and lyrics while reading and following the written text. Acting as a DJ, he then repeated not only the performer's words and expressions but also his accent. The girls also used similar strategies to Jamal's. During a picnic organized by a mixed group of males and females, for example, they listened to music while following the written text and reciting it (complete with accents) along with the singer. The girls' choice of music (e.g., Whitney Houston and Toni Braxton, who were quite significant in the pop scene at the time of the research) differed than the music chosen by boys in that it was predominantly rhythm and blues and contained mostly romantic themes. "We have to wonder," Amani (16, F, Somalia) explains, "why we try to really follow the model of the Americans who are Black? Because when you search for yourself, search for *identification*, you search for *someone who reflects you*, with whom you have something in common [italics added]" (group interview, French).

So, as I concluded elsewhere, one invests where one sees oneself mirrored (see Chapter Five). However, this investment is not without its history and social context. Investing in Black popular culture can easily be read as a resistant act to being excluded from the dominant public space in North America. As much as this investment opens doors and opportunities, it also closes others. This is clearly the case with continental African youths, where some doors were opened while others were closed, thus influencing their language learning and identity formation.

And Immigrants Will Continue Coming: Concluding remarks

Immigrants, it seems, are at our doors and the ocean tides have been washing them ashore at beautiful and normally tranquil beaches. Like the participants in my research projects, while some reach the shores, others succumb to the deadly silence of the ocean where no one is there to hear their pain and cry as they sink into the bottom. Those who make it, oddly enough to be called the "lucky ones," produce two things. On the one hand, they turn the familiar strange because they appear suddenly and en masse and, on the other, the incoming people are themselves "strangers." They are called strangers, to use Zygmunt Bauman's (2016) explanation, precisely because they "tend to cause anxiety... [they are] fearsomely unpredictable, unlike the people with whom we interact daily and from whom we believe we know what to expect; for all we know," Bauman continues, "the massive influx of strangers might have destroyed the things we cherished—and intend to maim or wipe out our consolingly familiar way of life" (p. 8). Cautiously articulated, there is a thin line, for Bauman, between anxiety and *mixophobia*: the "fear of the unmanageable volume of the unknown, untamable, off-putting and uncontrollable" (p. 9). The social imaginary' that I discussed earlier can easily slip into mixophobia, so one has to be extremely vigilant. As we see throughout this book, immigrants can easily turn into "harbingers of bad news" (p. 15). They are not expected to be "here," they are supposed to be over "there," overseas, in a distant land that we occasionally hear about but we do not feel, smell, or touch—and we most certainly do not know its language.

But, they are "here" now, filling out our malls and living next door to us. What I tried to do in this chapter and throughout this book is to paint, journal, and offer more details on the people who are coming in through our shores and showing up at our borders. This chapter portrayed the routes that continental African youths have taken in their journey of becoming. To become Canadian or American, I have concluded, is to become Black. This is directly related to who they identify with (North American Blackness), what they learn (BSE or BESL) and how they learn it (through Hip-Hop lyrical and linguistic style).

This chapter and the preceding chapter are examples where the dominant is no longer a site of cultural, social, and linguistic investment. Indeed, the opposite is true. For African youths, choosing the margin is simultaneously an act of investment, an expression of desire, and a deliberate counterhegemonic undertaking. Choosing Hip-Hop must be read as a deliberate act of resistance. This is because Hip-Hop has always been a voice for voicelessness and performed as a prophetic language that addresses silence, the silenced, and the state of being silenced. As such, the chapter is an attempt to link African youths' word (what they learn and what and how they speak) and world (the hegemonic racializing social imaginary they encounter every day). In a Freirean way, we are confronted with a pedagogical question: can we as teachers afford not to link students' identities and racial becoming with what we teach in our (ESL) classrooms? A fuller answer can be found in Chapter Ten, so I want to offer two conclusions out of the current chapter.

First, all texts are open to different readings and interpretations and this chapter is no different. However, my hope is to offer this chapter as an example of how the intersection of immigration, Blackness, and language learning might look. In part, my hope is to offer a partial answer to the question: What happens when Blackness meets the syntax of immigration, especially in North America? Second, retrospectively, this chapter should serve as a methodological chapter—an example where micro and macro analyses are used simultaneously and where language is linked, if not returned, to identity (namely Blackness in my case) and where identity is the governing apparatus of language learning. In it, I show the impact of the macro on the micro; that is, how the larger social identities (the rhizomatic process of becoming Black) form and transform our subject-or-selfhood which, in turn, influences our language learning processes and the linguistic norm we invest in and eventually learn. We are yet to desire "the true word" to be spoken, it seems, only then can we desire "the world" differently (Freire, 1993, p. 32).

References

Adichie, C. (2014). *Americanah*. Toronto: Vintage.
Barthes, R. (1983). *Elements of semiology*. New York: Hill and Wang. (Original work published 1967)
Bauman, Z. (2016). *Strangers at our door*. London: Polity.
Beneviste, E. (2000). Subjectivity in language. In P. du Gay, J. Evans, & P. Redman (Eds.), *Identity: A reader* (pp. 39–43). London: Sage.
Butler, J. (1999). *Gender trouble: Feminism and the subversion of identity*. New York: Routledge.
Coleman-King, C. (2014). *The (re)making of a Black America: Tracing the racial and ethnic socialization of Caribbean American youth*. New York: Peter Lang.
Cooper, A., & Ibrahim, A. (in press). *Black voices matter: Black immigrants in the United States and the politics of race, language, and multiculturalism*. New York: Peter Lang.
Dyson, M. (2012). Foreword: Orator in chief. In Alim, S. & Smitherman, G., *Articulate while Black: Barak Obama, language, and race in the U.S.* (pp. ix-xiv). Oxford: Oxford University Press.
Fanon, F. (1967). *Black skin, white masks*. New York: Grove Weidenfeld.
Foucault, M. (1980). *Power/knowledge: Selected interviews and other writings*. New York: Pantheon.
Freire, P. (1993). *Pedagogy of the oppressed*. New York: Coninuum.

Hall, S. (1996). Introduction: Who needs "Identity"? In Hall, S. & du Gay, P. (Eds.), *Questions of cultural identity* (pp. 1-21). London: Sage Publication.

Hall, S. (2002). *Race: The floating signifier* [Video]. Northampton, MA: Media Education Foundation.

Hall, Stuart. (2013). The work of representation. In Hall, S., Evans, J. & Nixon, S. (Eds.), *Representation* (pp. 1-59). London: Sage.

Ibrahim, A. (2000). "Hey, ain't I Black too?" The politics of Becoming Black. In R. Walcott (Ed.) *Rude: Contemporary Black Canadian cultural criticism*. Toronto: Insomniac Press, pp. 109-136.

Ibrahim, A. (2011). When life is off da hook: Hip Hop identity and identification, BESL, and the pedagogy of pleasure. In Higgins, C. (Ed.), *Negotiating the self in another language: Identity formation in a globalized world* (pp. 221-238). Berlin: Mouton de Gruyter.

Ibrahim, A. (2014). *The rhizome of Blackness: A critical ethnography of Hip Hop culture, language, identity, and the politics of becoming*. New York: Peter Lang.

Ibrahim, A. (2017). Immigration/flow, hybridity, and language awareness. In Cenoz, J., Gorter, D. & May, S. (Eds.), *Language awareness and multilingualism*. Amsterdam: Springer.

Kristeva, J. (1974). *La Révolution du langage poétique* [Revolution in Poetic Language]. Paris: Lautréament et Mallarmé.

Minh-ha, T. (2011). *Elsewhere, within here: Immigration, refugeeism, and the boundary event*. New York: Taylor & Francis.

Ng-A-Fook, N., Ibrahim, A. & Reis, G. (2016). *Provoking curriculum studies: strong poetry and the arts of the possible in education*. New York: Routledge.

Okpalaoka, C. (2014). *(Im)migrations, relations, and identities: Negotiating cultural memory, diaspora, and African (American) identities*. New York: Peter Lang.

Pinar, W. (2011). *The character of curriculum studies*. New York: Palgrave.

Prince, A. (2001). *Being Black*. Toronto: Insomniac Press.

Rose, J. (2000). Feminine sexuality. In P. du Gay, J. Evans, & P. Redman (Eds.), *Identity: A reader* (pp. 51–68). London: Sage.

Sartre, J.-P. (1980). *Being and nothingness: A phenomenological essay on ontology*. New York: Pocket Books.

Woodward, K. (Ed.). (1997). *Identity and difference*. London: The Open University.

Notes

1 Staying somewhere to familiarize oneself with the place, its people, and their ways of "being" in that space. In the school, these sites are informal, such as hallways, the schoolyards, the school steps, the cafeteria, and the gymnasium, where the people in them are comfortable enough to speak their minds. Elsewhere (Ibrahim, 2014), I called this "hanging out methodology."

CHAPTER SEVEN

The New *Flâneur*: Subaltern Cultural Studies, African Youth in Canada and the Semiology of In-betweenness

(REPRINTED WITH PERMISSION) Ibrahim, A. (2008). The new *flâneur*: Subaltern cultural studies, African youth in Canada, and the semiology of in-betweenness. *Cultural Studies* 22(2), 234-253.

> Situated within subaltern cultural studies, and building on the work of Stuart Hall, Homi Bhabha and Mikhail Bakhtin, this essay tells the story of the 'new flâneur', a recent immigrant and refugee group of continental francophone African youth, who are attending an urban French-language high school in south-western Ontario, Canada. In it, I offer an alternative cultural framework of 'translation' and 'negotiation' as a way of seeing that which is supposedly competing and conflicting is indeed re-de-and-transformed and negotiated into New ways that make them radically performed. Their radicalness stems, precisely, from the notation that displaced identities, the focus of the paper, are not oppositionally articulated; on the contrary, they are negotiated, translated, and re-born in a more complex and hybrid space: a third one. This hybridity, I will show, is habitually performed in and through language—in its broad semiological sense. As part of an ethnographic research project, the essay will show the different ways in which the new fla^neurs form and perform their identities. Here, the Old and the New are not ethnographically observed in competition; both are translated in the identity formation processes and in the process, they are negotiated so that both are found in the same sentence, in the same garments, at the same time to produce a third hybrid space.

To walk is to vegetate
To stroll is to live
Balzac

Keywords subaltern cultural studies; African youth; Canada; blackness; identity; hybridity; language

MOST OFTEN THAN not, subaltern cultural studies takes for granted that identity is best conceived in and within that complex intersection of multiple discourses of difference, subjectivity, language, history, memory, and power relations. Ethnographically, however, what does this mean? How do these discourses work, and how do we recognize their intersectionality? If identity is no longer, as Stuart Hall (2001) would argue, what does it mean *to become*? What is understood by language here and methodologically, how do I as an ethnographer access my research participants' subjectivities, their identities? Grounded on an interpretive linguistic ethnography, this paper is an attempt to answer these questions. As such, it is contextually signified, modestly concluded, and ethnographically conceived. In fact, I am employing an ethnographic approach precisely to avoid the pitfalls of over-generalization. Generally, the paper is a methodological, pedagogical, and discursive intervention into the memetic logic of identity, race, and becoming. It tells the story of the 'new *flâneur*,' a recent immigrant and refugee group of continental francophone African youth, who are attending an urban French language high school in south-western Ontario, Canada, and who find themselves within what Nietzsche calls a 'public gaze' where their bodies are already-always read and imagined as 'Black'. They are caught within *the spectre of 'and'*, being continental in Canada and possessing a body that is read in the dominant social imaginary as a diasporic African body. The spectre of 'and' is also about what it means to be Senegalese or Nigerian, for example, *and* Canadian. This gaze, this social imaginary, which is yet to be fully understood within what Handel K. Wright (2003a) calls 'cultural studies as praxis', is a borne' shift in rethinking the discourse of race, identity, and pedagogy and has three main implications. First, as I have argued elsewhere (Ibrahim 2004), these youth were not black in Africa; however, once in North America, they fall within 'the eyes of power' (Foucault 1980) where they *become black* – and where blackness is conceived as a performative category, a form of speech, an attitude, and a social location one takes up. Following Simone de Beauvoir, Monique Wittig (2003) argued that one is not born a woman, but that one becomes a woman. Accordingly, I am contending, one is not born black either. In fact, one becomes black. In this sense, blackness becomes a code, a language, a set of cloths, a hair-do, a bodily expression, and above all an experiential memory. Second, as Meaghan Morris (1997) has argued, language in cultural studies is increasingly arrested within discourses of *différance*, temporalization and play. My study attempts to free language by introducing the actual verbal utterance as both an expression of identity and a formation of it. Becoming black for African youth meant learning Black English which, in turn, meant becoming black. That is to say, they are learning Black English because they are becoming black, yet they are becoming black precisely because they are learning Black English. Lastly, reflective of and informed by Handel K. Wright (2003a, p. 806) conceptualization of cultural studies as both 'an inter/anti/post/ disciplinary approach to the study of culture' and 'an intervention in institutional, sociopolitical, and cultural arrangements, events and directions' (see also Cohen, 1997), and borrowing from textuality and ethnography, I introduce 'ethnography of performance' as an approach that allowed me to access the youth identities. For ethnographers, I conclude, identity is best accessed in the performed. Put simply, I have three objectives in this paper to: (1) rethink Homi Bhabha's (1994) notion of the 'third space,' (2) introduce ethnography of performance, and (3) through my research, rethink the relationship between race, identity and displacement.

Flâneurie: theorizing identity through cultural translation and negotiation

> [This] is the dream of translation as 'survival' . . . as *sur-vivre*, the act of living on borderlines . . . [Here] the migrant's dream of survival [is] . . . an empowerment condition of hybridity; an emergence that turns 'return' into reinscription or redescription; an iteration that is not belated, but ironic and insurgent. [T]he migrant's survival depends . . . on discovering 'how newness enters the world.' The focus is on making the linkages through the unstable elements of . . . life—the dangerous tryst with the 'untranslatable'—rather than arriving at ready-made names.
>
> (Bhabha 1994, pp. 226-227, original emphasis)

Clearly, we live in a time of *universal subjecthood*, where identities and cultures are more than ever 'elusive' (Yon 2000), where *sur-vivre*—the act of displacement, of *flâneur* and of living in-between cultures, languages, landscapes, and borderlines—has become a second nature. The universal subjects are ones who possess a symbolic, and to be specific, intellectual capital that allows them to be in Australia one year, Canada the following year, and Britain or Berkley, California, the year after. As a matter of fact, I stopped asking where Gayatri

Spivak, Wole Soyinka or Homi Bhabha are teaching now. However, these universal subjects are not always as privileged. In fact, most of the time they are not at all. They are forced to flee their 'home' lands because of economic situation, civil war, political ideology, religious persecution, gender mutilation or forced conscription and dictatorship. Voluntarily or not, they find themselves interstitially torn between here and now and there and memory. They had witnessed enough to see the need to hold on to the Old, but the everyday is reminding them of the need to go on living, to experience and enjoy the New.

Significantly, the Old and the New are conceived here as historical temporalities, ways of being and as social, cultural, national, geographic, and linguistic spaces. Thinking 'Of Other Spaces,' Foucault (1986) convincingly argued that we live 'in the epoch of space of simultaneity ... in the epoch of juxtaposition, the epoch of the near and far, of the side-by-side, of the disperse' (p. 22). It is this dispersedly heterotopic and semiotic space,[2] this *dialectique de triplicité* (Lefebvre 1974), third space, 'both-and-also' (Soja 1996), which is taking place beyond *and* in-between two (or more) cultures, languages, and geographies that I want to explore first. Focusing particularly on identity as an ongoing 'event' of translation and negotiation (Ibrahim 2000a), my interest is to look at the ethnography of sur-vivre, that is, the impact and the outcome of displacement, of *flâneurie*.

Framing the politics of identity within the post-structural language of cultural studies, Stuart Hall (1990) writes that, 'Identity is not as transparent or unproblematic as we think. Perhaps instead of thinking of identity as already accomplished fact ... we should think, instead, of identity as a "production," which is never complete, always in process' (p. 222). It is, he continues, an ongoing event that is best conceived at the borderland between the Self and the Other. It is a process, a split, 'not a fixed point but an ambivalent point' (Hall 1991, p. 11). Hall (2001) refers to this process of identity formation as the New Identity which he distinguishes from the Old Identity. The logic of the Old Identity is an expression of the Cartesian stable self where the subject is situated within essentialized and static discourses of history, self, and memory; whereas the New Identity discourse is more complexly different. It neglects neither history and the multiple discourses within which the subject finds herself and the contradictory nature of these discourses nor the power relations or the *politics of positioning*: that is to say, how our gendered, racialized, and classed bodies are read socially and historically and the outcome of these social positions.

The borderland between the Self and the Other is what Mikhail Bakhtin (2001) refers to as *dialogism*. Luminously conceived, perceived, and lived, dialogism is a language, a philosophy, a semiotic space where being is conceptualized as an event, human being as a project or a deed, and society as a simultaneity of uniqueness. That is to say, one finds oneself in and within a network, 'a matrix of highly distinctive economic, political, and historical forces a unique and unrepeatable combination of ideologies, each speaking its own language, the heteroglot conglomerate of which will constitute the world in which we act' (Holquist 2002, p. 167). To be able to act, for Bakhtin (2001), also means to be addressed by Otherness. 'It is only in that highly specific, indeed unique placement that the world may address us' (Holquist 2002, p. 167). In a very real sense, Holquist argues, this becomes our 'address' in existence, 'an address expressed not in numbers, but by our proper name' and it is, very significantly, 'only from that site that we can speak' (2002, p. 167).

It is largely through language, through the signature of my 'proper name', that I become an active actor, a subject. As such, I differ from the Other precisely because while I am here, the Other cannot. This, for Bakhtin (2001, p. 365), produces 'heteroglossia' and 'ideological translation,' where the self becomes 'an act of grace, a gift of the other' (p. 364). To be able to receive this act of grace, this gift, however, I must occupy a location, a unique place in the ongoing event of existence that is mine, where existence is an event and my place, my identity in it is understood not only within time and space, but also as an activity, an act, a deed. My identity, my subjectivity which is determined by language (Bakhtin 2001), therefore, is never singular. I belong as much to myself as I do to the Other, yet the signifier that is my body 'makes manifest the subject of its signification' (Lacan 1977, p. 207); it makes me unique. After all, I could sign my proper name, and 'it' only belongs to me.

The *moment of identification* in this dialectic relationship between the Self and the Other is of extreme importance. It impacts and guides the shape, the form, and the intensity of the ways in which the Self translates the Other and vice versa. The question of intensity is an issue of desire. Elsewhere (Ibrahim, 1998, 2000a, 2000b, 2001, 2003), I showed that my research participants' desire and identification with blackness has certainly influenced their translation of the new Canadian context, what they learned and how. They named and identified, somewhat unconsciously, African American popular culture and language as sites for investment and yearning. *Identification*, I argued, *is the starting point of identity formation.* When the process of naming takes place, one might conclude, the process of ideological translation is inaugurated and in the case of my research participants, a *third space* is given birth to.

The third space: a semiology of in-betweenness

My conceptualization of the third space is deeply indebted to Jean-Paul Sartre (1980), Edward Soja (1996) and Homi Bhabha (1990). Though Bhabha's usage of the term is relevant and directly related, as we shall see, it is different from mine. I ground my analysis in an attempt to ethnographically explore and 'see' the complex ways identities are formed and performed and ultimately link them to the processes of learning, whereas Bhabha's framework is an inter/textual analysis. In doing so, I differ from Bhabha in being contextually specific and also in addressing the play of power relation in the creation of the third space.[3]

In an interview with Jonathan Rutherford, Homi Bhabha (1990) advanced three notions that are relevant to the present discussion, and illuminous of the visuality and the make up of the third space. The first point distinguishes between what Bhabha calls 'a creation of cultural diversity' and 'a containment of cultural difference'. Bhabha argues that within the Western cultural practices, 'although there is always an entertainment and encouragement of cultural diversity, there is always a corresponding containment of it' (1990, p. 208). This containment usually takes place in a subtle way and through a process of normalization whereby the dominant culture becomes the normalizing gaze. In other words, 'a transparent norm is constituted, a norm given by the host society or dominant culture, which says that "these other cultures are fine, but we must be able to locate them within our grid"' (1990, p. 208).

Unsatisfied with this liberal distinction, Bhabha advanced his second point by introducing his notion of 'cultural translation'. It argues that 'no culture is plainly plenitudinous, not only because there are other cultures which contradict its authority, but,' he continues, 'also because its own symbol forming activity, its own interpellation in the process of representation, language, signification and meaning-making, always underscores the claim to an originary, holistic, organic identity.' Cultural translation then is:

> a way of imitating, but in a mischievous, displacing sense—imitating an original in such a way that the priority of the original is not reinforced but by the very fact that it can be simulated, copied, transferred,

> transformed, made into a simulacrum and so on: the 'original' is never finished or complete in itself. The 'originary' is always open to translation so that it can never be said to have a totalised prior moment of being or meaning—an essence. What this really means [Bhabha argues] is that cultures are only constituted in relation to that otherness internal to their own symbol-forming activity which makes them decentered structures. (Bhabha 1990, p. 210)

Cultural translation does not allow for an essentialization of what is known as the 'original' or 'originary' culture for the latter itself is, and always was, open to and for translation. It is only original in the sense of being anterior, Bhabha argues. He thus convincingly concludes that all forms of culture are 'continually in a process of hybridity' (1990, p. 211). However, Bhabha emphasizes, 'the importance of hybridity is not to be able to trace two original moments from which the third emerges, rather *hybridity ... is the "third space"'* (p. 211, emphasis added). Therein lies my different path from Bhabha. I deploy the third space as an ethnographic performance of two or more languages, cultures, and belief systems. Indeed, for me, the third space is a trace, a synthesis, a performative act, and an articulation of these two or more cultures and languages, and since these traces are corporeally articulated, they are thus ethnographically perceptible. However, in the articulation (Hall 1986), the Old and the New are now metamorphosed in forms that look neither fully like the former nor the latter, but the two: the Old *and* the New. The Saussaurean bipolar of *signifié/signifiant* is no longer useful. For me, moreover, the third space sees the body as the locus of embodiment where this semiosis is articulated. Tersely, my unease with Bhabha's definition stems from the fact that it does not subjectify, historicize, or make tangible the hybridization project. Where, for example, is the play of race, sexuality, gender, and class in the process of hybridization? In this process of hybridization, where are those who are historically marginalized from the 'centers' of power? How does hybridity ethnographically look? Here, the Bakhtinian 'ideological translation' responds better to these questions.

For Bakhtin, the result of cultural and ideological translation wherein two linguistic, ideological, and cultural systems are to be mixed is to give birth to an organic world view which, in turn, will be performed in New linguistic and cultural practices. The product of this mixture is or can be 'hybrid', and for me it is socio-linguistically detectable and ethnographically observable. 'It is of course true that even historical, organic hybridity is not only two languages but also two socio-linguistic (thus organic) world views that are mixed with each other,' Bakhtin asserts, 'but in such situations, the mixture remains mute and opaque, never making use of conscious contrasts and oppositions'. Bakhtin adds:

> It must be pointed out however, that while it is true the mixture of linguistic world views in organic hybrids remains mute and opaque, such unconscious hybrids have been at the same time profoundly productive historically: they are pregnant with potential for new world views, with new "internal forms" for perceiving the world in words. (2001, p. 360)

In other words, *the third space* is organic because it is historically situated and partially unconsciously executed. It is an indissoluble mixture of two, or more, linguistic, ideological, cultural, and belief systems. It is third because it is found in the inter-geographies, cultures, languages, and memories (see figure 1). It is indeed where the 'first' and the 'second' are produced in the same sentence, in the same syntax, in the same grammar, in the same garment, at the same time. In the case of African students in this research, the product of the ideological translation of the Canadian context which synchronously starts at the moment of identifying and naming Black America/Canada as a site of investment by African students is a third space. That is, the third space for African youth is a product of the memory, experience, and cultural and linguistic behavioral patterns they bring with them when coming into Canada and what they translate in the latter context. They seem to identify with a Canada that is black, thus making race a crucial category.

Nonetheless, borrowing from Bhabha (1990) the third space 'enables other positions to emerge. [It] displaces the histories that constitute it, and sets up new structures of authority, new political initiatives, which are inadequately understood through received wisdom' (p. 211). These emerging positions are unrecognizable because they are the product of that luminal space where the Old is already in the New and the 'different'. The Old and the New emerge and are born from longitudinal negotiations and translations. Bhabha (1990) refers to these negotiations as 'the process of cultural hybridity' which "gives rise to something different, something new and unrecognizable, a new area of negotiation of meaning and representation' (p. 211).

The New Flâneur

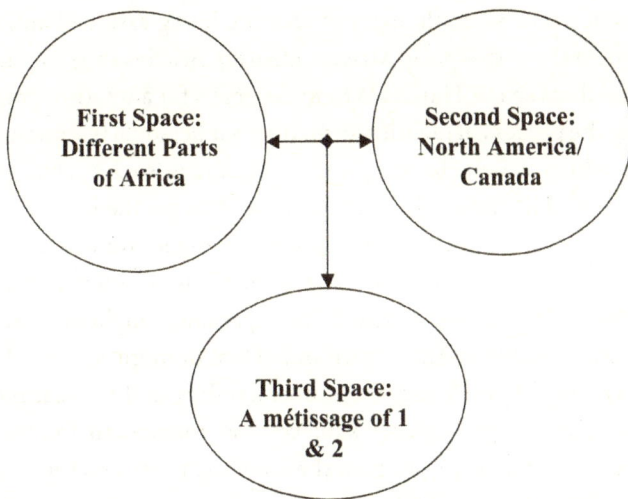

FIGURE 1: *The arrows between fast and second space are an expression of the dialectic nature between them, a product of translation and negotiation, whereas the arrow linking the latter with the third space is a product of this dialecticism. It is a hook, a story told in two tongues, a pipe receiving water from both sides (see Ibrahim 2005).*

It is the understanding of this semiotic 'new area of negotiation of meaning' that might illuminate our comprehension of identity formation processes, I contend, especially the identities of displaced subjectivities (including immigrants and refugees). To do so, Handel K. Wright (2003a) is worth quoting at length. Talking about his bodily experience as an African now living in North America, his displacement, and the different identities 'assigned' to him, Wright sees the tension of hybrid identities thus:

> [I]n the move from Sierra Leone to Canada and then the USA, I have been assigned and have taken up not only African identity but also 'black' identity. The complexity of identity [he continues] means that rather than being singular or merely replacing one form of identity with another (e.g. ceasing to be Krio and becoming 'black') identity is a series of complimentary and contradictory identifications operating simultaneously, with some coming to the fore or receding depending on context. I live and work in the USA but am not an American citizen; I am 'black' but not African American; I am simultaneously a continental and a diasporic African. (p. 811)

The third space is this simultaneity of tension, being assigned and taking up both 'continental *and* diasporic African' identity. Besides showing the dialogic nature of the third space, Handel Wright also calls for autoethnography in understanding the process of identity formation; for personal testimony, personal experience, which as Bell Hooks (1994) put it, can be 'such a fertile ground for the production of liberatory [praxis] because it forms the base of our theory making' (p. 70). My personal experience as a refugee from Africa now holding the Canadian passport and working in the US is no different than Handel Wright. Fearful of being essentialized, this experience taught me that displaced subjects find themselves in the borderland of two or more cultures, languages, and belief systems. In the process of understanding and translating the New context, subconsciously, displaced subjects also understand and translate the Old. We are located, I am arguing, in the landscape between the Old—which is part of us—and the New—which is becoming part of us.

When it comes to the African body in North America, as we shall explore subsequently, it is caught between two systems of signifying practices (see also Wright 2002, 2003a, 2003b). First, in Africa, I am tall, Sudanese, basketball player, academic, having different cultural, linguistic, tribal and ethnic lineages. Here, as Stuart Hall (1997) would argue, my blackness is outside the shadow of the other North American whiteness. However, second, as a refugee in North America, my perception of self is altered in direct response to the social processes of racism and the historical representation of blackness whereby the antecedent signifiers become secondary to my blackness, and I retranslate my being: I become black.

Elsewhere (Ibrahim 2003), I narrated a significant incident in my understanding of what it means to 'be' black in North America. It happened in May 16, 1999, the day I was officially declared 'Black', with a white policeman who stopped me in downtown Toronto, Canada, for no reason other than 'We are looking for a dark man with a dark bag,' as he uttered it. After questioning him about my 'darkness', he said, 'We are looking for a Black man with a dark bag'. There is no need to mention that my bag is actually light-blue and now, however, I am metamorphosed from 'dark' into 'Black'. Not that it matters either way, I reflected after, but some people either can not see or have 'color problem'. I am citing it here for two reasons. First, to frame the overall social context where my research participants circulate and form their identities; that is, to further our understanding of the everyday racism, human degradation, and general annihilation of black people

The New Flâneur

in North America. And second, to acknowledge how the present researcher is implicated in the research and the questions I am asking.

Just hanging out: the study and the ethnography of performance

Between January and June 1996, I conducted a critical ethnographic research[4] at Marie-Victorin (MV) High School[5] (Ibrahim 1998), which was then followed by short-term visits and informal observations in 2003. The research, which took place in an urban French-language high school in south-western Ontario, Canada, looks at the lives of a group of continental Francophone African youth and the formation of their social identity. Besides their gendered and raced experience, their youth and refugee status was vital in their, what I termed elsewhere, *moments of identification* (Ibrahim 2001): Where and how they were interpellated in the mirror of their society (cf. Althusser 1971, Bhabha 1994). Put otherwise, once in North America, I contend, very much similar to (Wright and) my experience earlier, these youth were faced with a social imaginary in which they were already Blacks. This social imaginary was directly implicated in how and with whom they identified, which in turn influenced what they linguistically and culturally learned and how they learned it. What they learned, I showed elsewhere (Ibrahim 1999), is Black English as a Second Language (BESL), which they accessed in and through black popular culture. They learned by taking up and repositing the Rap linguistic and musical genre and, in different ways, acquiring and rearticulating the Hip-Hop cultural identity.

In other words, continental African youth find themselves in a racially conscious society that 'asks' them to racially fit somewhere, where it is their racial identity that influences, if not determines their answerability. This dialogism, I also showed elsewhere (Ibrahim 1998), has strong influence in how African students 'see' and translate themselves as well as others, how they go about negotiating their identity formation, and the spaces they eventually occupy. For African students, moreover, these processes of translation and negotiation convert into a re-articulation of what it means "to be" black in a racially conscious society. Before their arrival to Canada, I argued, African students were not 'black', in the North American sense, although, like the speaking 'I' at this very moment, they had other adjectives that patch together their identities: 'Sudanese', 'Somali', 'intellectual', and so on. However, once in North America, these adjectives become secondary in their moments of identification. That is, soon after our arrival to North America, African students,

Wright and I were/are seeking spaces, identities, and representations with which we could say, 'We too are Black'. In their search for identification,[6] African youth took up the identifiable black Hip-Hop youth identity which in turn influenced what they learned and how. What they learned is BESL and how is by taking up and positing a Hip-Hop culture, especially Rap linguistic styles (Ibrahim 1998, 1999). African youths, in other words, started the odyssey of their identity formation, and heretofore blackness was/is the spatial representation of similitude, approximation, and affinity: thus *becoming* black.

To become black is not without its discursive politics of resistance. To say—using language, the body or any other media—"I too am Black" is to embody, perform, and ally oneself to and with the political category of blackness. That African youth locate themselves in/to the margin by taking up Rap and Hip-Hop and speaking BESL is by no means a coincidence. On the contrary, here, culture and language take on a different spin. They are no longer about language and culture *per se*, but become markers of desire and investment; an invocation of political, racial, and historical space. Downtown Toronto, and other metropolitan cities where African youth reside, is no longer a geographical space, it is also a language, an attitude, and a set of garments. '*Whassup homeboy?*' is no longer a simple linguistic expression nor about mastering a language. It is a 'space', a way of saying: 'I too am Black' or 'I too desire and identify with Blackness'. Baggy cloths and the myriad shades of sneakers, bicycle shorts, chunky jewelry, dreadlocks, braids, and other high fade designs become 'spaces' —downtowns?—which African youth perform and occupy very comfortably. They perform these inside and outside the school.

It is here that *ethnography of performance* has proven to be most useful. As a research methodology, ethnography of performance argues that ethnographers' best access to their research participants' inner-Selves is the latter's verbal and non-verbal performance. Put otherwise, the juxtaposition of what people actually and materially perform on and through their bodies, on the one hand, and what they say and think about those performances, on the other hand, give ethnographers the least distorted picture of their research subjects and their identities. Ethnography of performance is what might be called 'hanging out' methodology. That is, first, it acknowledges that there is no one method that would capture especially the essence of identity, so, second, one is required to use triangulation or multiple methods. Third, since identity is multiple and performed in multiples ways and sites, it requires multiple observations, in different sites and over an extended period of time. The objective is to see a macro-picture, a set of patterns. For this research, I literally 'hung out' with my research participants for six months almost everywhere: classrooms, hallways, school steps, gymnasium, their homes, picnics, night clubs, and parties, extracurricular school events, played basketball, and became the basketball coach. Simply put, I took thorough notes of their multiple identities: notes that allowed me to see patterns and hence reach certain conclusions. I then asked the participants to reflect on my own observations, notes and conclusions. My research findings therefore are not simply mine, based on my notes and interpretations, but a gift from the youth.

The site of the research, MV, was a small French-language high school (Grades 7-13) in south-western Ontario, with a school population of approximately 400 students from various ethnic, racial, cultural, religious, and linguistic backgrounds. Besides French, English, Arabic, Somali, and Farsi were also spoken at the school. I spent over six months there, as I already indicated. I attended classes at MV, talked to students, and observed curricular and extracurricular activities two or three times per week. Because of previous involvement in another project in the same school for almost two years, at the time of this research I was well acquainted with MV and its population, especially its African students, with whom I was able to develop a good communicative relationship. My background as a continental African also helped me to decipher their narratives and experiences. Clearly, we shared a safe space of comfort that allowed us to open up, speak and engage freely.

At the time of this research, students (or their parents) who were born outside Canada made up 70% of the entire school population at MV. Continental Africans constituted the majority within that figure and, indeed, within MV's population in general. They varied, first, in their length of stay in Canada (from 1-2 to 5-6 years); second, in their legal status (some were immigrants, but the majority were refugees) and, third, in their gender, class, age, linguistic, and national background. They came from places as diverse as Democratic Republic of Congo (formerly Zaïre), Djibouti, Gabon, Senegal, Somalia, South Africa, and Togo. With no exception, all of the African students in MV were at least trilingual, speaking English, French, and an African language, a mother tongue. Given their post-colonial educational history, significantly, most African youths in fact come to Franco-Ontarian schools already possessing a highly valued symbolic capital: *le français parisien* (Parisian French).

My research participants were part of this growing continental francophone African population in Franco-Ontarian schools. I chose 10 boys and six girls for extensive ethnographic observation inside and outside the classroom and inside and outside the school and interviewed all 16. Of the 10 boys, six were Somali speakers (from Somalia and Djibouti), one was Ethiopian, two were Senegalese, and one was from Togo. Their ages ranged from 16-20 years. The six girls were all Somali speakers (also from Somalia and Djibouti), aged 14-18 years. Because some interviews were conducted in French, I translated them all into English.

Performing it through language

The New Identity, Stuart Hall has argued above, neglects neither history nor memory. This was true in the case of African youth. Taking up the 'New', its linguistic and cultural practices was not done in opposition to their own 'Old' culture and language. On the contrary, both cultures and languages, that is to say the historical, linguistic and cultural memories that African students brought with them to Canada, and what they took up/learnt once here (namely, black popular culture and BESL), are found in the same sentence, in the same garment, on the same body and at the same time. The following is an excerpt, among many others, from my focus-group interview with male students. In it, we see that Sam[7] and Jamal[8] are not citing black stylized English in opposition to their Somali and French language. There is certainly a space of in-betweenness, of simultaneity, of 'inter' language, culture, and subjectivities:

> Sam: I don't rap man, c'mon give me a break. [laughs] Yo. A'ait a'ait you know, we just about to finish the tape and all clat. Respect to my main man. So, you know, you know wha'm mean, I m reprezi'in Q7. One love to Q7, you know wha 'm mean and all my friends back in Q7. Even
>
> though you know I haven't seen them for a long time you know, I still I got love for them you know who 'm mean. Stop the tapin boy.
>
> Jamal: Kick the free style. [I am translating here from the Somali language] Get me the tape man.
>
> Sam: A'ait this is Sam reprez'in AQA where it's born, reprez'in you know wha 'm mean? I wonna say whassup to all my niggers, you know, peace and one love. You know wha ' mean Q7 represin forever. Peace (rap music).

Jamal: crank it man, 'm coming up (rap music).

Sam: Je reviens man, you know. It's from Mecca yo, e reprezin you know, Mecca a'ait. You ask [laughs]. [In Somli] Put the music up, wallahi bellahi [in the name of Allah]. [In Somali] Look at this, a'ait a'ait.

Expressions such as 'a'ait,' 'reprez'in Q7,' 'boy,' 'kick the free style,' 'whassup to all my niggers' 'peace and one love' are all very common in Rap sphere (Ibrahim 1998, chapter 7, Smitherman 2000). Since Rap itself is a contemporary black cultural form, re/citing it by African students is in fact a performance of where they want to locate themselves politically, racially, culturally, and linguistically. However, the desire to locate oneself to and with 'Black' history and memory is espoused and entangled with the students' embodied/embedded identities, history, culture, and language. The Somali language was not put off in the advantage of another. It is code-switched in the same sentence with French and (black stylized) English. Here, there is no either-or, there is on the contrary this *and* that. And metaphorically, but also literally, this is how cartography or demarcation of space is indicated, how we tell others who we are or what we have become.

In my focus-group interview with male students, I asked them in French to meditate on my earlier observation. Here are two significant responses:

Musa: Here, we are in Canada, you see. We are going to keep our culture, but at the same time there is the new technologies, the new musics. There is also glamour and modernization of the cities and towns.

Mukhi: The way we dress, the way we talk, we are in Canada . . . The small Angolot you know, the small cloth we put around [the bottom], it is like the way we dress backhome. We need to mix in different genres of dress here. Backhome, for example, we put on Boubou and all that. But, I don't find it embarrassing to go out like that.

'We are going to keep our culture, but at the same time . . .' This is precisely the performance of tension between the Old and the New, which should be perceived as normal in the third space because there is a continuous *code-switching* between the two. Mukhi better expressed this idea of tension in his notion of 'mix'-ing. This mixing is not done in favor of one or the other: 'But I don't find it embarrassing to go out like that,' i.e. in Boubou. The Boubou becomes a signifier of national identity, but an ambivalent one since it is not put on by itself but 'mixed' with a touch of Hip-Hop. There is no culture shock. Instead, there is simultaneity, parallelism and dialogism.

Are these really moments of contradiction?

The following are two illustrative moments of the interstitiality, inbetweenness and their ethnographic observability. Again, the significance of these moments stems from the contention that they can be (read as) moments of contradictions. The language of the third space is developed, precisely, to argue otherwise, to make the reading of identity more complex. They may be moments of contention and tension, but, as we shall see, not of contradiction. As displaced subjects (including myself) who encountered new social, cultural, and linguistic spaces and practices, I will argue that African youths *have become*. They have become a negotiated product of the translated Old and New. To negate one or the other is to obliterate part of what has become. Since the third space is a language of inbetweenness, it does not have a fixed shape or form. Its shapes and forms depend on the socio-historical conditions and on power relation. Edward W. Said, Salman Rushdie, Stuart Hall, Gayatri Spivak, Samuel Beckett, Julia Kristeva, Joseph Conrad, Jacques Derrida (the list is too long to be continued and too complex to get into each of these individuals) are a sample of what the third space might look like. They are products of inbetweenness, an ambivalent product. The two moments cited later, which are excerpts from my observation notebook, are meant to show the ambivalent nature of in-betweenness, the third space. Here are the two moments:

> (1) The day was April 12, 1996. It was during lunch and early evening time. The lunch time: I was sitting in the foyer of the school just under the board of the recognized best students by the school. Should I be surprised that all the names, except for two, sounded very French? Dare I say that they brought whiteness to mind? After four months at the school, I am forced to say No to the first and Yes to the second. Najat[9] and a group of seven African young girls were holding a tape-recorder which they brought with them. They stopped in the middle of the foyer in their way from the gymnasium to the library; two girls were having the hijab -veil- on. 'Whassup Awad? Man School sucks',

Najat talked to me in English. At the beginning of her second sentence, one of the girls plugged in the tape-recorder: it was Cool J who was rapping. Najat turned around and spoke to one female in Somali and hereafter everyone joined in the dance. Hands were moving, bodies were swinging and the girls were talking in Somali, French, and English. Two of the girls, as already cited, were putting on Islamic *hijab*, others were dressed in Somali national dress: a Boubou, others were dressed in baggy Hip-Hop dress.

(2) The second illustrative moment was on the some day around 5:30 p.m. It was a moment of loosening and relaxation after a very busy schedule of practice at the school cafeteria/stage. Everybody was busy practicing for Black History Month activities. The same afternoon group of girls I have just talked about earlier, plus everyone else, mostly girls, joined the music that was playing on the sound system. It was again Cool J followed by Queen Latifa followed by Toni Braxton followed by African music from Zaire, Egypt, and Somalia. Yusuf (the 19-year old, organizer of the Black History Month gathering—there was no teacher to help and no institutional support) was the DJ. Most girls, including mostly the subjects of my research, were dressed either in costume for the practice or Hip-Hop 'mixed' with traditional African dress from South Africa, Somalia, Zaire, among others. Those who knew the songs—most of the crowd—seem to mimic and recite them. The hairstyles seem to vary from dyed to dreadlocks to African braids. During and after the practice, during and after this described episode, everyone was code-switching between English, French, and students' own languages.

Male and female students, as we can see, did enter the third space. However, given the patriarchal history and prescribed social and Islamic religious 'tradition', the background of almost all research participants, the female body seems to fall under stricter rules and policed more rigidly and systematically. Whereas males seem to enjoy what the Canadian context can offer, including dating, females are mostly denied this privilege (Ibrahim 1998, p. 248). Clearly gender plays a major role in the intense experience of the third space.

Dialectique de triplicité: an epilogue

> You know in any culture, there are advantages and disadvantages, strong points and weak points. I will keep the strong points and leave the rest, there are points we love about our culture and others we don't like. So, it's about your choices, do you accept the weak points or don't you? But that doesn't mean I am rejecting my culture when I choose a new one, I keep what's valuable in my culture. (Amani, 17 year old, female)

Perceptibly noticeable, nonetheless, are the ways in which the New and the Old intermingle in this complex third space. For African youth, to be is to become: to become a double-edged product, an ambivalent one. To become is to be answerable to more than one site. We answer through language, which is no longer an abstract category. On the contrary, it is a performed event in and through which identities are articulated. If identities are multiple, shifting and always in the making, as Stuart Hall (2001) and Judith Butler (1999) rightly tell us, then there are no pre-constructed identities that we just slip into (Welcome to the constructed New Identity!). Moreover, it is certainly in language that identities are complexly performed. Code-switching then is not just about language, it is also, literally and metaphorically, about subjectivities that are code-switched depending on who is talking to whom, in what context, and for what purpose. The complex identity formation of displaced subjects, immigrants as well as refugees as I have shown, stems from the fact that once they are in the New socio-and-geo-cultural context, they endeavor to look for spaces of identification. African youth 'chose' blackness through arduous, complex and, mostly, subconscious processes of 'translation' and 'negotiation'. However, this was not done in opposition to, or in competition with their embodied memories and histories. The two, Old and New, are put forth in the same sentence, in the same garment, in the same space, at the same time.

Since I situated the language of the third space in a socio-historical moment and within power relations, it is blackness that becomes a site of identification for African youth. They identified with a black Canada and this was 'declared' through language and culture, by invoking ritual expressions and bodily performances. Here, their blackness highlights the extent of their racialized experiences and shows that the black body speaks a language of its own, a language that is not fully theirs nor is it under their control. On their part, as we have seen, African youth have little difficulty in performing their culture and language along the translated New 'Canadian' context. 'Competition' and 'entitlement', even 'being' and 'becoming', for me, therefore, have to be situated not in their abstract discourses, but rather in their contextual discursive space where to speak is to say – 'I can also be partial, ambivalent, and a product of two'. The final question then is what are the possibilities of this partiality, ambivalence, and interstitiality to be named as such? The question, in other words, is multiple subjectivities and not singular ones since to be is to become, and to become in the *dialectique de triplicité* is to be forever born in two.

References

Althusser, L. (1971) *Lenin and Philosophy*, London, New Left Books.
Bakhtin, M. (2001) *The Dialogic Imagination: Four Essays*, Austin, TX, University of Texas Press.
Bhabha, H. (1994) *The Location of Culture*, London, Routledge.
Bhabha, H. (1990) 'The third space: interview with Homi Bhobha', in *Identity Community, Culture, Difference*, ed. J. Rutherford, London, Lawrence & Wishart, pp. 26-33.
Bourdieu, P. (1991) *Language and Symbolic Power*, trans. G. Raymond & M. Adamson, London, Polity Press.
Butler, J. (1999) *Gender Trouble: Feminism and the Subversion of Identity*, New York, Routledge.
Cohen, T. (1997) '"Along the watchtower": cultural studies and the ghost of theory', *MLN*, vol. 1, pp. 400-430.
Foucault, M. (1986) 'Of other spaces', *Diacritics*, vol. 10, no. 3, pp. 22-27.
Foucault, M. (1980) *Power/Knowledge: Selected Interviews and Other Writings*, New York, Pantheon.
Hall, S. (2001) 'Introduction: who needs "identity"?', in *Questions of Cultural Identity*, eds S. Hall and P. du Gay, London, Sage, pp. 1-17.
Hall, S. (ed.) (1997) *Representation: Cultural Representations and Signifying Practices*, London, The Open University.
Hall, S. (1991) 'Ethnicity: identity and difference', *Radical America*, vol. 13, no. 4, pp. 9-20.
Hall, S. (1990) 'Cultural identity and diaspora', in *Identity, Community, Culture, Difference*, ed. J. Rutherford, London, Lawrence & Wishart, pp. 222-237.
Hall, S. (1986) 'On postmodernism and articulation', *Journal of Communication Inquiry*, vol. 10, no. 2, pp. 45-60.
Holquit, M. (2002) *Dialogism: Bakhtin and His World*, London, Routledge.
Hooks, B. (1994) *Teaching to Transgress: Education as the Practice of Freedom*, New York, Routledge.

Ibrahim, A. (2005) 'There is no alibi for being (Black)? Race, dialogic space, and the politics of trialectic identity', in *Claiming Space: Racialization and Spatiality in Canadian Cities*, ed. C. Teelucksingh, Waterloo, ON, Waterloo University Press, pp. 20-32.

Ibrahim, A. (2004) 'One is not born Black: becoming and the phenomenon(ology) of race', *Philosophical Studies in Education*, vol. 35, pp. 77-87.

Ibrahim, A. (2003) 'Marking the unmarked: Hip-Hop, the gaze and the African body in North America', *Critical Arts: A Journal for Cultural Studies*, vol. 2, no. 1, pp. 15-24.

Ibrahim, A. (2001) '"Hey, Whadap Homeboy?" Identification, desire, and consumption: Hip-Hop, performativity, and the politics of becoming Black', *Taboo*, vol. 5, no. 2, pp. 85-102.

Ibrahim, A. (2000a) 'Trans-framing identity: race, language, culture, and the politics of translation', *Trans/forms: Insurgent Voices in Education*, vol. 5, no. 2, pp. 120-135.

Ibrahim, A. (2000b) '"Hey, ain't I Black too?" The politics of becoming Black', in *Rude: Contemporary Black Canadian Cultural Criticism*, ed. R. Walcott, Toronto, ON, Insomniac, pp. 109-136.

Ibrahim, A. (1999) 'Becoming Black: Rap and Hip-Hop, race, gender, identity, and the politics of ESL learning', *TESOL Quarterly*, vol. 33, no. 3, pp. 349-369.

Ibrahim, A. (1998) *"Hey, whassup homeboy?" Becoming Black: Race, Language, Culture, and the Politics of Identity. African Students in a Franco-Ontarian High School*, unpublished PhD dissertation, University of Toronto, OISE.

Jenks, C. (1995) 'Watching your step: the history and practice of the flaneur', in *Visual Culture*, ed. C. Jenks, New York, Routledge, pp. 2-15.

Lacan, J. (1977) *Écrits: A Selection*, New York, Norton.

Lefebvre, H. (1974) *La production de l'espace*, Paris, Éditions Anthropos.

Morris, M. (1997) 'A question of cultural studies', in *Back to Reality? Social Experience and Cultural Studies*, ed. A. McRobbie, Manchester, Manchester University Press, pp. 102-120.

Sartre, J. P. (1980) *Being and Nothingness: A Phenomenological Essay on Ontology*, New York, Pocket Books.

Simon, R. I. & Dippo, D. (1986) 'On critical ethnography work', *Anthropology & Education Quarterly*, vol. 17, pp. 195_202.

Smitherman, G. (2000) *Black Talk: Words and Phrases from the Hood to the Amen Corner*, Boston, MA, Houghton Mifflin.

Soja, E. (1996) *Thirdspace: Journeys to Los Angeles and Other Real-and-Imagined Places*, Cambridge, MA, Blackwell.

Yon, D. (2000) *Elusive Culture: Schooling, Race, and Identity in Global Times*, New York, State University of New York Press.

Wittiq, M. (2003) 'One is not born a woman', in *Identities: Race, Class, Gender, and Nationality*, eds L. Alcoff and M. Eduardo, Oxford, Blackwell, pp. 159-164.

Wright, H. K. (2003a) 'Cultural studies as praxis: (making) an autobiographical case', *Cultural Studies*, vol. 17, no. 6, pp. 805-822.

Wright, H. K. (2003b) 'Editorial: whose diaspora is this anyway? Continental Africans trying on and troubling diasporic identity', *Critical Arts*, vol. 17, no. 1 & 2, pp. 1-16.

Wright, H. K. (2002) 'Editorial: notes on the (im)possibility of articulating continental African identity', *Critical Arts*, vol. 16, no. 2, pp. 1-18.

Wright, H. K. (1998) 'Dare we de-centre Birmingham? Troubling the origin and trajectories of cultural studies', *European Journal of Cultural Studies*, vol. 1, no. 1, pp. 33-56.

Notes

1   I am using *flâneur* in its nomadic sense, where nomads, especially desert nomads, do not walk aimlessly as the original meaning suggests. They have a destiny and have a macro- and micro-knowledge and understanding of what surrounds them geographically, culturally and linguistically. The new *flâneur*, however, are still learning, they are ethnographers and translators of that which surrounds them. One might refer to them as the post-modern nomads who can easily travel corporeally and intellectually from South to North and vice versa thanks to digital technology and accessibility of transportation. For this paper, I am interested in the physical displacement, the actual corporeal move. As we shall see, the new *flâneurs* I am talking about here are not the most privileged, they moved to the North, namely Canada, because of war and civil unrest. Privileged or not, their identities, I conclude, are best understood within what Stuart Hall (1991) calls New Identity [see Chris Jenks (1995) for other definitions of the *flâneur*].

2   I understand semiotic space as a symbolic market of exchange or a field (Bourdieu 1991) of language, culture, history and memory where identities are both formed and performed. It is a space of symbolic signs where the value of any sign is not determined in relation to a pre-existing entity or a concept, but by their relationships with others in a system. Corollary, signs are both producers and a product of a system of meaning and representation; and language, signs and their meaning are historically, culturally and socially produced. As I conceive it, the semiotic space of in-betweenness is an operative psychic space that allows one to function in two separate, yet interrelated systems of culture, language, history and sociality. And thanks to translation and negotiation, as we shall see, it enables the subject to function in, and *articulate* (Hall 1986), two semiotic systems that, on the surface, have no points of connection. Canada and Somalia, for example, I will show, have the strongest connection within the 'third space,' the *articulation* of trialectic identity.

3   Modestly, my intent is not to create a dichotomy between textuality and reality, but to be contextually specific. My approach to this debate is closer to Handel Wright (1998, 2003a, 2003b). Talking about African orature, literature, and cultural studies, Wright (2003a) convincingly argued that, we 'need to acknowledge

and incorporate traditional African orature, new media and popular culture text, the expertise of non-academic teachers (e.g. traditional griots), an emphasis on performance and the utilization of literature in African development. The result is a discourse and praxis that obfuscates borders between text and lived culture, the academy and the community, the canonical and the popular, the literary and the socioeconomic electronic and traditional texts' (pp. 810-811). This is why my study is influenced as much by textuality as by ethnographic 'reality.' It is to be found in what Stuart Hall (1997) calls 'dirty intersection' of text and context.

4 For Simon and Dippo (1986, p. 195), *critical ethnographic research* is a set of activities situated within a project that seeks and works its way towards social transformation. This project is political as well as pedagogical, and who the researcher is and what his or her racial, gender, and class embodiments are necessarily govern the research questions and findings. The project, then, according to Simon and Dippo, is 'an activity determined both by real and present conditions, and certain conditions still to come which it is trying to bring into being' (1986, p. 196). The assumption underpinning my project was based on the assertion that Canadian society is 'inequitably structured and dominated by a hegemonic culture that suppresses a consideration and understanding of why things are the way they are and what must be done for things to be otherwise' (p. 196).

5 All names are pseudonyms.

6 Here is Amani's (17-year-old, grade 12, from Somalia) reflection during my focus group interview with female students on the contention that identification is the starting point of identity formation: 'We have to wonder why we try to really follow the model of the Americans who are Blacks? Because when you search for yourself, search for identification, you search for someone who reflects you, with whom you have something in common'. Amani seems to name blackness as a site of interpellation (Althusser 1971), the Other that entered the Self only to become part of it.

7 A 19-year-old male from Djibouti who has been at the school since grade 8; he is the school rapper and 'the Jordan' of the basketball court.

8 A 20-year-old male from Djibouti who was 'pushed out' of school; he presently hosts a show at CUIT, a local radio station in Toronto, where he airs rap in French and English.

9 A 15-year-old Djiboutian girl and amongst the African girls Najat is the most 'popular' girl in the school and the most identifying with Hip-Hop culture.

CHAPTER EIGHT

Don't Call Me Black! Rhizomatic Analysis of Blackness, Immigration, and the Politics of Race without Guarantees

(REPRINTED WITH PERMISSION) Ibrahim, A. (2017). Don't call me Black! Rhizomatic analysis of Blackness, immigration, and the politics of race without guarantees. *Educational Studies* 53(4), 511-521.

Abstract

What happens when the syntax of race meets immigrants whose bodies are assumed to be "Black" in North America but who either do not have the history or the conception of Blackness in North America or are not familiar with the North American Black-White dichotomy? Dealing with three empirical studies and a novel, in the present review essay, I answer this complex question by entering a rhizome and a cartography (Deleuze & Guattari, 1987) where race is a complicated, nuanced and ever-shifting/ed category; an identity politics without guarantees; whose outcome is so contingent and tentative that it is unpredictable (Hall, 1992). I will conclude with a sketch of a critical pedagogy that attempts to decolonize the unidimensional nature of Blackness as currently existing in North America.

Keywords: African and Caribbean Immigrants, Blackness, Rhizome.

A Prologue

In a recent article, contextually in the U.S., Zahida Sherman Ewoodzie (2014) called for a complicated notion of Blackness, one where, first, we need to acknowledge the diversity of and within Blackness and, second, Caribbean and continental Africans need to question both their understanding and relation to African Americanness and African Canadianness. I want to do two things in this short article. First, I want to have a conversation with Ewoodize about how we might have 'the talk' around the complexity of Blackness in the context of Black immigrant communities while keeping in mind how that conversation might be perceived as, "please don't call me Black." As part of this conversation, second, I want to offer a rhizomatic analysis of Blackness (Ibrahim, 2014a; Deleuze & Guattari, 1987). By rhizomatic analysis, I am referring to a nuanced, ever-complicated, never-fixed, ever-to-become category of Blackness. Here, I will draw a cartography, a critical pedagogy where there are and at the same time there are no borders of/for Blackness. That is the tension of a rhizomatic analysis of Blackness, a politics of race without guarantees. According to Stuart Hall (1992), a politics of race without guarantees is when there is nothing inherent, set, and fixed about race; where Blackness, for example, becomes a sociohistorical category, like all other categories, that is open to the best as much as it is susceptible to the unfortunate and the ugly. Not only that, Hall continues, but constructing positive image of Blackness does not 'guarantee' a positive response from its audience. Black is forever-to-become, positively and negatively. So, opening up the category of Blackness as a multi-dimensional and historically specific category—a category that is taken up and performed in multiple ways by different people and in different places—is the main argument I am putting forth in this review essay. As we shall see in the studies under review herein, even though it is experienced in somewhat similar fashion, Blackness in Canada is not the same category as Blackness in the United States (U.S.). Blackness is louder in the U.S. than in Canada (Walcott, 2000)—both in its presence and human cost (one only needs to bear witness to the level of murder of Black people in the U.S. by the police); but in both contexts, as it will become clear, Blackness is caught under the spectre of Whiteness (see also Wright, 2012).

Being Caught in the Zone

Dear Non-American Black, when you make the choice to come to America, you become black. Stop arguing. Stop saying I'm Jamaican or I'm Ghanaian. America doesn't care. So, what if you weren't "black" in your country? You're in America now. We all have our moments of initiation into the Society of Former Negroes. Mine was in a class in undergrad when I was asked to give the black perspective, only I have no idea what that was. Adichie (2014, p. 273)

When the Black body encounters the syntax of (im)migration and displacement, a 'complicated conversation' (Pinar, 2007; Ng-a-Fook, Ibrahim & Reis, 2016) seems to come into existence. Adiche's novel, as we shall see, is an exemplar of this complicated conversation, but the present essay is provoked firstly by Zahida Sherman Ewoodzie's 2014 bold and provocative opinion article: *"Don't' call me Black": Black identity, diaspora, and American dreaming in college.* In this complicated conversation, Ewoodzie situates herself and her discourse as an insider, as someone who has experiential knowledge with different *categories* of Blackness, namely African Americans (her own background: "[the] Black folks up-from-slavery kind" (n.p.)), continental Africans (being married to one) and "Caribbean people." Since the latter category was not de-essentialized, Ewoodzie's article assumes an equation between Caribbeanness and Blackness. In her article, Ewoodzie also makes reference to two studies. One sociological, where the author (Ogunipe, 2011) shows that the general American audience perceive differences in social status, education level and salary based on whether the person identifies herself or himself as "Black" or "African American." When confronted with this 'social imaginary' (Ibrahim, 2014a) where the former is considered lower than the latter, continental African and Caribbean immigrants, especially in college, tend to think highly of themselves and may go as far as to say, "Don't call me Black." This sentiment, Ogunipe (2011) explains, stems from the fact that first and second-generation Black immigrants (a category I will complicate later) constitute 12-13% of the overall U.S. Black population, yet they constitute 41% of Black first-year students in Ivy League.

The other study that Ewoodzie cites is a psychological study conducted by Dr. David R. Williams and his associates on the "mental health of Black Caribbean immigrants" (2007, n.p.). The study found that, "Increased exposure to minority status in the United States was associated with higher risks for psychiatric disorders among Black Caribbean immigrants, which possibly reflects increased societal stress and downward social mobility associated with being Black in America" (n.p.). In other words, as Ewoodzie (2014) put it, "racism-related stress increases the longer [Black Caribbean immigrants] live in the US" (n.p.). In the U.S., it seems, White supremacy makes sure Black immigrants fall into the zone, into the discursive space and social imaginary of Black America: with its negative history and ill treatment. "Oh, they all look like Blacks to me" has proven to be violent social imaginary and racial profiling has proven to be deadly for both Black Americans and Black immigrants. For Ewoodzie, this calls for "an empowering Black solidarity," one where, "whether we came to this country [U.S.] by choice or by force, our institutions are showing us that our fates are inextricably linked."

Blackness, in sum, has become "a unifying tool to demand that America live up to its promise to all of us" (n.p.).

In what follows, I will introduce and discuss three empirical studies that attempt to complicate Ewoodzie conversations. The first study is by Chonika Coleman-King (2014): *The (re)making of a Black America: Tracing the racial and ethnic socialization of Caribbean American youth.* The second is by Chinwe L. Ezueh Okpalaoka (2014): *(Im)Migrations, relations, and identities: Negotiating cultural memory, diaspora, and African (American) identities.* The last study is mine (Ibrahim, 2014a): *The rhizome of Blackness: A critical ethnography of Hip-Hop culture, language, identity, and the politics of becoming.* The irony of reviewing one's own work is not lost on me, but interesting to note, all three books and studies are published in Peter Lang's book series: Black Studies & Critical Thinking.

"In [North] America, You Are Black, Baby":
In the beginning was Americanah

Before discussing these three empirical studies however, Chimamanda Ngozi Adichie's (2014) novel *Americanah* deserves as much attention, especially in light of the argument in this review essay, which is an attempt to gather some of the most recent studies that link continental African and Caribbean immigrants and their experience with Blackness. Even though a novel, *Americanah* has some of the most perceptive proses on what it means to be Black *and* immigrant in the United States. In *Americanah*, we are introduced to two terms, which I will use interchangeably throughout this article—"Black immigrants" and what Adichie calls "non-American Blacks"—to talk about people of African descent who immigrate to the United States.

Using episodic style, Adichie makes her reader bear witness as her characters walk through, so to speak, what it means to become Black (Ibrahim, 2014a). Set in the triangle of New England, Washington DC and Philadelphia, the novel is a *tour de force* narrated by a Nigerian female blogger, Ifemelu, who blogs primarily about race and immigration, namely what it means to 'become (Black) American.' Part of becoming American, Ifemelu concludes in one of her blogs, is the realization that "in America, you are black, baby." "America doesn't care" if you are Ghanaian, Jamaican or from Jamaica New York, Ifemelu explains, because in the case of Black immigrants, becoming American means 'becoming Black.' Throughout the novel, Ifemelu assumes a non-Black American who either does not know or new to the process of becoming Black. In one of her blogs, and with an incredible pedagogy of humor, Ifemelu didactically explains what it means to become Black (and she is worth quoting at length):

> You must show that you are offended when such words as "watermelon" or "tar baby" are used in jokes, even if you don't know what the hell is being talked about… You must nod back when a black person nods at you in heavily white area. It is called the black nod. It is a way for black people to say "You are not alone, I am here too." In describing black women you admire, always use the word "STRONG" because that is what black women are supposed to be in America. If you are a woman, please do not speak your mind as you are used to doing in your country. Because in America, strong-minded black women are SCARY. And if you are a man, be hyper-mellow, never get too excited, or somebody will worry that you're about to pull a gun. When you watch television and hear that a "racist slur" was used, you must immediately become offended. Even though you are thinking "But why won't they tell me exactly what was said?"… When a crime is reported, pray that it was not committed by a black person, and if it turns out to have been committed by a black person, stay well away from the crime area for weeks, or you might be stopped for fitting the profile. If a black cashier gives poor service to the non-black person in front of you, compliment that person's shoes or something, to make up for the bad service. If you are in an Ivy League college and a Young Republican tells you that you got in because of Affirmative Action, do not whip our your perfect grades from high school. Instead, gently point out that the biggest beneficiaries of Affirmative Action are white women. If you go to eat in a restaurant, please tip generously. Otherwise the next black person who comes in will get awful service… If you're telling a non-black person about something racist that happened to you, make sure you not bitter. Don't complain. Be forgiving. If possible, make it funny. Most of all, do not be angry. Black people are not supposed to be angry about racism… This applies only for white liberals, by the way. Don't even bother telling a white conservative about anything racist that happened to you.

Because the conservative will tell you that YOU are the real racist and your mouth will hand open in confusion (pp. 273-5).

For Adichie, Blackness becomes a second language and Adichie is its translator. For non-American Black, it seems, to speak Blackness is become aware of its syntax, which includes the smallest acts: the head nod, using the word 'strong' every time one speaks about a Black woman, tipping generously, brushing off the accusation that one got into an Ivy League college because of Affirmative Action when one is the top of his/her class, etc. Moving from the episodic to the methodical, we will see in the following sections how others have experienced empirically what Ifemelu has experienced in the novel.

Becoming Black: Immigration, displacement and identities

In general, we will hear the echoes of Ifemelu didactic instructions in the three studies under investigation. I will begin with Chonika Coleman-King (2014) study as it was the first to be published among the three. Coleman-King begins with the passionately autobiographical, as someone who was born in the U.S. to Jamaican parents. This creates a moment of simultaneity where she feels like being of two worlds, "but not belonging completely to one or the other" (p. 1). Matriculating through the public school system in New York City, she was marked by invisibility in the school curriculum. Interestingly enough, part of her invisibility was the fact that she could not fully internalize the U.S. history of Black-White binary and dichotomy. Coleman-King was also marked by a household where there was an exceptional economy of hospitality and love, but at the same time a household that was overly strict when it came to the value and deep respect for education. This early childhood experience shaped not only her understanding of herself but who she had become as an adult, educator, and now a professor/researcher. As all passionate researchers (Ibrahim, 2014b), Coleman-King's body and experiences were smuggled into the research only to become part of the ethno-graphically observable and the discursively speakable. For passionate researchers like Coleman-King, there is no dichotomy between the epistemological and the ontological. That is to say, who we are, our embodied/embedded identities and our experiential knowledge should not and cannot be separated from the research we produce and the conclusions we reach.

Like Ifemelu, Coleman-King then enters the difficult terrain of labeling and language. What name should we give 'Black immigrants'? In the case of the Caribbean immigrants, Coleman-King refers to them as 'Caribbean immigrants' or 'Caribbean Americans' (vs. 'native-born Blacks' or 'Black Americans'). Again, like Ifemelu, "In my blackness," Coleman-King (2014) writes, "the experience of American racism deeply resonates with me, and as a person of Caribbean descent my experience is often marginalized and misunderstood" (p. 4). A central reason for this misunderstanding and marginalization is the facile reading of race without ethnicity. That is to say, essentializing people based on their 'race' (basically phenotypes) without reference, among others, to cultural, national, linguistic, class, gender, education and historical backgrounds. This is a crucial theme that cuts across all three studies, as we shall see.

At the heart of the Caribbean immigrants' identity development and integration processes in the U.S. for Coleman-King is the formation of a dialogic space where the history and perspectives of Caribbean immigrant parents directly impact the identity development of their children. However, this dialogic space simultaneously initiates a unique identity formation where Caribbean American youth have their own unique experience, especially with race and racism. As a result we see in Coleman-King a non-static, ever-shifting and ever-complex American Caribbean youth identity, one where "experiences and messages shared at home and school [are] informed by multiple historical and sociopolitical spheres [that] shape [Caribbean immigrants'] understandings regarding race, racism, and ethnic identity" (p. 11).

To understand the intersection among race, ethnicity, nationality, socioeconomic status and historical context, Coleman-King looked at how racial socialization, among other ecological factors, can and does influence the identity development of youth. Using life narrative as a method for data collection, she asked three significant questions:

(1) "how do Caribbean immigrant parents socialize their children with respect to race and ethnicity?

(2) What do Caribbean American youth learn about U.S. racism through experiences in a mixed-race, middle-class school?

(3) How do socialization experiences at home and school influence youth's understanding of themselves as racial and ethnic minority in the United States" (pp. 8-9).

Her research participants were ten middle school students. Of the ten, two were 1.5-generation (i.e., came to the U.S. at the age of 2 and 9) and eight were second-generation (i.e., U.S.-born) Caribbean American students. Beside being middle school students, they all lived in a middle-class, mixed-race, and suburban community just outside a large city in the northeastern United States. Seven out of the ten parents came from Jamaica—which speaks to the overrepresentation of Jamaicans among the Caribbean immigrants in the U.S.—all of whom are professionals.

Coleman-King's main finding is that, it is almost impossible to disentangle race, class, and citizenship. She offers the life narrative of Kerry Ann Fisher, mother of Bryce, who was one of the participants in the study (pp. 62-67). Kerry Ann came to the U.S. at the age of 16 from a rural, subsistence farming and exceptionally humble background, not to say poor. Even though she became a Certified Public Accountant with "a rather large home" (p. 64), that is to say a comfortable U.S. middle-class life, her humble background not only influenced her work ethics and what she expected of herself, but also what she "demanded" of her son Bryce. This type of life narrative is found throughout Coleman-King's study.

Her findings can be summarized as such: first, the experience of Caribbean immigrants with school has lots of successes, but also has hardships, sacrifices, and failures. Second, building on other literature as well, White supremacy seems to be an unforgiving poison that creates a distressing situation for Caribbean immigrants. Rather than achieving upward mobility over the course of several generations (as is the case with White immigrants), the progeny of Black immigrants experience a downward trend. Third, the process of Americanization is synonymous with racialization: *to be become American means to become Black American*. Fourth, as part of becoming Black American, the research participants had to contend with interpersonal racism, negative images and eventually, as Coleman-King put it, "Black immigrant groups succumb to... pressures as they are made into "Black Americans" and forced to exist at the margins of society" (p. 22). Fifth, in the face of this racial hegemony, parents seem to emphasize ethnic rather than racial socialization, with modest results. That is to say, White supremacy with its binaries (Black/White) has proven to be more hegemonic. Sixth and finally, the narrative of parents, which was informed by transnational, class, and early immigration perspectives and experiences, became significant in creating an alternate space for youth to re-define their identities (p. 205). This is why, Coleman-King concludes, we as educators, researchers, and critical pedagogues need to complicate and interject ethnic socialization with racial socialization. Part of this complication is to call for a more nuanced analysis rather than reductive Black/White and post/not-post-racial binaries.

With the second study by Chinwe L. Ezueh Okpalaoka (2014), we enter the domain of the spiritual where—because of the ugliness of racism, making us almost insane—we need to recapture our mental health and repossess our own bodies. Okpalaoka's study is a poetic exploration of these essential questions: "Who is an African? Which group of people can rightly lay claim to an African identity? Is an African identity the sole right of a particular group of people?" (p. 1). To answer these questions, Okpalaoka weaves the autobiographical with the biographical with the ethnographic with the poetic. By the end of the book, what we have is an unsettling picture where the imaginary of Black African immigrants is already stereotyped, not to say colonized, by negative images about African Americans even before their arrival to the U.S. (p. 7). African Americans, on the other hand, are also not immune to negative media(ted) and Hollywood representations, like Tarzan, where the African immigrant is assumed to be hungry, poor, diseased, and uncivilized.

What becomes clear in Okpalaoka's study is that these two imaginaries can no longer afford to be side by side. That is, given the mass migration of Black African immigrants—constituting 12-13% of U.S. Black by 2010—Black African immigrants are rubbing shoulders with African Americans everywhere, in schools, workforce, colleges, etc. This situation, for Okpalaoka, requires new naming and new paradigm shift. In collaboration with Cynthia Dillard, Okpalaoka begins by troubling the very term, African American. She puts "American" in parenthesis to mark and designate those who were born of African people brought to the U.S. during the Middle Passage and the transatlantic slave trade. So, she writes it thus: African (American). As part of the paradigm shift, we move from 'descent' to 'ascent.' Instead of talking about 'African descent,' Okpalaoka is proposing to use 'African ascent' because "ascendency implies a progressive movement that calls on us to consider a different language or discourse for the ways we talk about people of African origin.

Looking within ourselves and our common history to (re)member who we are," Okpalaoka writes, "is critical to confronting dominant discourses that seek to define us. But remembering who we are," she concludes, "means that we have to address the dearth of knowledge about Africa, Africans, and the African (im) migration experience in our society and in our schools" (pp. 2-3). Okpalaoka begins with a powerful premise that African people have always been on the move, hence ascend is a better descriptor that descend:

> The play on the word "ascend" connotes an upward, progressive movement: always in motion, always fluid, and always becoming. As far back as has been documented by historians, African people have been on the move, sometimes of their own volition but historically as a result of forced removal from the place they call or once called home (p. 119).

Invoking what Cynthia Dillard calls 'endarkened feminist epistemology,' where the emphasis is on the historical roots of global Black feminist thought, Okpalaoka interviewed a group of Nigerian and Ghanaian American girls to understand how home and school experiences shape the ways they "navigate their world as girls who are Black, African, African American, and American all at once and in various combinations of these identities" (p. 54). An understanding of the girls' stories, Okpalaoka argues, "might teach us about their educational and sociostructural needs and would allow educators to accommodate their needs in schools" (p. 54). Unfortunately, we are never told how many girls were interviewed, for how long or their location in the United States.

Nonetheless, three broad themes emerge out of these interviews. First, given how White supremacy ranks "the African" at the lowest level in the racial hierarchy, Okpalaoka found that the girls emphasized their ethnicity and nationality in an effort to de-emphasize their race as defined by American stereotypes (p. 13). Second, Okpalaoka discusses the power of language, especially naming ourselves using endarkened feminist epistemology (EFE). EFE argues that the oppression of Black women—e.g., the girls in Okpalaoka's study—is a worldwide phenomenon and it does not concern only Black women. It should concern everybody. Here, the girls' African names (that are sometimes unpronounceable in the Anglo tradition, which is used two or three syllable names) should be approached with sacredness and respect. Names are containers of memories that witness and testify to our geographic, national, historical and cultural locations. Names send us back to the notion of ascent, community, lineage and aboveall to the notion of Ubuntu: "I am because we are" (p. 38). The diploma that one earns, according to Ubuntu, does not belong to the individual, it "belongs to us" (the community) (p. 55). Third and finally, the girls' Africanness becomes a stored wisdom, a cultural memory and a source of strength that helps negotiate and construct new identities in the diaspora while actively seeking to remember and maintain old ones. In this sense, they are never a finished product, they are always to become.

Blackness North of the 49th Parallel

The three texts I dealt with thus far are talking about the Black immigrant experience in U.S., so what about the Black immigrant experience in Canada, north of the 49th parallel? To answer this question, I will introduce and discuss my own study (Ibrahim, 2014a). My study, *The rhizome of Blackness*, is a meta-reading and meta-analysis of three studies I conducted in late 1990s, 2007 and 2011. All three studies were 'critical ethnographic projects' and studied groups of continental African youth (not the "blacks folks up from slavery kind"). By critical ethnographic project I am referring to a set of activities situated within a political and pedagogical project that sought and worked its way towards social transformation. In other words, these studies were an intervention into the dominant hegemonic culture that suppressed, and continues to suppress, a consideration and understanding of why things are the way they are and what must be done for things to be otherwise (p. 16). Contrary to Okpalaoka and Coleman-King, however, my studies were conducted in Canada, in different regions (within the province of Ontario) and with two linguistic communities (French and English).

The first study was conducted in a small French-language high school in a large city in southwestern Ontario, and the other two studies were conducted in a large city in English-language high schools. If Okpalaoka study was about using the stories of the girls to understand their educational and sociostructural needs, and Coleman-King study was about racial and ethnic socialization, mine was about 'how,' in their daily activities and ways of being, continental African youth *become Black*. I was interested in what they spoke and how they spoke it, what they wore and how they wore it, and what music they listened to and why they listened to it, etc. In short, I was interested in the feast of the everyday, the theatre of the marvelous: their lives inside the school and outside the school.

To understand the script of this theatrical play, I developed what I called 'hanging out methodology.' In a true ethnographic spirit, one 'hangs out' in a place to get the full picture, if ever that is possible, of the place, the people, the culture, and the sense of being and becoming in it. This is especially true with young people. The aim of the hanging out methodology is to investigate what young people actually do, say, and perform on their bodies and, in turn, what their doings 'say' about who they are, and their identities, desires, and futures. Put simply, I lived with these young people for at least six months in each location. I went to classes with them, I played basketball with them, I helped them academically, I went to picnics with them, and I even visited their homes. Very significant to note, in being with the students in varieties of places and at different times, my hanging out methodology was an attempt to understand the complex through the banal, the structural through the everyday, the infinite possibilities of identities through the daily utterances, performances and doings (p. 19).

In 1990s, I 'hung out' with 16 students, 10 boys and 6 girls. That is to say, I followed them very closely for at least three days a week inside and outside the school for 6 months. In 2007 and 2011, I decided simply to 'hang out' in the schools without following a particular group of students. Students were all high school students, most of whom were Canadian-born, while some were 1.5 generation (i.e., arrived in Canada at a young age). Over 90% of their parents were born outside Canada, coming from at least 9 countries from Sub-Saharan Africa; so they had different national and cultural background and they spoke, beside English and/or French, different African languages.

These are my conclusions. First, what Philomena Essed (1991) (see also Essed & Goldberg, 2002) calls 'everyday racism' is very much alive and kicking in these three schools and the Canadian society at large. It is so much alive that, in one school, students went on a strike requesting one physical education teacher be removed from the school. Second, similar to Coleman-King, where to become American for Caribbean immigrants means becoming Black American; in my study, becoming Canadian means becoming Black Canadian. However, unlike Coleman-King, I offer a thick description of what I am calling the *rhizomatic process of becoming Black*. Referencing Deleuze and Guattari (1987), the rhizomatic process of becoming Black is a complex, complicated, fluid, multiple, and multiplying, and forever becoming. Unlike the U.S. dichotomous experience of Black-White, in Canada, the rhizomatic process of becoming Black is both possible and it is a constant flow or movement of de-territorialization. It is a way of becoming and a constant move between the old (the African) and the new (the Canadian). The end result of this de-territorializaiton is a *rhizomatic identity*: an "assemblage" that is welcoming sociality, with everything that it brings (the good and the ugly), but with no guarantees as to what it might look like or what maze it has to go through to get there; thus living Stuart Hall's (1992) prophecy of a politics of race without guarantees (see also Wright, 2016). The rhizomatic process of becoming Black, I have shown, is a tree that is welcoming the sun, the rain, the snow, and so on, whose branches and leaves are growing horizontally. There are no certainties about what shape or form they will take, or how green they will turn out to be. This rhizomatic identity—African-Canadianness—thus finds itself in a constant state of flow, deterritorization, and multiplicity (p. 50).

Third, unlike Okpalaoka or Coleman-King, and to differentiate further the American and the Canadian experience and context, I make a distinction between being and becoming Black. Being Black is an accumulative memory, an understanding, a conception, and an experience with which individuals interact with the world around them. It is like a mother tongue, one can never fully master it, but one is comfortable within it that she/he can recognize that which is beyond language, the implicit. Like learning a second or foreign language, becoming Black is the process of building this memory—experience. In my study, especially with the newly arrived, some continental African youth were not familiar with the North American Black-White dichotomy. They never thought of themselves as 'Black' before their arrival in North America, specifically in Canada. Other adjectives used to patch together their identities, such tall, academic, Yoruba, basketball player, etc. However, once in North America, these adjectives become secondary to their Blackness. They re-translate themselves, hence becoming Black.

Fourth, Black popular culture, namely music, more specifically Hip-Hop emerges as a crucial site of identification and language learning. Among all the choices available, continental African immigrant youth invest into a Hip-Hop identity that is mediated by their identity formation. The end result is, instead of learning English as a second language (ESL), they learn Black English as a second language (BESL), which they access in and through Hip-Hop. Put otherwise, they are learning BESL precisely because they are becoming Black, but they are becoming Black precisely because they are learning BESL. Fifth and finally, however, complicated by gender and social class, this Black Canadian identity sits side-by-side with an African identity, thus creating a rhizomatic and hybrid third space. Similar to Okpalaoka, a decolonized and realistic Africa becomes a source of strength and a cultural memory that helps these youth walk through the ugly scene of White supremacy in search for a better future. I concluded my study by calling for a critical pedagogy of the imaginary, one where Blackness is already-always multidimensional, multicultural, multilingual, multiethnic and multinational.

By way of Concluding: An Epilogue

As Okpalaoka (2014) makes clear, there is a "dearth of knowledge about Africa, Africans and the African (im)migration experience" in the current literature" (p. 3; see also Ibrahim & Abdi, 2016). The three studies presented here are an attempt to fill in that gap. The three studies, taken collectively, give us a discursive framework where we get some clues to the general deep structure of the system in which Black immigrants live, think, learn, and circulate their desires and identities. It is clear that this system is not linear, but heterogeneous; it is not simplistically organizational, but complexly rhizomatic. The three studies show us that the process of becoming Black is a story, a narrative, and a plot. The narrative in these studies exposes what Trinh-Minh-ha (2011) calls "the (ugly) nature of the system" (p. 42). Here, Whiteness and White supremacy become a rigid map and a clearly demarcated cartography against which Black immigrant experience is mapped, categorized, and signified. To counter this arborescent and rigid space, immigrants of African ascent have to be given the endarkened epistemological tools to dismantle this unidimensional, and colonial and limiting social imaginary (Ibrahim, 2014a, p. 37). We need a critical pedagogy that attempts to decolonize, re-imagine, re-make and re-mark Blackness in general, and Black immigrant experience in particular, differently. Only then can we hope for a true vocation of becoming human, where humanity is expressed with full agency, desire, and located subjectivity (McKitrick, 2014; Ibrahim, 2014b). Only then can the Caribbean Black immigrants—youth or otherwise, and continental African immigrants—men or women/rich or poor, link their word with their world.

Pedagogically, we need to arm our students so that they can gaze back at this "ugly nature of the system," as Trinh-Minh-ha (2011) calls it, a system where they are already represented, imagined, and talked about. To reach this point, we as critical teachers and critical pedagogues need to do two things simultaneously. We need to open up and disrupt the one-dimensional representation of Blackness and at the same time be mindful of the danger of doing so. To explain, White supremacy has the historical and structural power to represent and write Blackness one-dimensionally. It has been doing that since Carolus Linnaeus in mid-1700s (Bonilla-Silva, 2014). In this colonizing and violent writing, the nuanced, multiple, shifting, social, historical, and contingent nature of Blackness is reduced to only one dimension: a cartography and a tableau that is already drawn, with a persistent tilt towards negativity. Critical pedagogues need to enter this colonizing cartography and look into its actual, ever-shifting, and becoming nature. As we do that, however, we need a heightened level of attention not to essentialize Blackness, as White supremacy has been doing, and not to fall into the quibble between Black-vs-Black: African American/African Canadian vs. African/Black immigrants. We need an epistemic path that will ensure the possibility of the struggle against White supremacy, on the one hand, and the creation of Black-and-Black alliance, on the other. I hope the rhizomatic analysis of Blackness that I briefly introduced here and fully discussed elsewhere (Ibrahim, 2014a) might be one path to take. There, full agency, subjectivity, desire, hope, and investment are all essential parts of what it means to become Black, where students are empowered enough to locate themselves in time and history—with their infinite possibilities—and at the same time question the adequacy of that location. Only then, can we talk about a different imaginary and a pedagogy of hope, where a decolonized, less violent, and multi-dimensional category of Blackness is possible.

Reference

Adichie, C. (2014). *Americanah*. Toronto: Vintage.

Bonilla-Silva, E. (2014). *Racism without racists: Color-blind racism and the persistence of racial inequality in America*. Lanham, MD: Rowman & Littlefield.

Coleman-King, C. (2014). *The (re)making of a Black America: Tracing the racial and ethnic socialization of Caribbean American youth*. New York: Peter Lang.

Deleuze, G. & Guattari, F. (1987). *A thousand plateaus: Capitalism and schizophrenia*. Londong & New York: Continuum.

Essed, P. & Goldberg, D. (2002). *Race critical theory*. Malden, MA: Blackwell.

Ewoodzie, Z. (2015, January). *"Don't' call me Black": Black identity, diaspora, and American dreaming in college*. Retrieved from http://www.forharriet.com /2015/01/dont-call-me-black-black-identity.html#axzz3saaWzNvw.

Hall, S. (1992). What is this "Black" in Black popular culture? In Dent, G. (Ed.), *Black popular culture* (pp. 21-33). Seattle, WA: Bay Press.

Ibrahim, A. & Abdi, A. (2016). *The education of African Canadian children: Critical perspectives.* Montreal: McGill-Queen's University Press.

Ibrahim, A. (2014a). *The rhizome of Blackness: A critical ethnography of Hip-Hop culture, language, identity, and the politics of becoming.* New York: Peter Lang.

Ibrahim, A. (2014b). Research as an act of love: Ethics, émigrés and the praxis of becoming human. *Diaspora, Indigenous and Minority Education 8*(1), 7-20.

Deleuze, G. & Guattari, F. (1987). *A thousand plateaus: Capitalism and schizophrenia.* London & New York: Continuum.

Essed, P. (1991). *Understanding everyday racism: An interdisciplinary theory.* Thousand Oaks, CA: Sage.

Minh-ha, T. (2011). *Elsewhere, within here: Immigration, refugeeism and the boundary event.* New York: Taylor & Francis.

Ng-A-Fook, N., Ibrahim, A. & Reis, G. (2016). *Provoking curriculum studies: Strong poetry and the arts of the possible in education.* New York: Routledge.

Ogundipe, V. (2011). *The development of ethnic identity among African-American, African immigrant and diasporic African immigrant university students* (Unpublished doctoral dissertation). Georgia State University: Georgia.

Okpalaoka, C. (2014). *(Im)migrations, relations, and identities: Negotiating cultural memory, diaspora, and African (American) identities.* New York: Peter Lang.

Pinar, W. (2007). *Intellectual advancement through disciplinarity: Verticality and horizontality in curriculum studies.* Rotterdam: Sense.

Walcott, R. (2000). *Rude: Contemporary Black Canadian cultural criticism.* Toronto, ON: Insomniac Press.

Williams, D., Haile, R., Gonzalez, H., Neighbors, H. Baser, R. & Jackson, J. (2007). The Mental Health of Black Caribbean Immigrants: Results from the National Survey of American Life. Retrieved from http://www.ncbi.nlm.nih.gov/pmc/articles/PMC 1716238/.

Wright, H.K. (2012). Is this an African I see before me? Black/African identity and the politics of (Western), academic knowledge. In Wright, H. & Abdi, A. (Eds.), *The dialectics of African education and Western discourses: Appropriation, ambivalence and alternatives* (pp. 180-192). New York: Peter Lang.

Wright, H. (2016). Stuart Hall's relevance for the study of African blackness. *International Journal of Cultural Studies, 19*(1), 85-99.

McKitrick, K. (Ed.) (2014). *Sylvia Wynter: On being human as praxis.* Durham, NC: Duke University Press.

CHAPTER NINE

When Neoliberalism Meets Race, Post-colonial Displacement and Immigration, It Creates Americanah: A Teacher Education Complicated Conversation

(REPRINTED WITH PERMISSION) Ibrahim, A. (original, not published). When neoliberalism meets race, post-colonial displacement and immigration, it creates *Americanah*: A teacher education complicated conversation.

Abstract

This article reads the novel, *Americanah*, against the backdrop of what I am calling a 'teacher education complicated conversation.' While doing so, the article shows that *Americanah* can be an exceptional pedagogical tool to decipher neoliberalism and map its intersection with race, post-colonialism, displacement, and immigration.

The world was defined as known and finite, a principle agreed up by science and theology. Hence the chief way for a nation to promote or achieve its own wealth and happiness was to take them away from some other country.

William Appleman Williams (cited in J. W. Smith, 2003, p. 4)

For one to succeed, it seems, others have to be crushed, not to say outright colonized, in order for wealth to be accumulated. This is Adam Smith's principle of 'mercantilism' at its zenith, which according to J. W. Smith has foregrounded all neoliberal thinking. In the citation above, Williams is indeed expounding what has become the theological notion of mercantilism. However, J. W. Smith (2003) explains, when this notion became too naked, that is, "When the injustice of mercantilism was understood, it became too embarrassing and was replaced by the supposedly just Adam Smith free trade. But free trade as practiced by Adam Smith neo-mercantilists was far from fair trade" (p. 5). According to Anup Shah

(2010), Adam Smith's mercantilism, which was later dubbed as free trade and free enterprise, which Pierre Bourdieu (1998) referred to as "the essence of neoliberalism" (n.p.), was the dominant philosophy and the primary economic theory, especially in the United States (U.S.) and Britain, particularly in the 1930s. For it to succeed at that time, Shah shows, the U.S. and Britain had to depend on a geopolitical apparatus where imperialism, colonialism and subjugation of others had to be at its core in order to have access to the resources required to produce such vast wealth. For Shah, this apparatus is still not only alive but actually flourishing. The election of Donald J. Trump as the U.S. president, with his racist, sexist, abilist, xenophobic, Islamophobic, and homophobic remarks (Epstein, 2016), is only the latest evidence showing the veracity of Shah's argument.

My intent in this article is to show how novels and textuality in general can be a great way to explain neoliberalism, on the one hand, and show its limits, on the other. I will use Chimamanda Ngozi Adichie's novel *Americanah* (2013) as an example of/for what I am calling 'a teacher education complicated conversation.' For Pinar, Reynolds, Slattery, and Taubman (1995), a complicated conversation is non-linear, bottom-up, built on the lived, and made up of a continual series of moments shifting from the mundane to epiphanal. To deserve its name, first, a complicated conversation does not escape history or sociality, it makes use of social categories (race, class, gender, etc.) in the praxis of teaching and learning. Second, it has the courage and audacity to engage, look for and think through the "blind impresses," the gaps and the blind spots of thoughts, ideas, and practices (Rorty, 1989, p. 43). The blind impresses are the difficult knowledges – problems, if you like – that society prefers not to face, be it racism, sexism, xenophobia, ethno-supremacy, or homophobia. Third, and finally, a complicated conversation is a call for a critical pedagogy of imagination, humanism, and becoming (Rautins & Ibrahim, 2011). This is a pragmatist pedagogy that begins by acknowledging the historical moment in which we live: a startling world of uncertainty, a world saturated by unknown complexities of future sustainability, interdependence, and human possibility (Greene, 1995); a world where the educational landscape is shifting as it attempts to grapple with global issues (especially that of migration, war, and displacement), and where we, as critical pedagogues, provoke global citizenship and wakefulness in our students (O'Hara, 2006). Clearly, perturbing social conditions (terrorism, poverty, violence, and economic and environmental crises) and educational challenges (standardized testing, discipline/punishment, and oppressive pedagogy) are now especially profound. Yet, Greene (2008) dares to ask: "How can we commit ourselves to [teaching and] learning in times like these?" (p. 18).

My hope is to offer a partial answer to Greene's question. Deploying the idea of a complicated conversation within a teacher education context while reading *Americanah*, we get to understand neoliberalism on the one hand and see its limits on the other. To state that *Americanah* is a novel, hence a fiction and a work of total imagination, is tautological. Novels, Richard Rorty (1989) argues, can be exceptionally perceptive and may even serve as a witness and a testimony to its time. In *Americanah*, as we shall see, race, post-colonialism, displacement, and immigration stare neoliberalism in the face. To better understand this background, a brief discussion on neoliberalism itself is necessary.

Grounded both in politics and the economy, for Susan George (1999) and Anup Shah (2010), neoliberalism at its core is about making trade possible and easier regionally, nationally and internationally. It is about freer movement of enterprises, people, goods, and resources, always seeking cheaper resources and maximizing profits and efficiency. To achieve this objective, neoliberalism requires the removal of all that which is considered (perceived or real) as barriers to free trade, such as restriction of capital flows, regulations, tariffs, certain laws, standards, and regulatory measures. Here, the so-called market is given the pulse of a thinking being which understands the pressures of the market and hence 'naturally' regulates itself. Put almost in theological terms, this is the only way to have a successful market-based economy. To use Margaret Thatcher's terms, There Is No Alternative (or TINA, see Gilroy, 1991) to this neoliberal philosophy, where the market rules, public expenditure (including education and health) is reduced to its bare minimum, deregulation and privatization are the only guarantees for prosperity, and the public and community good is radically shifted to individualism and individual responsibility where those on the top inhale too deeply in their success and those at the bottom consider their wretched of the earth plight as a verdict on them and their place in the world.

Discussing this philosophy as a question of the Left and the Right, crisscrossed by Authoritarianism and Libertarianism, Shah (2010) found that fascism (the Right) represents Authoritarianism and anarchism (i.e. liberal socialism) represents Libertarianism (the Left). On the other hand, socialism and communism represent the Left while neoliberalism at its zenith represents the Right (see Figure I on following page).

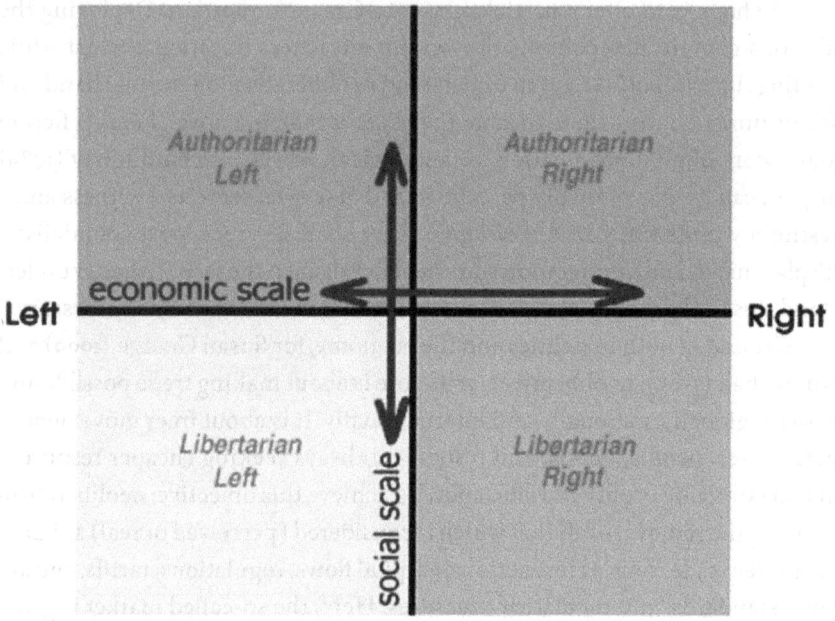

Figure I: Political Compass
Source: www.politicalcompass.org (cited in Shah, 2010, n.p.)

However, as we shall see with *Americanah*, these sharp, colonial, linear, and straight lines and diagrams collapse. We need a complicated conversation if we ever to understand how people live through the chaos in/of their daily lives. In *Americanah*, we are left with rhizomes and cartographies where lines of flight and possibilities (Deleuze & Guattari, 1987) are not linear, hence taking the contour shapes where borders are complicated and messy. Race, culture, and displacement become more salient than economic models. Of course, this is not meant to suggest a rift between the economic and the cultural but to argue that, when it comes to immigration, post-colonialism, displacement and race, neoliberalism with its theological formula can only serve the colonial at the expense of the post-colonial and the im/migrant. In many post-colonial contexts, immigration is not a matter of choice but of necessity; it is not for leisure but for peace, safety and a better future. This is well shown in *Americanah*.

It is all about the hair stupid: The story of Ifemelu

> And now here she was telling him it was over. "Why?" he asked. He taught ideas of nuance and complexity in his [university] classes and yet he was asking her for a single reason, the *cause*. But she had not had a bold epiphany and there was no cause; it was simply that layer after layer of discontent had settled in her, and formed a mass that now propelled her. She did not tell him this, because it would hurt him to know she had felt that way for awhile, that her relationship with him was like being content in a house but always sitting by the window and looking out.
> *Americanah* (Adichie, 2013, pp. 8-9, original emphasis)

It is a rhizomatic moment—a complex, multi-layered, ever-shifting and contingent moment—when the story of an African, a Nigerian woman to be specific, starts at Princeton University. We first meet Ifemelu in her late-twenties, waiting for a train to take her to braid her hair. "But she did not like that she had to go to Trenton to braid her hair. It was unreasonable to expect a braiding salon in Princeton," the narrator explains, "the few black locals she had seen were so light-skinned and lank-haired she could not imagine them wearing braids— and yet as she waited at Princeton Junction station for the train, on an afternoon ablaze with heat, she wondered why there *was* no place where she could braid her hair" (pp. 3-4, original emphasis).

Getting off the train in Trenton, Ifemelu took a taxi, whose driver was a Caribbean man, to find herself in Mariama African Hair Braiding salon. While at the salon, first, we are exported humorously to West Africa by a group of hairdressers who came from Mali, Sénégal and Côte d'Ivoire. They discuss what it means to be an African in America, which Ifemelu ends labeling "Non-American Black" (NAB), and how coming to the U.S. was not a question of choice but—given the political, social and economic "mess" where they came from—of necessity if life was to become worthy of living (p. 16). At the salon, second, we discovered that Ifemelu had been in the U.S. over thirteen years, during which she became a U.S. citizen, finished her undergraduate studies and had had a fellowship at Princeton, which was about to finish and that she had "decided to move back to Nigeria" (p. 19). While at the salon, finally, we came to know that Ifemelu was in a long-term relation with Blaine, an African American professor at Princeton, which she ended for absolutely no reason other than, she decided so.

Poetically, this decision was then used as a junctural moment in the novel—a radical, transformative and significant moment (Hall, 2013)—that took us back to Nigeria to meet Obinze, an ex-boyfriend and a childhood friend. Presented as a shadow against which Ifemelu has had to negotiate every aspect of her life, we also met her parents. Her mom was a God-fearing Catholic who went to church every Sunday and who one day declared, "I am saved… this afternoon … I received Christ. Old things have passed away and all things have become new. Praise God" (p. 50). Bemused by his wife, her father on the other hand always declared, "I am an agnostic respecter of religion" who went to church only for weddings and funerals (pp. 50-51). Ifemelu's father was a civil servant "who wanted a life different from what he had, who had longed for more education than he was able to get." So, he "talked often of how he could not go to university because he had to find a job to support his siblings, and how people he was cleverer than in secondary school now had doctorates" (p. 57). Her father, we are told, was a "typical overzealous colonial subject" who used "big words" to impress his then missionary teachers, but he did not know where to draw the line; so during her childhood he would scold Ifemelu "for being recalcitrant, mutinous, intransigent, words that made her little actions seem epic and almost prideworthy" (p. 58).

As for Obinze, he was an usual teenager. He was "a fine boy even if he was short" (p. 66). He lived with his single mom, a university professor of English, who "had fought with a man, another professor at Nsukka [a city in Nigeria], a real fight, punching and hitting, and she had won, too, even tearing his clothes, and so she was suspended for two years and had moved to Lagos until she could go back [to her teaching job at the university]" (p. 66). By all means, we are told, this was an usual story because "market women fought, mad women fought, but not women who were professors" (p. 66). What was intriguing for Ifemelu was that, knowing all this, when she met Obinze—for the first time in high school—he was none of that. He was calm, neat, and inward—qualities that made him extremely seductive and "mesmerizing" (p. 85). Human connections happened between Ifemelu and Obinze and teen lovemaking in the novel was almost graphic.

After high school, Ifemelu and Obinze ended up going to separate universities, one in Nigeria (Obinze) and one in the U.S. (Ifemelu). Distance seemed to have its curse, so they broke up their relationship because of physical distance, which turned into emotional distance. This break up was one of the reasons why Ifemelu applied for Princeton fellowship after her undergraduate studies in the U.S.. Yet, they met again after Ifemelu moved back to Nigeria. Obinze by then was a married man with a beautiful wife and a happy child. Intentionally and methodically Ifemelu rekindled the relationship again, unfortunately to the detriment of Obinze's marriage. For unexplained reason, Ifemelu was psychically cold and emotionally unapologetic in destroying Obinze's marriage. In an epic formula, the novel ended with Obinze chasing Ifemelu and coming to her apartment one more time, where he was asked to *come in*. Here, we are left to assume that he was asked to 'come in' back in Ifemelu's apartment and life, hence achieving what she wanted. These were the last lines of the novel:

> He paused, shifted. "Ifem [that is what Obinze used to call Ifemelu], I am chasing you. I'm going to chase you until you give this [coming back in the relationship] a chance."
>
> For a long time she stared at him. He was saying what she wanted to hear and yet she stared at him.
>
> "Ceiling," [that is what she used to call him] she said, finally. "Come in" (p. 588).

Saying the unsaid and the unsayable

What is not said thus far is that, in the U.S., Ifemelu is actually a blogger with thousands of followers. This is how she made her living. The blog was called, *Raceteenth or Various Observations About American Blacks (Those Formerly Known as Negroes) by a Non-American Black*. It is this series of blogs that I want to focus on now. They are spread throughout the novel and they serve as a compass into the complexity and the different directions into, particularly, race and immigration. They are discussed here for three reasons. First, they serve as a preamble for what I am calling later the intersectionality of race, post-colonialism, displacement, and immigration. Second, they serve as literary devices that the reader might find helpful. Third and finally, through them, neoliberalism and its limits become clear and the idea of free movement of people and goods is just that, an idea. Here, as Ifemelu calls it in her blogs, being an 'American-African' (a continental African living in or immigrant to the U.S.) or 'African-American' ("which is what we call our brothers and sisters whose ancestors were slaves" (p. 172)) is an identity that one chooses as much as it is an identity that is chosen for us. In their totality, these blogs create some of the most observant and perceptive meta-analysis of what happens when neoliberalism rubs shoulder with race, immigration and post-colonialism. (It is neither the time nor the space to enter this debate, but I am using 'post-colonialism' in its plain sense of post-independence from direct colonial rules.)

One of the first blogs we read was about a dreadlocked White[1] man who sat next to Ifemelu on a train, with a ponytail and a "tattered shirt worn with enough piety to convince her that he was a social warrior" (p. 4). When he came to know that Ifemelu was a blogger, he surprised her by asking, "Ever write about adoption? Nobody wants black babies in this country, and I don't mean biracial, I mean black. Even the black families don't want them." The blog went on, "he [the white man] and his wife had adopted a black child and their neighbors looked at them as though they had chosen to become martyrs for a dubious cause" (p. 5). As someone who was not familiar with the history of what it meant *to be* Black in the U.S. and as someone who did not grow up with the U.S. Black-and-White dichotomy, this was one of Ifemelu's earliest experiences with the rhizomatic and ever-shifting meaning of race (Ibrahim, 2014; Hall, 2002). Another blog on the same topic of the ever-shifting and complicated nature of race in the U.S. was about Alma. Had she met Alma in Lagos, Ifemelu reflected in her blog, "she would have thought of her as white, but she [Ifemelu] would learn that Alma was Hispanic, an American category that was, confusingly, both an ethnicity and a race" (pp. 128-9). That blog was titled: "Understanding America for the Non-American Black: What Hispanic Means" and it is worth quoting at length:

> Hispanic means the frequent companions of American blacks in poverty rankings, Hispanic means a slight step above American blacks in the American race ladder, Hispanic means the chocolate-skinned woman from Peru, Hispanic means the indigenous people of Mexico. Hispanic means the biracial-looking folks from the Dominican Republic. Hispanic means the paler folks from Puerto Rico. Hispanic means the blond, blue-eyed guy from Argentina. All

you need to be is Spanish-speaking but not from Spain and voilà, you're a race called Hispanic (p. 129).

From the two blogs above, it was clear that race had already poked its ugly head in Ifemelu's life (as a new 'American-African' in the U.S.); and despite people having full agency, their movement (racial or otherwise) was not as free as claimed neoliberalism. Complicated by immigration and transnational movement, we read a blog about an "Igbo Massachusetts Accountant," which was also the title of the blog and, again, it is worth quoting at length:

> He [the Igbo Massachusetts Accountant, who also wrote online] had not been back to Nigeria in years and perhaps he needed the consolation of those online groups, where small observations flared and blazed into attacks, personal insults flung back and forth. [I] imagined the writers, Nigerians in bleak houses in America, their lives deadened by work, nursing their careful savings throughout the year so that they could visit home in December for a week, when they would arrive bearing suitcases of shoes and clothes and cheap watches, and see, in the eyes of their relatives brightly burnished images of themselves. Afterwards they would return to America to fight on the Internet over their mythologies of home, because home was now a blurred place between here and there... (pp. 143-4).

By this blog, Ifemelu started to show a deeper understanding of the struggle of what it meant to be a post-colonial subject and a displaced immigrant who was seeking a sense of home in a supposedly neoliberal climate where his/her whole struggle throughout the year was to save some money, as was the case with the Igbo Massachusetts Accountant, so that he could go see his family for a week. The general conclusion from Ifemelu's blog is that, immigrants live an aching nostalgia that is leaving them neither here nor there, in a constant state of psychic displacement and social learning. A significant learning curve for Ifemelu was about dress in the U.S., especially dressing well—a significant cultural phenomenon in most post-colonial Africa (Bong, 2015). One blog explained the dress code in the U.S. thus:

> When it comes to dressing well, American culture is so self-fulfilled that it has not only disregarded this courtesy of self-presentation, but has turned that disregard into a virtue. "We are too superior/busy/cool/not-uptight to bother about how we look to other people, and so we can wear pajamas to school and underwear to the mall" (pp. 157-8).

At the university, Ifemelu was a member of the African Students Association, where students from Nigeria, Uganda, Kenya, Ghana, South Africa, Tanzania, Zimbabwe, Congo, and Guinea got together. "They mimicked what Americans told them," we were told: "You speak such good English. How bad is AIDS in your country? It's so sad that people live on less than a dollar a day in Africa" (p. 170). With this association, Ifemelu "felt a gentle sense of renewal… she did not have to explain herself" (p. 171).

One of the most significant blogs was found on page 227 in the novel. It was a reworking of Figure I above. The "Political Compass" of neoliberalism in this blog was called "American Tribalism" (the title of the blog), and it had four pillars: class, ideology, region, and race. Class, the blog explains, refers to "rich folk and poor folk"; ideology refers to liberals and conservatives who "don't merely disagree … on political issues, [but] each side believes the other is evil"; region refers to North and South where the "North looks down on the South [and] the South resents the North"; and race where there is "a ladder of racial hierarchy in America." By the time we got to this blog, Ifemelu's maturity with the U.S. Black-and-White dichotomy was becoming evident. However, in this same blog, she got a shock that complicated her understanding of race. She told a story of a visiting speaker during her undergraduate studies. Ifemelu overheard "a classmate whispers to another, ""Oh my God, he looks so Jewish," with a shudder, an actual shudder. Like Jewish was a bad thing. I didn't get it. As far as I could see," Ifemelu wrote, "the man was white, not much different from the classmate herself. Jewish to me was something vague, something biblical. But I learned quickly. You see, in America's ladder of races, Jewish is white but also some rungs below white" (pp. 227-8). For Ifemelu, the Jewish question then opened up the category of race to an ever-complex and complicated conversation, especially in a supposedly neoliberal time when people were supposed to be judged by what they did, not who they were (gender, race, etc.).

When Neoliberalism Meets Race 151

Ifemelu's staring neoliberalism in the face continued, particularly when her dad told her on the phone from Nigeria, "I have no doubt that you will excel. America creates opportunities for people to thrive" (p. 253). By then, she has become *wide-awake* (Greene, 2005) of the vulgarity of race as one of the pillars of neoliberal tribalism in the U.S.; that is to say, deeply aware and conscious of how race impeded (and continues to impede) people's life chances. This wide-awakeness was then translated in the second of three most significant blogs in the novel (the first was the one I discussed above and found on page 227 in the novel). It was titled: "Understanding America for the Non-American Black: What Do WASPs Aspire To?," and it is worth quoting at length:

> Professor Hunk has a visiting professor colleague, a Jewish guy with a thick accent from the kind of European country where most people drink a glass of antisemitism at breakfast. So Professor Hunk was talking about civil rights and Jewish guy says, "The blacks have not suffered like the Jews." Professor Hunk replies, "Come on, is this the oppression olympics?"
> Jewish guy did not know this, but "oppression olympics" is what smart liberal Americans say, to make you feel stupid and to make you shut up. But there IS an oppression olympics going on. American racial minorities – blacks, Hispanics, Asians, and Jews – all get shit from white folks, different kids of shit, but shit still. Each secretly believes that it gets the worst shit. So, no, there is no United League of the Oppressed. However, all the others think they're better than blacks because, well, they're not black. Take Lili, for example, the coffee-skinned, black haired and Spanish-speaking woman who cleaned my aunt's house in a New England town. She had a great hauteur. She was disrespectful, cleaned poorly, made demands. My aunt believed Lili didn't like working for black people. Before she finally fired her, my aunt said, "Stupid woman, she thinks she's white." So whiteness is the thing to aspire to. Not everyone does, of course... but many minorities have a conflicted longing for WASP whiteness or, more accurately, for the privileges of WASP whiteness. They probably don't really like pale skin but they certainly like walking into a store without some security

dude following them. Hating Your Goy and Eating One Too, as the great Philip Roth put it. So if everyone in America aspires to be WASPs, then what do WASPs aspire to? Does anyone know? (pp. 253-4)

Two things to take away from this blog. First, race is very much alive and kicking in the U.S. (the context of the novel)[2] and any neoliberal suggestion that race "is totally overhyped these days, [and] black people need to get over themselves" (Adichie, 2013, p. 5) is nonsensical. Second, Ifemelu's rhetorical question is worthy of an answer. What WASPs aspire to is a reproduction of a system that works so well for them, a system where in the novel, the only person who has land inheritance and a family summer vacation house was Curt, a Republican WASP who has his own apartment in Baltimore and he is only in his twenties. Curt and Ifemelu dated for awhile and he simply showered her with gifts, including an overnight trip to Paris. Epistemically, Foucault (2009) had shown, we tend to (re)produce what we already know; as such, we should not be surprised that Curt and his likes would loudly – if not violently – call for the reproduction of neoliberalism, which Ifemelu calls 'American tribalism.' Why should we expect them to do otherwise?

The third and very significant blog was titled, "To My Fellow Non-American Blacks: In America, You Are Black, Baby." This blog captured not only the four pillars of neoliberal tribalism discussed in the novel but also Shah's Left/Right and Authoritarianism/Libertarianism intersection as shown in Figure I. It is worth noting that the blog started with this conditional sentence, "when you make the choice to come to America" (p. 273). However, for most post-colonial subjects in war torn areas like North or East Africa, for example, coming to America or the West in general is not a question of choice. All one needs to do is to look at the recent 'boat people' crossing from Libya (North, East and Sub-Saharan Africa) into Europe. People are risking their lives to get to safe shores. When these immigrants and refugees arrived at the shores of America, the blog argued, they entered what I have termed elsewhere *becoming Black* (Ibrahim, 2014, 2016). This is an extremely complicated process of identity reconfiguration, where those who are not familiar or do not know intimately the North American Black-and-White dichotomy go through an initiation process that gets them to know what it means *to be* Black in North America. *To be* and *to become* are intersected yet different processes. To be

Black is like speaking one's mother tongue (where one is naturally comfortable in it, it is a second nature), while becoming Black is like speaking a second language (where one is still learning what words mean, how to put sentences together and how to pronounce certain words). Ifemelu was becoming Black in that she was starting to speak the 'language of Blackness' as defined in North America. To use Adichie's (2013) terms, becoming Black meant starting to "sound American," that is perfecting "the blurring of the *t*, the creamy roll of the *r*, the sentences starting with "so," and the sliding response of "oh really"" (p. 213, original emphasis). The blog is long but it is worth quoting at length:

To My Fellow Non-American Blacks: In America, You Are Black, Baby

Dear Non-American Black, when you make the choice to come to America, you become black. Stop arguing. Stop saying I'm Jamaican or I'm Ghanaian. America doesn't care. So what if you weren't "black" in your country? You're in America now. We all have our moments of initiation into the Society of Former Negroes. Mine was in a class in undergrad when I was asked to give the black perspective, only I had no idea what that was. So I just made something up. And admit it—you say "I am not black" only because you know black is at the bottom of America's race ladder. And you want none of that. Don't deny now. What if being black had all the privileges of being white? Would you still say "Don't call me black, I'm from Trinidad"? I don't think so. So you're black, baby. And here's the deal with becoming black: You must show that you are offended when such words as "watermelon" or "tar baby" are used in jokes, even if you don't know what the hell is being talked about... You must nod back when a black person nods at you in heavily white area. It is called the black nod. It is a way for black people to say "You are not alone, I am here too." In describing black women you admire, always use the word "STRONG" because that is what black women are supposed to be in America. If you are a woman, please do not speak your mind as you are used to doing in your country. Because in America, strong-minded black women are SCARY. And if you are a man, be hyper-mellow, never get too excited, or somebody will worry that you're about to pull a gun. When you watch television and hear that a "racist slur" was used, you must immediately become offended. Even though you are thinking "But why won't they tell me exactly what was said?"…

When a crime is reported, pray that it was not committed by a black person, and if it turns out to have been committed by a black person, stay well away from the crime area for weeks, or you might be stopped for fitting the profile. If a black cashier gives poor service to the non-black person in front of you, compliment that person's shoes or something, to make up for the bad service. If you are in an Ivy League college and a Young Republican tells you that you got in because of Affirmative Action, do not whip out your perfect grades from high school. Instead, gently point out that the biggest beneficiaries of Affirmative Action are white women. If you go to eat in a restaurant, please tip generously. Otherwise the next black person who comes in will get awful service… If you're telling a non-black person about something racist that happened to you, make sure you are not bitter. Don't complain. Be forgiving. If possible, make it funny. Most of all, do not be angry. Black people are not supposed to be angry about racism… This applies only for white liberals, by the way. Don't even bother telling a white conservative about anything racist that happened to you. Because the conservative will tell you that YOU are the real racist and your mouth will hand open in confusion (pp. 273-5).

Becoming Black, it seems, flies in the face of neoliberalism. It means, first, there is no free floating signifier (Hall, 2002), Blackness is a fixed category whose meaning is already deciphered; second, in becoming Black, one has to face the weight of what it means *to be Black* in the U.S. with its negative history and 'racial ranking'; third, contrary to neoliberal thinking, becoming Black sends us back to Michael Young's (1958) original meaning of 'meritocracy,' which is a dystopia filled with racism, negativity and denial of history; fourth and finally, to resist this dystopia, according to neoliberal thinking, can only mean self-suicide because all negative things that happen to you are your own doing, no one else to blame but yourself. To explain, according to the original meaning of 'meritocracy' which is first coined by Young, one has to surrender and accept their 'fate,' where rich people are rich because morally they deserve to be there and therefore deserve the reward the society lavishes on them; and poor people are poor not only because of their own doing but their misfortune is a verdict on their own failure. This is neoliberalism at its zenith, with social places where winners and losers are sorted out and wealth is accordingly allocated, where one does not have any obligation towards other fellow citizens other than profit, and where respectability is a question of how much wealth one has accumulated (Rawls, 2005; Sen, 2009; Taylor, 1994). For Susan George (1999), this is a *cul-de-sac* and it requires a severe jolt to be escaped.

Rethinking Neoliberalism: *Americanah* as a Teacher Education Complicated Conversation

> To ask whether a society is just is to ask how it distributes the things we prize—income and wealth, duties and rights, powers and opportunities, offices and honors. A just society distributes these goods in the right way; it gives each person his or her due. The hard questions begin when we ask what people are due, and why (Sandel, 2008, pp. 15-6).

From the discussion above, it is clear that *Americanah* raises a number of very significant themes. I have used this novel since 2013 within a required teacher education social foundations course, which I have taught (and continue to teach) both in Canada and the United States for over 15 years. Teaching different iterations of this course for this long, I have found the theme of neoliberalism persistently difficult for teacher education students to grapple with. The conceptual, not to say the abstract, nature of the topic seems particularly difficult. It is worth noting, students' difficulty with neoliberalism is not new. In fact, reaching similar conclusions to mine, for Sandra Beth Schneider's students, neoliberalism is a "seemingly amorphous, inaccessible, and invisible framework" (Schneider, 2015, p. 284). So, pedagogically I needed to make the invisible visible in neoliberalism, and the intangible tangible, hence my thinking of using this novel. I have found over the years that textuality in general, particularly stories and novels, as one of the best pedagogical tools that make students remember and see concepts I am dealing with in my classes.

Before the introduction of this novel, I used to make students read a number of articles and book chapters on the topic, with special focus on the ethics of how neoliberalism has turned (public) education into a commodity, hence stripping it from its critical and necessary democratic ideals and community. The list of reading included Martinez and Garcia (1997), Bourdieu (1998), J. Smith (2003), Duvall (2007), Schneider (2015), among others. In constructing it this way, neoliberalism became a stand-alone topic and made the invisible scripts of race, class, gender, and orientation even more invisible.

Starting 2013, I revamped that section in my course. Now, I first introduce and accentuate more vividly the concept of intersectionality—where race, class, gender, etc. cannot be separated from each other and from the social context in which they are found. As a result, I call this module in my course, 'Race, Displacement, Post-colonialism, and Neoliberalism: An Intersectionality.' Second, I introduce *Americanah* as an example of intersectionality. Before we read the novel, however, we still read the authors above. Pedagogically, I now introduce neoliberalism in a form of a debate and divide the class into two teams: for and against neoliberalism. Putting the onus on the students, and using the list of references and resources I initiated as a starting point, each team is to research their position and present it in class. With my help, a third group acts as judges, weighing the logic and the convincing nature of the arguments presented.

Using these resources and arguments, I then ask the class individually to read *Americanah* against the backdrop of neoliberalism. This assignment is called Reading and Inquiry (R & I), where students are expected to do free-style reading notes, and where there are no right and wrong readings but there are convincing readings. The themes addressed above are some of the themes that students come back to time and again. Beside those themes, in reading the novel, recently one White female student used Elizabeth Martinez and Arnoldo Garcia (1997) classic definition of neoliberalism and its five themes: deregulation, privatization, abandonment of the public and common good, free-market reign, and eradication of social services. Her main arguments are thus: 1) calling for a relative equal distribution of wealth is not an act of generosity, but an act of necessity if Ifemelu must not feel the need to immigrate to the U.S. and actually stay and contribute to

Nigeria's social, intellectual, and economic prosperity; and 2) equal distribution of wealth is a necessity if 'boat people' (my term for the people the student was describing in her paper) do not feel the obligation to sacrifice their lives crossing the Mediterranean Sea in search of peace in Europe; if Black people in the U.S. are judged by what they do not by the car they drive; if "oppression olympics" (using Sandel, 2008, term) is no longer needed as marginalized groups are jostling to be ranked as the most oppressed; and, finally, if we can propose a notion of 'radical love' (my term, which I will address soon).

A female student of color focused on the theme of intersectionality in Ifemelu's thoughtful blog, "Job vacancy in America – National arbiter in chief of "who is racist"" (Adichie, 2013, p. 390). In the blog, Ifemelu argues that, "In America, racism exists but racists are all gone. Racists belong to the past" (p. 390). So, humorously suggested, we need an arbiter, Ifemelu writes, "Somebody needs to get the job of deciding who is racist and who isn't" (p. 390). Even though it is suggested with humor, the student argues, *everyday racism* (Essed, 1991, a concept which students are familiar with in my course) is hard to pin down and hence hard to name. Here, using the language of the blog, if one is not lynched or if one is not a "bloodsucking monster," then one cannot be called a racist (p. 390). This same female student then turned to another blog that dealt with a similar manifestation of racism at a global level, which was called "Traveling while black." The blog was talking about the "recognizable black," not "those folk who look Puerto Rican or Brazilian" (Adichie, 2013, p. 410). The blog was about a trip which "a friend of a friend" took to Egypt where an "Egyptian Arab guy" called him "a black barbarian." This is supposed to be Africa, the blog wonders, so Blackness seems to be negatively perceived at a global level. Contrary to neoliberal ideology, the female student contends, where social categories are supposed to be free floating signifiers, the Black body is already read and a tableau that is locked into negativity.

Following the intersection of race and poverty, a White male student focused on a blog that talked about "white privilege," and where a White "Appalachian hick" described his plight as "fucking poor in West Virginia" and whose family "is on welfare" (Adichie, 2013, p. 429). The blog was about imagining that Appalachian hick as a "black guy." "Check the stats," the blog explains. "The Appalachian hick guy is fucked up, which is not cool, but if he were black, he'd be fucked up plus" (p. 429). Another White male student focused on a blog on language, or "what things really mean" (Adichie, 2013, p. 435). Apparently, the blog argues, "Americans are most uncomfortable with race," that is, if they say, "Oh, its' simplistic to say it's race, racism is so complex," this means "they just want you to shut up already" (p. 435). If a White person says, "a neighborhood is diverse, they mean nine percent black people. (The minute it gets to ten percent black people, the white folk move out.) If a black person says diverse neighborhood, they are thinking forty percent black" (pp. 435-6). "Mainstream film" means "white folks like it or made it," "urban" means "black and poor" and "racially charged" means "we are uncomfortable saying "racists"" (p. 436).

"The White Friend Who Gets It" is one of the last blogs that deals with what the blog calls the best gift that people of color, especially Black people, can have in their fight against racism. A White female student decided to deal with that blog. The "White Friend Who Gets It," the blog goes, can say "shit" that you cannot say as a Black person, or should not be saying. "Shit" like "since the beginning of America, white people have been getting jobs because they are white," and that "the American Black deal is kind of like you've been unjustly imprisoned for many years, then all of a sudden you're set free, but you get no bus fare. And, by the way, you and the guy who imprisoned you are now automatically equal" (pp. 448-9).

Complicating the Complicated Conversations:
A Call for Equality and Radical Love

Having implemented this module of 'Race, Displacement, Post-colonialism, and Neoliberalism: An Intersectionality' almost five times now, I continue to improve on it. However, using the notion of intersectionality, doing the reading for this module, and having the debate in class are a good climax that anchors the reading around neoliberalism and makes the invisible visible and intangible tangible. *Americanah* shows students the limits of neoliberalism. In the face of this "crazy" (Adichie, 2013, p. 360) situation of racial injustice, as Ifemelu argues above, first, we need to be courageous. That is, in the face of unequal distribution of wealth, the burden of history, the ugly head of racism and post-colonialism, the global crisis of immigration and refugees—especially the torturous process of 'becoming Black' in North America—White privilege and neoliberal ideology of meritocracy, we need to confront and take our ignorance seriously. Second, we need to find psychic ways that help us confront the pain and agony of racism, experienced on a daily basis by what Ifemelu calls 'American Blacks' and 'Non-American Blacks.' Third, we need to confront our shortcomings when it comes to race, economic deprivation and historical inequalities. Talking about her relationship with Curt (her White ex-boyfriend), Ifemelu talked about these shortcomings as an utter surprise, in that sometimes Curt was extremely (if not over) attuned with racism, his own privilege as a wealthy, handsome, and educated WASP; yet in many occasions, he was "tone-deaf" to what is clearly for Ifemelu an act of racism. The narrator of the novel put it thus:

> It was not that they avoided race, she [Ifemelu] and Curt. They talked about it in the slippery way that admitted nothing and engaged nothing and ended with the word "crazy," like a curious nugget to be examined and then put aside. Or as jokes that left her with a small and numb discomfort that she never admitted to him. And it was not that Curt pretended that being black and being white were the same in America; he knew they were not. It was, instead, that she did not understand how he grasped one thing but completely tone-deaf about another similar thing, how he could easily make one imaginative leap, but be crippled in the face of another (pp. 360-1).

It is clear that we cannot talk about, imagine or even teach we do not know. What is a second nature and lived experience of racism for Ifemelu is inconceivable and totally foreign for Curt. Curt may even deny or accuse Ifemelu, as he did, with over reading or being too sensitive to race. This is why Ifemelu in one blog advised Non-American Blacks to be careful about how, when and where to put race on the table because the readily available discourse of "playing the race card" or "reverse discrimination" can backfire (p. 359). So, Ifemelu argues, the privileged, especially those in positions of power, have to be extremely careful about not judge the world using only their lens and lived experience. Like all experiences, their experiences are limited by time and space. To make this point, Ifemelu narrates an experience she has had at a dinner party in Manhattan, a day after Barack Obama became the Democratic Party's candidate for President of the United States. A balding White man said, "Obama will end racism in this country" (p. 359). Back and forth with the party attendants, some of whom have argued that race would no longer become an issue after Obama's election, Ifemelu told the crowd:

> The only reason you say that race [would not become] an issue is because you wish it was not. We all wish it was not. But it's a lie. I came from a country where race was not an issue; I did not think of myself as black and I only became black when I came to America. When you are black in America and you fall in love with a white person, race doesn't matter when you're alone together because it's just you and your love. But the minute you step outside, race matters. But we don't talk about it. We don't even tell our white partners the small things that piss us off and the things we wish they understood better, because we're worried they will say we're overreacting, or we're being too sensitive. And we don't want them to say, Look how far we've come, just forty years ago it would have been illegal for us to even be a couple blah blah blah… [And] when we come to nice liberal dinners like this, we say that race doesn't matter because that's what we're supposed to say, to keep our nice liberal friends comfortable (pp. 359-360)

As a teacher, I make sure I check what I say in moments like these. So, instead of making statements or declaring my own position, I continue to invite students to speak and hence turn 'teaching' into a pedagogical 'invitation into a conversation.' Yet, unapologetic however, I offer my comments. I do so normally at the end of the conversation or in the last moments of class. So, in responding to the shortcomings above, I invoked the philosopher Martin Buber (2002) and what he had to say in a different context. Buber argues for what he calls "genuine dialogue," which he proposes against "monologue disguised as dialogue" where one listens to his/her own echo or him/herself, and "technical dialogue" where one "is prompted solely by the need of [so-called] objective understanding" (p. 22). For Buber, genuine dialogue is one where not only one ethically cares (Noddings, 1992) and genuinely listens, but one "where each of the participants really has in mind the other or others in their present and particular being and runs to them with the intention of establishing a living mutual relation between himself and them" (Buber, 2002, p. 22). The logical result of this genuine dialogue is what Jesus Gomez (2015) calls "radical love," where people communicate out of love and not for instrumental purposes. Radical love, Gomez (2015) argues, "seeks the equality of difference in terms of identity, fights against discrimination, and develops values of solidarity" (p. 64). Here, structures and subjectivity are in a constant state of dialogue, thoughts and feelings "are united in the search for identity and meaning in the network society" (pp. 64-5). For Gomez (2015), radical love can only happen with the existence of agency and between equals. Radical love, he writes, "may be achieved through communication and dialogue in a context that is more horizontal, flexible, and comprehensive" (p. 65). In radical love, we become the protagonists and the authors of our own lives, which increases, on the one hand, "our opportunities to make choices," and "the margins of our freedom and our decision-making ability," on the other (pp. 65-6). Eventually, this will help us bring into existence a meaningful life and enable us to combat the racism, sexism, abilism, and other forms of discrimination, marginalization and social stratification.

In *Americanah*, ironically, we had a glimmer of this radical love in the biracial relationship between Ifemelu and Curt. In it, we see some shape of radical love, where love is communicated through the verbal act (i.e. linguistically) and through that which is purely emotional and beyond language (i.e. sacramentally). Facing head-on what Ifemelu calls "the problem of race in America," we also bear witness to moments of genuine dialogue and a radical economy of listening and communication. In a neoliberal context, the survival of such radical love is not meant to be sustained, hence the break up between Ifemelu and Curt. Writing about the dark side of the non-sustainability of such radical love, Ifemelu contends in one blog:

> The simplest solution to the problem of race in America? Romantic love. Not friendship. Not the kind of safe, shallow love where the objective is that both people remain comfortable. But the real deep romantic love, the kind that twists you and wrings you out and makes you breathe through the nostrils of your beloved. And because that real deep romantic love is so rare, and because [neoliberal] American society is set up to make it even rarer between American Black and American White, the problem of race in America will never be solved (pp. 366-7)

Despite this context, to continue calling for radical love is to hold on to radical hope, especially in the present situation of hopelessness, where neoliberalism is writ large. With the election of Trump, neoliberalism has found a king(dom), any notion of public good has become a sin, and the role of government is reduced to garbage collection. It is exactly in this historical moment that we need *wide-awakeness* (Greene, 2005; Rautins & Ibrahim, 2011). In such a critical moment, we as critical pedagogues are called on to become witness, to speak truth to power, to propose alternative subjectivities and possibilities, and to educate—and radically. As Maxine Greene (2005) articulates it, we are entrusted with a consequential task:

> The... educator must be awake, critical, open to the world. It is an honor and a responsibility to be a teacher in such dark times—and to imagine, and to act on what we imagine, what we believe ought to at last be (p. 80).

If we do not take such ethical responsibility seriously, we will most likely fall into the neoliberal trap of meritocracy, which will continue the persistent situation of marginalization, exclusion and silencing of certain minoritized groups (of students). My approach to intersectionality and my use of *Americanah* is a small crack of hope in this dark time. Without this small crack, people will find themselves in and within an economy where people can only produce what they already know, hence those with intellectual imagination, and social, cultural and linguistic capital and competency will find themselves in a social and educational system that will advantage them over those who have little or none of these competencies. For Maxine Greene (2005), this type of economy ultimately silences. This silencing, Greene writes, "may be like that of being in a closed room with the windows shut against the "world" others are seeing and accepting" (p. 78). Therefore, it is imperative for teachers, especially those who are calling for radical love, to unbar the "doors" and "windows" of their classrooms and accompany students on the road to consciousness, imagination, pluralism, and the meaningful pursuit of knowledge and discovery. Contrary to neoliberal ideology of laissez-faire, critical pedagogues of wide-awakeness, of radical love, of radical hope are called on more than ever to raise consciousness in our students and to unmask oppression and liberate the capacity to learn, imagine, act, and openly dialogue with the world. Complicated conversations are more than ever urgent and, for me, *Americanah* has opened up many conversations that my classes would not have had, especially as it relates to the intersection of race, post-colonialism, displacement, and neoliberalism. I hope with this module I was able to bring into existence a meaningful life, a contingent life that is worthy of living.

Reference:

Adichie, C. (2014). *Americanah*. Toronto, ON: Vintage.

Anup, S. (2010). *A primer on neoliberalism*. Retrieved from: http://www.globalissues.org/article/39/a-primer-on-neoliberalism.

Bond, P. (2015). Contradiction in consumer credit: Innovations in South African super-exploitation. *Critical Arts* 2(29), 218-239.

Bourdieu, P. (1998). The essence of neoliberalism. *Le Monde Diplomatique*. Retrieved from http://mondediplo.com/1998/12/08bourdieu.

Buber, M. (2002). *Between man and man*. New York, NY: Routledge.

Coleman-King, C. (2014). *The (re)making of a Black America: Tracing the racial and ethnic socialization of Caribbean American youth*. New York: Peter Lang.

Deleuze, G. & Guattari, F. (1987). *A thousand plateaus: Capitalism and schizophrenia*. Londong & New York: Continuum.

Derrida, J. (2000). *Of hospitality*. Stanford: Stanford University Press.

Duvall, E. (2007). What a difference an ideology makes: An alternative pedagogical orientation to neoliberal values in education. In Alanen, R. & Poyhonen, S. (Eds.), *Language in action: Vygotsky and Leontievian legacy today* (pp. 124–160). Newcastle, UK: Cambridge Scholars.

Epstein, J. (2016). *Here's the proof of Donald Trump's racism, sexism & anti-gay rhetoric you've been asking for, trolls*. Retrieved from: http://www.thenewcivilrightsmovement.com/joshuaepstein/trump.

Essed, P. (1991). *Understanding everyday racism: An interdisciplinary theory*. Los Angeles, CA: Sage.

Foucault, M. (2009). *Naissance de la Clinique*. Paris: Quadrige /Presses Universitaires de France.

George, S. (1999). *A short history of neo-liberalism*. Retrieved from: http://www.zmag.org/CrisesCurEvts/Globalism/george.htm.

Gilroy, P. (1991). *"There ain't no black in the Union Jack": The cultural politics of race and nation*. Chicago, IL: University of Chicago Press.

Gomez, J. (2015). *Radical love: A revolution for the 21st century*. New York: Peter Lang.

Greene, M. (1995). *Releasing the imagination: Essays on education, the arts, and social change*. San Francisco: Jossey-Bass.

Greene, M. (2005). Teaching in a moment of crisis: The spaces of imagination. *The New Educator* 1, 77-80.

Greene, M. (2008). Commentary: Education and the arts: The windows of imagination. *Learning Landscapes* 1, 17-21.

Hall, S. (1992). What is this "Black" in Black popular culture? In Dent, G. (Ed.), *Black popular culture* (pp. 21-33). Seattle, WA: Bay Press.

Hall, S. (2013). The work of representations. In Hall, S., Evans, J. & Nixon, S. (Eds.), *Representation* (2nd ed.) (pp. 1-59). Los Angeles, CA: Sage.

Ibrahim, A. (2014). *The rhizome of Blackness: A critical ethnography of Hip-Hop culture, language, identity, and the politics of becoming.* New York: Peter Lang.

Ibrahim, A. (2016). "Who owns my language?" African Canadian youth, post-coloniality and the symbolic violence of language in a French-language high school in Ontario. In Ibrahim, A. & Abdi, A. (Eds.), *The education of African Canadian children: Critical perspectives* (pp. 145-163). Montreal: McGill-Queen's University Press.

Noddings, N. (1992). *The challenge to care in schools: An alternative approach to education.* New York: Teachers College Press.

O'Hara, M. (2006). In search of the next enlightenment? The challenge for education in uncertain times. *Journal of Transformative Education 4*, 105-117.

Okpalaoka, C. (2014). *(Im)migrations, relations, and identities: Negotiating cultural memory, diaspora, and African (American) identities.* New York: Peter Lang.

Rautins, C. & Ibrahim, A. (2011). Wide-awakeness: Toward a critical pedagogy of imagination, humanism and becoming. *International Journal of Critical Pedagogy 3*(2), 24-36.

Rawls, J. (2005). *Political Liberalism.* New York: Columbia University Press.

Rorty, R. (1989). *Contingency, irony, and solidarity.* Cambridge: Cambridge University Press.

Sandel, M. (2008). *Justice: What's the right thing to do?* New York: Farrar, Strauss & Giroux.

Schneider, S. (2015). Teaching Neoliberalism, in the Context of Corporate Reform, in the Undergraduate Social Foundations Classroom. *Educational Studies 51*(4), 284–299.

Sen, A. (2009). *The idea of justice.* New York: Belknap Press.

Smith, J. W. (2003). *Cooperative capitalism: A blueprint for global peace and prosperity.* London: The Institute for Economic Democracy.

Taylor, C. (1994). The politics of recognition. In D. Goldberg (Ed.), *Multiculturalism: A critical reader* (pp. 75-106). Oxford, UK: Blackwell.

Young, M. (1958). *The rise of the meritocracy: 1870-2033.* London: Thames & Hudson.

Notes

1 APA requires the capitalization of Black and White, I shall observe that. However, the novel does not. I will quote the novel in its original version.

2 For empirical studies in the U.S., see Coleman-King (2014) and Okpalaoka (2014) and in Canada, see Ibrahim (2014).

CHAPTER TEN

Operating Under Erasure: ~~Hip-Hop~~ and the Pedagogy of Affect

(REPRINTED WITH PERMISSION) Ibrahim, A. (2004). Operating under erasure: ~~Hip-Hop~~ and the pedagogy of affect. *Journal of Curriculum Theorizing, 20*(1), 113-133.

> *The black pathfinder is offset by the crazy gold trim. Moving down 52nd Street, cruise style. There is a super phat sound emanating from the other side of glory. Neither Milton's paradise regained or lost. It's just paradise in and of itself.*
>
> SPADY (1993, P. 96)

> *Anything you wanted to know about the [L.A.] riots was in the records before the riots... I've given so many warnings on what's gonna happen if we don't get these things straight in our life... Armageddon is near. How close is near.*
>
> ICE CUBE

Jouissance—and affective in general—seems to invariably be cheated in language. It is always-always in the excess, that which can only be accessed in and through the performed, that which can not be fully captured in language, something about it is always left over (Butler, 1999; Grossberg, 1992; Hall and du Gay, 1996; Kristeva, 1982; Lacan, 1977, among others). My interest in this paper is to navigate through this cultural space of left over, namely Black popular culture, Hip-Hop to be specific, and link it to a larger framework of pedagogy and learning. Affective, Grossberg (1992) explains, is "the unrepresentable excess—the sublime?—which defies images and words, which can only be indicated" and popular culture, especially when operating within an affective sensibility, "is a crucial ground where people give others ... the authority to shape their identity and locate them within various circuits of power" (p. 83).

On their part, Giroux and Simon (1989a) argued that, "Popular culture represents a significant pedagogical site that raises important questions about the relevance of everyday life, student voice, and the investments of meaning and pleasure that structure and anchor the why and how of learning (p. 5). If this is so, it is surprising then how little attention the intersection of pedagogy, affective/investment, and popular culture within school sites has received. Here, my focus is on ethnography in general and critical ethnography in particular (see Simon and Dippo, 1986 for full discussion). I shall therefore begin with a theoretical framework—pedagogy of affective—then discuss my research and offer a conclusion on the need to rethink the connection between Black popular culture, which is currently operating under erasure, the curriculum, identity investment, and the process of critical teaching and learning.

Mapping What Matters

The complexity of studying popular culture *ethnographically* stems from the fact that it works at the notoriously difficult plane of affect. Why we love a particular music, read a genre of novels, or watch "sleeze TV," Grossberg (1992) explains, might be explained, but never fully. All we feel emotionally is that quasi-orgasmic rush, *juissance*, running through our veins. However, I want to argue, this rush is neither neutral nor without its *politics of identification* (Ibrahim, 2003), which eventually influences (if not determines) what we learn and how we learn it. That is, the rush is not simply ideological (where we as consumers are manipulated by a ruling class) nor simply affective or emotional; after all our emotions have their own (rational?) structure and language (Bourdieu, 1984; Williams, 1979). It is at this intersection of the consciously rational, willful, committed, and the unconsciously emotional, passionate, pleasurable, and volitional that I want to locate popular culture.

Mapping what matters within popular culture is a "mattering map" (Grossberg, 1992), where no investment is haphazard and where people's identities and everyday lives are formed and performed. Popular culture is increasingly pervasive and powerful force not only economically (think about how many millionaires rap has created), but, more importantly, pedagogically and educationally. It is where people and youth in particular socialize their identities and thus envision the possibilities of their existence. Popular culture can be defined as a durable, transposable disposition, structured *champ*[1] (Bourdieu, 1984) or a discursive formation (Foucault, 1977) whose meaning is only possible within a theory of articulation (Hall, 1986). The latter argues that diverse elements or formations, which have no intrinsic, historical or apparent connection, can be connected, accumulated and articulated together to produce a new event, be it identity, musical, or otherwise. For example, the articulation of dance hall music, DJing, MCing, break dancing, R&B, sound system, graffiti, and fashion produced what we know now as Hip-Hop.

Such articulations, Grossberg (1992) argues, create a series of "alliances" which in turn make "a number of different positions available to different groups" (p. 71). That is, different cultural articulations invade, populate and incorporate different bodies differently, and in the process effectively guarantee their singular sensibility, investment and engagement. However, no alliances are absolute and each has its own circuits of power that either empower or disempower. They do so because people affectively authorize them. As Grossberg (1992, pp. 83-4) aptly put it,

> People actively constitute places and forms of authority (both for themselves and for others) through the deployment and organization of affective investments. By making certain things matter, people "authorize" them to speak for them, not only as a spokesperson but also as a surrogate voice... People give authority to that which they invest in; they let the objects of such investments speak for and in their stead. They let them organize their emotional and narrative life and identity.

To affectively authorize a discursive formation to "speak" on our behalf is to enter the plane of belonging and identification (where identities are formed through interpellation (Althusser, 1971), and insofar as these moments of identification are fragmented and dispersed, identities are similarly dispersed). To affectively authorize a discursive formation is to find ourselves "at home," at least temporarily, with what we care about, "partly because there seems to be no other space available, no other terrain on which [we] can construct and anchor [our] mattering maps" (Grossberg, 1992, pp. 84-5). Hence they become sites of empowerment. On the other hand, however, affective relations can also be disempowering because "They render ideological and material realities invisible behind a screen of passion." They blind and position "people in ways which make them particularly vulnerable to certain kinds of appeals, and, most frightening, they can easily be articulated into repressive and even totalitarian forms of social demands and relations" (Ibid., p. 87). For example, misogyny and homophobia in Hip-Hop, which originally emerged as a subaltern creative cultural space of resistance, are cases in point. So there is no affective investment, and for that matter no popular cultural form, that is not complexly contradictory.

For Grossberg (1992), "mattering maps" are like "investment portfolios" where changing investments matter as much as where, how, and the intensities and degrees of investment. They "define different forms, quantities and places of energy, They "tell" people how to use and how to generate energy, how to navigate their way into and through various moods and passions, and how to live within emotional and ideological histories" (p. 82). Mattering maps, he continues, "also involve the lines that connect the different sites of investment; they define the possibilities for moving from one investment to another, of linking the various fragments of identity together. They define not only what sites … matter but how they matter" (p. 84). Put otherwise, it is these mattering maps that regulate not only our passion, investment, and texture of our affective, but eventually our identities, identification, and the possibilities of we could become. In the following section I want to propose a larger "articulation" between race, curriculum, and investments as they relate to the above framework of affective and mattering maps.

Race, Curriculum, and Mattering Maps

"I still remember," I wrote in my field-notes diary, "on my first day at the high school where I am conducting my research, while standing in the middle of the foyer, the 14-year old girl Najat came running to embrace me in a manner of a lost old friend. She then wondered in French if I was coming to school to teach. "Non," I responded in French, but I was equally curious why she wanted me at the school. "Just because there is nothing Black in this school. All you see is white, white, white," she responded in English." First, I knew Najat since I was working in another research project in the same French-language high school for almost two years and second, I want to argue, in these non-identificatory spaces where self-consciousness undergoes the experience of desire to be reflected, seen and recognized, other spaces of identification, mattering maps will emerge: Black popular culture. In this case, Black popular culture—and diasporic Black hybrid identities in general—will emerge not only as sites of identification, but also as curriculum sites where learning can and does take place. I intend to show that, in the present research, when Black/African youth were unable to participate in dominant ("white, white, white") spaces, Black popular culture emerged as a mattering map of investment, learning and desire. Hence creating a "null curriculum"; by which I am referring to the sites of affective and pedagogical investment that are directly implicated in youth identity formation, but are not formally acknowledged in their schooling/learning processes (cf. Eisner, 1979).

This raises a number of research and pedagogical questions, two of which will be addressed here. First, where (and how) do our youth form their identities if not within and in relation to the realm of popular culture, which is negated most often within formal education settings (Dimitriadis and McCarthy, 2001; Giroux and Simon, 1989 a&b) and, second, what are the implications of this negation in reframing and reconceptualizing critical curriculum studies? Put otherwise, I want to ask, do social identities, especially race and gender, and their formation processes have any significant role in the process of learning; how do we engage these identities; and how can critical educators bring student-based and student-produced knowledge into the classroom, not to be consumed but rather to be critically engaged, deconstructed? This, furthermore, raises questions of voice and experience. How do we acknowledge previous experience as legitimate content and challenge it at the same time? How do we affirm student voices while simultaneously encouraging conscientization (Freire, 1993): the interrogation of such voices? And how do we avoid the conservatism inherent in simply celebrating personal experience and confirming what people already know? (cf. Eisner & Powell, 2002; Giroux and Simon, 1989a; Quinn & Kahne, 2001).

These questions can not be understood separately from a diagnosis of the modern condition of what Dimitriadis and McCarthy (2001) call "the age of difference." It is a temporal, poststructuralist and globalized historical moment where desire, agency, identification, and identity count and, indeed, where the politics of identity is the center of teaching and learning. A moment where identity itself is mediated by technological media, on the one hand, and by its relation to the Other, on the other. A moment where movements of goods, ideas, arts, and bodies are ever made easier; a moment where postcolonial subjects are increasingly forming part of the metropolitan centers. In this moment, Dewey's (1916, p. 6) classic notion of "formal education" which was defined as "the deliberate educating of the young" would miss a wide range of aspects of learning that go on in sites other than classrooms. Such may include homes, hospitals, factories, night clubs, sport sites, concerts, museums, and so on (see Beer and Marsh, 1988; Cremin, 1976; Giroux, 2000; Nieto, 2000), as well as school sites such as hallways and gyms. The tension between what goes on in the hallways and gyms where learning can and indeed does take place and where students identities are formed (Giroux and Simon, 1989b; Ibrahim, 1998, 1999, 2000a&b), on the one hand, and classroom pedagogies and practice strategies, on the other, is scarcely dialogued about within the field of curriculum studies; at least not until recently (see also Dimitriadis and McCarthy, 2001; Goldberg, 1997; Kelley, 1998). There is therefore a need to rearticulate that tension and, as I shall do, show the potency of popular culture, more specifically Black popular culture, in the process of students' identity formation, cultural and linguistic practice. Here, the question of what I term *the politics of embodiment*: sexualized, gendered, abled, classed, and racial/ized identities that students bring with them to the classroom and how these identities are formed is vitally important to the praxis of imaginative critical educators.

Unfortunately, the age of difference is also the age of boundary maintenance, quick fixes, moral panic, competence measurement, unthreatening forms of multiculturalism, "accountability," "clientele," and the language of panacea and technique (what Dimitriadis and McCarthy, 2001 call "technicist discourse"). It is an age of what Nietzsche called "ressentiment" (resentment), a "practice by which one defines one's identity through the negation of the other" (Dimitriadis and McCarthy, 2001, p. 4). This ressentiment, Dimitriadis and McCarthy (2001) explain, is pronounced more clearly in how difference, multiplicity, and heterogeneity are dealt with in educational settings; how knowledge formation, mattering maps, genres of representation, and bodily encounters are all regulated by ressentiment. The Other is here capitalized, absolutized and rancourly put either in the inner-city or "overthere" in the Third World. The identity of social victim, interesting enough, especially in the United States, is claimed by the professional middle-class dwellers of the suburb. "In so doing, the suburban professional class denies avenues of social complaint to its other, the inner-city poor." This in turn projects the "suburban worldview as the barometer of public policy, displacing issues of inequality and poverty with demands for balanced bugets, tax cuts, and greater surveillance and incarceration of minority youth" (Ibid., pp. 4-5).

In education, the politics of ressentiment, especially as expressed by mainstream (conservative?) educational theorists, tends to "draw a bright line of distinction between the established school curriculum and the teeming world of multiplicity that flourishes in the everyday lives of youth beyond the school" (Dimitriadis and McCarthy, 2001, p. 2). Nowhere in the U.S. is this narcissistic line (and its moral panic) more drawn than against Black popular culture in general and Hip-Hop in particular.[2] The conservative TV host Bill O'Reilly of *The O'Reilly Factor* on the Fox News Network single handedly forced Muppets and Pepsi Company to drop the rappers Snoop Dogg and Ludacris, respectively, from their advertisements and as their commercial representatives. Ironically, Ludacris was replaced by the Osbornes. Race as much as political agenda determine who gets to be represented and how and, in education, they regulate and govern who gets to be included in the curriculum—the "main text,"[3] as Maxine Greene (1992, p. 2) refers to.

For Eisner (1979) the "main text" can be divided into three typologies: implicit, explicit, and null curriculum. In the explicit curriculum, students enter a discourse[4] and culture whose common signifier is "schooling," with publicly sanctioned goals. These goals are usually presented as ideologically neutral and pedagogically necessary if one is to become a "functional citizen." In the implicit curriculum, also known as the "hidden curriculum" (Apple, 1990, 1982), students are expected to conform and follow certain patterns of cultural practices of schooling that are not stated explicitly. "Take, for example, the expectation that students must not speak unless called on," Eisner (1979, p. 76) explains, "or the expectation that virtually all of the activities within a course [or a class] shall be determined by the teacher, or the fact that schools are organized hierarchically." For Eisner, what the school is doing through these implicit but firmly expected cultural practices is preparing "most people for positions and contexts that in many respects are quite similar to what they experienced in school," that is "hierarchical organization, one-way communication, routine; in short, compliance to purposes set by another" (1979, p. 77).

The "null curriculum" is defined as "what schools do *not teach*" (Eisner, 1979: 83; original emphasis). It is a configuration of knowledge, a mattering map that is linked to students' identities and ways of knowing and learning but not directly addressed in their schooling processes. Eisner argues that most subject matters that are now taught in school systems are taught out of habit. That is, schools teach geography, math, chemistry, and so on, for no reason other than that these were always taught (Eisner, 1979, p. 88). It is of course unwarranted to suggest that Eisner is negating their importance as subjects of study. To the contrary, he is reminding us of this question, which is rarely asked in educational settings: Why are we teaching what we are teaching? Hence, Eisner concludes, "we ought to examine school programs to locate those areas of thought and those perspectives that are now absent in order to reassure ourselves that these omissions were not a result of ignorance but a product of choice" (1979, p. 83).

It is here, I argue, that we should locate Hip-Hop, the cultural space or mattering map which accommodates both internal tensions and dynamic cultural ciphers, mediating the corrosive discourse of the dominating society while at the same time functioning as a subterranean subversion.[5] Hip-Hop is a null curriculum that is so subtle and subterranean that Ice-T likened it to a home invasion. "Homes are being invaded by hip-hop theories and Hip-Hop flavors. White kids are being injected with black rage and anger. People like KRS-One, Public Enemy, Cube are stimulating kids to question authority. And moms says, 'My home has been invaded by these new ideas. How did it get here?' It comes through the walkman. These homes are being invaded by us. And they know it. They know we are in their homes" (cited in Spady, 1993, p. 95).

But this home as well as school invasion and bombardment of popular culture images, Greene (1997) warned us, frequently has the (negative) effect of freezing the imaginative thinking of youth, thus potentially whirling them into "human resources" as opposed to "centers of choice and evaluation" (57). For critical educators, the latter will happen only when, on the one hand, we as critical pedagogues recognize the temporal and non-static nature of youth identities and when the youth themselves, on the other, are able to gaze back at these images and consciously "read" (through) them, a "conscious participation in [the art]work, a going out of energy, an ability to notice what there is to be noticed" (Greene, 1997, p. 58). Following Greene, my interest in the null curriculum is a recall to emphasizing the intersectionality between identity, politics, experience, and pedagogical dis/engagement and the process of learning. Building on this, I want to show below that students do appropriate and develop aspects of "null curriculum" as part of their identity formation; and in the case of Black popular culture, such a curriculum can be utilized in and as a form of critical pedagogy and praxis. This way, I conclude, we may contribute to bringing in Black students' previously unwarranted and non-validated forms of knowledge, address the feeling of alienation that Black students have in relation to Eurocentric curricula, and contribute to a more relevant, engaging and integrative anti-racist curriculum (Dei, 1996).

Against Temporality: Race-ing the Everyday

"The everyday"[6] (Nietzsche, 1977) was quite a feast for my research participants, a group of continental francophone African youths. It was both a space of contradiction and confrontation. It was where they encountered the overdeterminded racial (racist?) gaze and it was, interestingly, their rendezvous with the *jouissance* of identification, investment, and desire. The former is linked to their Blackness. Here, all individuals who possess the Black body and who either live or immigrate to the West enter, so to speak, this "overdetermined gaze," what Gilroy (1997) calls "ethnic absolutism." This was well expressed by Frantz Fanon (1967, p. 116) when he talked about himself as a Black *Antillais* coming to the metropolis of Paris, "I am the slave not of the "idea" that others have of me but of *my own appearance* [my emphasis].... I progress by crawling. And *already* [my emphasis] I am being dissected under white eyes, the only real eyes." There is no métissage here, no creolization, no hybridity: just one lump sum category, and one that is *already* determined, defined: Black. As a result, ironically, Blackness and its cultural and linguistic expression emerge for African youth as sites of bond, investment, and learning. The research data clearly shows that African youth choose[7] Black popular cultural forms as sites of identification (Ibrahim, 1998, 2000a&b, see also below). They do so as part of their identity formation processes and their search for what it means to be Black in North America. As well, depending on their age and gender, they variably perform, enact the North American Black-stylized English and Hip-Hop identity. Hence, they create a null curriculum; color the everyday "little things" (Nietzsche, 1977); and heretofore begin the odyssey of *becoming Black*.

Being is being distinguished here from becoming Black (see also Ibrahim, 1999). The former is defined as an accumulative memory, an experience, an understanding and an apprehension upon which one interacts with the world around her/him, whereas the latter is the process of building this apprehension, this memory. For example, as a continental African, I was not "Black" in Africa, though I had other adjectives that used to bricolage my identity, such as tall, Sudanese, basketball player, etc. That is, my Blackness was not "marked," as Stuart Hall (1997) would argue, since it constituted part of the norm which was taken for granted, it was outside the shadow of the dominant North American Other. However, as a refugee in North America, my perception of self was altered in direct response to the social processes of racisms and the historical representation of Blackness whereby the antecedent signifiers became secondary to my Blackness, and I retranslated my self: I became Black (Ibrahim, 2000a).[8]

Similarly, the research findings point to the fact that continental African youth are constructed and positioned, much like Fanon, and thus treated as "Blacks" by North American hegemonic discourses, representations and dominant groups, respectively. This positionality offered to continental African students in exceedingly complex ways through interlocking representational discourses does not and is unwilling to acknowledge students'—ethnic, language, national and cultural—identity difference. Blackness, as I already noted, becomes the encompassing category and the umbrella under which African youth find themselves. This racialized perception and treatment is enforcing and simultaneously enforced by a social imaginary, a discursive space where Blackness is projected further into negative historical memory and representation (Smedley, 1999; West, 1993). Elsewhere I show that this cartography of Blackness[9], influences students' sense of identity, which, in turn, influences what they linguistically and culturally learn and how (Ibrahim, 1998, 1999, 2000a&b). What they learn, I will outline below, is Black-stylized English, which they access in Black popular cultural forms, such as films, newspapers, magazines and, more importantly, rap, reggae, pop, R&B, and other types of music.

The Study: Site, and Participants

This paper is part of a larger critical ethnographic research (Ibrahim, 1998) that was guided by the following questions. How and in what way does race social identity difference enter the process of learning? What is the role of race and racism in students' identity formation? How are continental African youth positioned and constructed in and out of school? What are the implications of this construction in their social identity formation, and how are these identities formed and performed?

The site of the research is a small, urban Franco-Ontarian high school, which I will refer to as Marie-Victorin (MV)[10] and which is located in southwestern Ontario, Canada. Being a Franco-Ontarian school, the official language is French, however, the language spoken often in corridors and hallways is English. Besides English and French, Arabic, Somali, and Farsi can also be heard at other times. MV has a population of approximately 400 students, from different ethnic, language, religious, and national backgrounds. One-third to one-half of the 400 are students of colour. Despite this disproportionate percentage, all teachers, administrators and staff are White.

When continental African students arrived en mass at MV from their homelands starting in 1991, they constituted from one-third to one-half of the school population. They came from cultural and linguistic backgrounds as diverse as their countries of origin: Somalia, Djibouti, Democratic Republic of Congo (formerly Zaïre), Togo, South Africa, Gabon, and Senegal. The Somali speakers make up the majority within this group. The continental African youth vary in age, gender and class. Most come from a middle-class or affluent background; their ages range from twelve to twenty; and they spread from grade seven to thirteen. Some came to Canada as landed immigrants, the majority however came as refugees.

I knew the school and its population very well since I worked in another research project in the same school for almost two years. With permission from the school administration, I restarted to visit the school and to "hang out" with African students at least once a week, and in most cases, two or three times from January to June of 1996. I took the role of a participant-observer, keeping regular notes and diaries. Having determined what they could offer to my research, I chose for extensive observation sixteen students—ten boys and six girls—between the ages of fourteen and twenty. The girls were Somali-speakers form Somalia and Djibouti. Of the ten boys, six were Somali-speakers—from Somalia and Djibouti, two Senegalese, one Ethiopian and one Togolese. I observed them in and out of the classrooms as well as in and out of school. With the consent of students and their parents, I interviewed them. I videotaped and audio-taped interactions and exchanges among students. I attended soirées, plays, basketball games, and graduations; and was delighted to be invited to their residences. I transcribed the interviews and some of the videotapes, and analyzed the data by grouping them by theme, category and subject.

Whassup With Hip-Hop? Enacting Black Hybrid Identities

The identification of continental African students with Hip-Hop culture needed no second observation after six months of being at MV. This identification with Hip-Hop, which is a Black male cultural practice, seemed to cut across all ages for the boys. Depending on their age, the situation with the girls was somewhat different. Girls in grade twelve and thirteen tended to be more postmodernly eclectic in their dress: oscillating between Parisian, eloquent North American middle-class, Hip-Hop and traditional national dress. Some of them, for example, dressed in traditional Somali dress for the multicultural celebration day. Conversely, like the boys, the younger girls of grades seven, eight and nine dressed in Hip-Hop and spoke Black-stylized English. On one afternoon, these younger girls, while behind the scenes preparing for an African dance performance scheduled as part of the Black History Month celebration and also while wearing the Islamic *hijab* (veil), were rapping to a recording of the African American rapper Cool J.

Hip-Hop cultural expressions, as performed (Butler, 1999) and enacted by continental male and female African students at MV, have three distinctive but interlocking features. Hip-Hop can be described as a way of dress, walk, and talk. Hip-hop dress is eloquently described by Rose (1991: 277) in talking about a New York City summer party. Picture this: "Thousands of young Black folks milled around waiting to get into the large arena. The big rap summer tour was in town, and it was a prime night for one to show one's stuff." Rose then describes what I see as Hip-Hop dress at MV: "Folks were dressed in the latest "fly gear": bicycle shorts, high-top sneakers, chunk jewelry, baggy pants, and polka-dotted tops. The hair styles were a fashion show in themselves: high fade designs, dread, corkscrews, and braids." Hip-Hop walk, on the other hand, usually involves moving the hands simultaneously with the head and the rest of the body as one is walking or talking. The talk is what generally referred to as "Black English" or "Black talk" (Smitherman, 2000), which I refer to as Black-stylized English (Ibrahim, 1999).

Since continental African students have limited or no contact with African Americans, their source for "Black" (read African American) linguistic and cultural practices is Black popular culture, specifically rap music; referred to in some circles as "urban music" (Walcott, 2000; Powell, 1991). Hence continental African students tend to "pick up" expressions and ways of talking and rapping that encompass stylistic and lexical features and not grammatical ones.

For example, African students use expressions such as "yo yo" [appellation to pay attention], "whassup," "whadap," "wadap" [what is up/what is happening], "homeboy," and "homie" [my cool friend]. In so doing, they are stylistically and lexically allying themselves with and translating what they conceive as "Black linguistic practice." This translation/imitation/citation/enactment is expressed in and through students' speech, is a performance of Black-stylized English (BSE).

BSE is Black English (BE) with style; it is a subcategory. BE is what some have referred to as *Black talk* (Smitherman, 2000), which has its own structure, syntax and grammar. BSE, on the other hand, refers to ways of speaking that do not depend on a full mastery of the language (Ibrahim, 1999). It banks more on *ritual expressions* such *whassup, whadap*, etc., which are more an expression of politics, moments of identification with Hip-Hop cultural identity and a desire for it than they are of language per se. They become the youth way of saying: "I too am Black," and "I too desire Blackness."

For continental African youth, significantly, these lexical expressions are new linguistic and cultural practices they learn, take up or "enter." Adopting Hip-Hop, making it a mattering map influences not only their identity formation but also how they position themselves and how they are positioned by others (Foucault, 1977). This is because when continental African students chose African American cultural and linguistic practices, they in fact chose an identification with a language and historical memory as well as a political and social stance.

I asked students in all of my interviews with African students, "Où est-ce que vous avez appris votre anglais?" (Where did you learn English?). "Télévision," they unanimously responded. However, within this *télévision*, there is a particular representation that seems to interpellate African youth identity and identification: Black popular culture. I asked Najat (14, F, Djibouti),[11] for example, about the last movie she had seen:

Najat: I don't know, I saw *Waiting to Exhale* and I saw what else I saw, I saw *Swimmer*, and I saw *Jumanji*; so wicked, all the movies. I went to *Waiting to Exhale* wid my boyfriend and I was like "men are rude" [laughs].

Awad: Oh believe me I know I know.

Najat: And den he [her boyfriend] was like "no, women are rude." I was like we're like fighting you know and joking around. I was like, and de whole time like [laughs], and den when de woman burns the car, I was like, "go girls!" You know and all the women are like "go girl!" you know? And den de men like khhh. I am like, "I'm gonna go get me a popcorn" [laughs]. (individual interview, English)

Two issues are of particular interest in Najat's example. The first is the influence of Black English in using *de, den, dat,* and *wicked* instead of *the, then, that,* and *really really good*, respectively. The second is embedded in this notion: Youths do not read, relate to and identify with texts disembodiedly. That is, their agency and subjectivities bear witness and influence their reading of the text. For example, two subjectivities influenced Najat's reading of *Waiting to Exhale* were her race and gender identities. It is the Black/woman in burning her husband's car that interpellates Najat.

This interpellation or hailing, using Althusseur's (1971) terms, or *moments of identification,* using my own, point to the process of identification. This is a subconscious process which takes place over a period of time and it functions by internalizing that which is meaningful to us, hence determining our mattering maps, that which deserves our desires and investment. Omer (18, M, Ethiopia) expresses the different ways in which African youth enter, so to speak, this process of identification when he contends:

> Black Canadian youths are influenced by the Afro-Americans. You watch for hours, you listen to Black music, you watch Black comedy, Master T.,[12] the *Rap City*, there you will see singers who dress in particular ways. You see, so. (individual interview, French)

For Omer and all the students I spoke to, their identification with Black popular culture is in large measures connected to their inability to relate to dominant groups and their cultural capital. As a result, Black popular culture emerges as a site of identification. Exploring this contention, Mukhi (19, M, Djibouti) contends:

> We identify ourselves more with the Blacks of America. But, this is normal... We can't, since we live in Canada, we can't identify ourselves with Whites or country music you know [laughs]. We are going to identify ourselves on the contrary with people of our colour, who have our lifestyle you know. (group interview, French).

Operating Under Erasure

The impact of these moments of identification was felt not only in the identity formation processes, but also in the course of second language learning. Here, rap was a significant site. And the fact that rap language was more spread in the boys' narratives raises the question of the role of gender in the process of identification and learning. The following are two of the many occasions on which students articulated their identification with and desire for Black America through the re/citation of rap linguistic styles.[13]

Sam: One two, one two, mic check. A'ait [alright], a'ait, a'ait.

Juma: This is the rapper, you know what 'm meaning? You know wha 'm saying?

Sam: Mic mic mic; mic check. A'ait you wonna test it? Ah, I've the microphone you know; a'ait.

Sam: [laughs] I don't rap man, c'mon give me a break. [laughs] Yo! A'ait a'ait you know, we just about to finish de tape and all dat. Respect to my main man [pointing to me]. So, you know, you know wha 'm mean, 'm just represen'in Q7. One love to Q7 you know wha 'm mean and all my friends back to Q7... Stop the tapin' boy!

Jamal: Kim Juma, live! Put the lights on. Wordap. [Students talking in Somali] Peace out, wardap, where de book. Jamal 'am outta here.

Shapir: Yo, this is Shapir. I am trying to say peace to all my Niggaz, all my bitches from a background that everybody in the house. So, yo, chill out and this is how we gonna kick it. Bye and with that pie. All right, peace yo.

Sam: A'ait this is Sam represen'in AQA [...] where it's born, represen'in you know wha 'm mean? I wonna say whassup to all my Niggaz, you know, peace and one love. You know wha 'm mean, Q7 represen'in foreva. Peace! [Rap music]

Jamal: [as a DJ] Crank it man, coming up. [rap music] (group interview, English)

Of interest in these excerpts is the use of Black-stylized English (BSE), especially the language of rap: "Respect for my main man," "represen'in Q7," " kick the free style," "peace out, wardap," "'am outta here," "I am trying to say peace to all my Niggaz, all my bitches," "so, yo chill out and this is how we gonna kick it," "I wonna say whassup to all my Niggaz," "peace and one love." As important, when Shapir deploys terms like "Niggaz" and "bitches," he is first reappropriating the word *Nigger*, an appellation common in rap and Hip-Hop culture which is invoked without its traditional racist connotation; and, secondly, however he is using the sexist language that exists in rap (Ibrahim, 1999). This language has been challenged by female rappers and was critiqued by male and female students (Ibrahim, 2000a, p. 126).

Clearly, the boys were investing in Black popular culture, especially rap, as both a site of desire and of language learning. Depending on their age, on the other hand, the girls were either fully investing in rap and Hip-Hop like the boys or being postmodernly eclectic. In spite of this, I detected the following three features of Black English (BE) in both the older and the younger girls' speech: 1) the absence of the auxiliary *be* (19 occasions, e.g., "they so cool," "I just laughing" as opposed to *they are so cool* and *I am just laughing*); 2) BE negative concord (4 occasions, e.g., "all he [the teacher] cares about is his daughter you know. If somebody just dies or if I decide to shoot somebody you know, he is *not* doing *nothing* [italics added]"; the expression would be considered incorrect in standard English because of the double negative); and 3) the distributive *be* (4 occasions, e.g. "I be saying dis dat you know?" or "He be like 'Oh, elle va être bien' [she's going to be fine]"). These BE markers are, first, expressions of the influence of Black Talk on the girls' speech and, second, performances of the girls' identity location and desire. The girls had no illusion on where they saw themselves mirrored and where to invest. Amani (16, F, Somalia) contends:

> We have to wonder why we try to really follow the model of the Americans who are Blacks? Because when you search for yourself, search for identification, you search for someone who reflects you, with whom you have something in common. (group interview, French)

In a group interview, I asked Mukhi, in English, "But do you think that that [listening to rap] influences how you [African youths] speak?" He responded,

> "How we dress, how we speak, how we behave."

Supporting both Mukhi and Amani, Hassan (17, M, Djibouti) argued:

> Yes yes, African students are influenced by rap and hip-hop because they want to, yes, they are influenced probably a bit more because it is the desire to belong maybe.
>
> Awad: Belong to what?
>
> Hassan: To a group, belong to a society, to have a model/fashion [he used the term *un modèle*]; you know, the desire to mark oneself, the desire to make, how do I say it? To be part of a rap society, you see. It is like getting into rock and roll or heavy metal. (individual interview, French)

In the same interview, Hassan found it unrealistic to expect to see Blackness allied with rock and roll or heavy metal, as they are socially constructed as White music. Similarly, he argued that African youths would have every reason to invest in basketball—constructed as a Black sport—but not hockey, for example. Clearly, *one invests where one sees oneself mirrored*, and African students had no doubt where their investment lay: an investment that is considerably influenced by who they are or what they have become.

In a racially conscious society, Hall (1991) argues, being Black means one is expected to be Black, act Black, and so be the Other. Becoming Black, on the other hand, I have shown, was a significant cartography not only in how African students were positioned in and outside the school, but also in how they saw, formed, and performed their identities, subjectivities, investments and desires (see also Yon, 2000). This *politics of positionality*—how one is imagined, constructed and represented and the impacts of these on how one sees oneself, I contended, was directly implicated in students' political, linguistic, and cultural choices. The effects of this politics are eloquently delineated in Fanon's *Black skin/White mask*. Fanon (1967, p. 116) shows how the gaze of the Other fixes him in an identity: "When people like me, they tell me it is in spite of my colour. When they dislike me, they point out that it is not because of my colour. Either way, I am locked into the infernal circle." Again, when the child pulls her finger and points at him exclaiming "Look momma, a Black man," Fanon writes, "I was fixed in that gaze"—the gaze of Otherness (Hall, 1991).[14] This example is probably too descriptive causing one to cast a doubt on the subtle and the almost completely unconscious experience within which identities are formed and performed, which in turn make certain maps matter.

Taking up, identifying with, enacting, imitating or citing Hip-Hop and rap means learning the cultural as well as linguistic practices that are introduced to continental African students through Black popular culture. They enter representational discourses of Blackness and Hip-Hop by learning a new style of dress and new ways of walking and of talking. Hence, students enter a "null curriculum," with which they do identify; a curriculum that at least partially reflects their own subjectivities; a curriculum that influences who they are and the future they desire.

This is not a Conclusion: Affective and the Pedagogy of Hip-Hop

> Hiphopness—the dynamic and constant sense of being alive in a hip hop, rap conscious, reality based world—is actually where many young black people are today. As we enter [the 21st Century], it becomes even more important to realize that significant changes are taking place in the rapidly growing hip hop world. To stand back, wack crack style is to succumb to the inertia of the past. And yet, to become a participant in this highly fluid, ritualized space is to exercise an act of freedom that may very well change your constitutive being (Spady, 1993, p. 96).

The issues at stake in this paper are as follows. First, there seems to be two contradictory "texts"—tendencies, if you like—in education today. They are best described by Greene (1997, p. 64), "one has to do with shaping malleable young people[15] to serve the needs of technology in a postindusturial society; the other has to do with educating young people to grow and to become different, to find their individual voices, and to participate in a community in the making." The pedagogy of Hip-Hop I am proposing, which is a pedagogy of affective, oscillates towards the latter, emphasizing a "politics of choice." Here the cartography of African students' null curriculum would be the starting point, if not the base, for a critical inclusive curriculum. A curriculum that, 1) deconstructs "culture" as static category, with hierarchical arrangements, undermining the multiplicity of cultural identity, difference, and community (Yon, 2000); 2) sees students' lives as providing the basis for reconceptualizing history as dynamic cultural, and social productions; 3) notes that what might constitute reality for students may not be the teacher's reality; 4) draws on students' creative use of Black stylized English; 5) investigates Black popular cultural forms as part of hybrid diasporic cultural expressions that draw on a plurality of Black histories and politics;[16] and 6) sees gender differences of identity enactments or a global understanding of them as part of a critical inclusive curriculum (hence, they need serious engagement and deconstruction).

Second, we know that students do not come to classrooms as generic disembodied individuals. On the contrary, racial and gender identities formed outside the classroom are crucial in the learning processes. Specifically, I showed and pointed to the fact that, Black popular culture, defined as a "null curriculum," is and can be on-and-off-school site where learning can and indeed does take place. If this is so, the notion of learning and worthwhile knowledge then needs to be reproblematized and broadened to include a variety of forms. Accordingly, learning may mean learning and appropriating hybrid cultural and linguistic practices that are not valued by the hegemonic dominant culture or outside the "main text." Significantly however, this raises the question: Why do African youth, for example, choose linguistic and cultural forms that are marginalized by the dominant group's narratives and cultures? The answer lies in part in what might be called the "politics of ethnic absolutism of Blackness," that is, how students are positioned by hegemonic discourses as "Blacks."

Third, this positionality needs to be deconstructed and new formulations that link on-and-off-school identities to classroom praxis need to be articulated and seriously engaged (see also Diamond and Mullen, 1999; Morgan-Fleming, 1999). Here, there is an urgent need for a praxis that links "formal" education/learning with the popular, "informal." If those "who have been denied their primordial right to speak their word" are ever to speak it, Paulo Freire (1993, p. 69) argued, their world has to be linked to their word. Here, I am suggesting rap to be incorporated in classrooms, particularly English classrooms and especially English as a Second Language (ESL). There, rap can be studied as a genre, style and content, or it can be used simply to expose students to different linguistic variations and accents.

Fourth, rap and Black popular culture in general can create spaces where not only women and gender issues are brought to the forefront, but also racial, class, ability, and other forms of oppressions. Elsewhere (Ibrahim, 2002), I cited the multiple times in which students expressed their dissatisfaction with the "main text." One female student, it was her fifth year in the school, complained about doing the same language arts exercise for four consecutive years with the same teacher. When I asked her, as part of a group interview, whether she would like to study Hip-Hop/rap, the whole group applauded and answered, "Bien sûr! Ce serait bien agréable, très bon" [Of course! It would be really great, really good]. For these young people, rap as an aesthetic and oral narrative could be a curriculum that brings their concerns about sexuality, racism, sexism, and homophobia to the center. Also as a space for knowledge production, rap can be envisioned as a borderland which creates a language of critique that goes hand in hand with a language of possibility and hope (Anzaldua, 1987; hooks, 1994; Giroux, 1994; Simon, 1992).

Fifth and finally, proposing Black popular culture as a curriculum site is not an end in itself. I see it as either a starting point from which one moves into the "main text" or as a "text" used within the borders of the "main text." This proposition is also a call to centralize and engage marginalized subjectivities, their voices, and their ways of being and learning. It is a proposition which entails, first, a legitimization of a form of knowledge otherwise perceived as illegitimate and, second, a disruption to the one-dimensional representation of Blackness, a hybrid category which is *de facto* multicultural, multilingual, and multiethnic (Ibrahim, 2000a). It is also a proposition where rap and Hip-Hop can constitute sites of possibilities and hope. A hope that those who do not see themselves represented in the curriculum, those who can not relate to the curriculum, those who are wittingly or unwittingly kept silent, may find a subject matter they can relate to and identify with; a subject matter that brings their experience to the forefront so it can be valued and not uncritically engaged. A hope that educators will not stuck in the notion that they do not know much about Hip-Hop, and hence it is better kept dormant. A hope that they will engage the different mattering maps where students invest their identities, learning, and desires. In the case of African youth, one must ask, whose identity are we assuming if we do not engage Hip-Hop and rap in our classroom activities? "By ignoring the cultural and social forms that are authorized by youth and simultaneously empower

or disempower them," Giroux and Simon (1989a, p. 3) argue, "educators risk complicitly silencing and negating their students."
This is unwittingly accomplished by refusing to recognize the importance of those sites and social practices outside of school that actively shape student experiences and through which students often define and construct their sense of identity, politics, and culture. (Giroux and Simon, 1989a, p. 3)

The issue at stake, then, is not only to motivate and empower students but, more importantly, to enable them to locate themselves in time and history and at the same time critically interrogate the adequacy of that location.

References

Althusser, L. (1971). *Lenin and Philosophy*. London: New Left Books.
Anzaldua, G. (1987). *Borderlands/La Frontera: The New Mestiza*. San Francisco: Spinter/Anut Luter
Apple, M. (1990). *Ideology and Curriculum*. New York: Routledge.
Apple, M. (1982). *Education and Power*. Boston: Routledge and Kegan Paul.
Beer, V. and Marsh, D. (1988). A Non-School Curriculum Model Illustrated in a Museum Setting, *Journal of Curriculum and Supervision*, Vol. 3, No. 2, pp. 221-239.
Butler, J. (1999). *Gender Trouble: Feminism and the Subversion of Identity*. New York: Routledge.
Bourdieu, P. (1993). *The Field of Cultural Production*. New York: Columbia University Press.
Bourdieu, P. (1984). *Distinction: A Social Critique of the Judgment of Taste*. Cambridge: Harvard University Press.
Dei, G.J.S. (1996). *Anti-racism: Theory and Practice*. Halifax: Fernwood Publishing.
Dewey, J. (1916). *Democracy and Education*. New York: The Free Press
Diamond, C. T. P. and Mullen, C. A. (1999). *The Postmodern Education: Arts-Based Inquiries and Teacher Development*. New York: Peter Lang.
Dimitriadis, G. and McCarthy, C. (2001). *Reading the Postcolonial: From Baldwin to Basquiat and Beyond*. New York and London: Teachers College Press.
Eisner, E. and Powell, P. (2002). Art in Science? *Curriculum Inquiry*, Vol. 32, No. 2, pp. 131-159.
Eisner, E. (1979). *The Educational Imagination On the Design and Evaluation of School Programs..* New York: Macmillan Publishing Co., Inc.
Fanon, F. (1967). *Black Skin White Mask*. New York: Grove Weidenfeld.
Foucault, M. (1977). *Language, Counter-memory, Practice*. Translated by D. Bouchard and S. Simon. New York: Cornell University Press.
Freire, P. (1993). *Pedagogy of the Oppressed*. New York: Continuum.

Gilroy, P. (1997). Diaspora, Utopia and the Critique of Capitalism. In Gelder, K. and Thornton, S. (Eds.). *The Subcultures Reader*. New York: Routledge, pp.340-349.

Giroux, H. (2000). *Stealing Innocence: Youth, Corporate Power, and the Politics of Culture*. New York: St. Martin's Press.

Giroux, H. (1994). Living Dangerously: Identity Politics and the New Cultural Racism. In Giroux, H. and McLaren, P. (Eds.) *Between Borders: Pedagogy and the Politics of Cultural Studies*. New York: Routledge, pp. 29-55.

Giroux, H. and Simon, R. (1989a). Schooling, Popular Culture, and a Pedagogy of Possibility. In Giroux, H. and Simon, R. (Eds.) *Popular Culture, Schooling, and Everyday Life*. Massachusetts: Bergin & Garvey Publishers, Inc. pp. 219-235

Giroux, H. and Simon, R. (1989b). Popular Culture as a Pedagogy of pleasure and meaning. In Giroux, H. and Simon, R. (Eds.) *Popular Culture, Schooling, and Everyday Life*. Massachusetts: Bergin & Garvey Publishers, Inc. pp. 1-29.

Goldberg, M. (1997). *Arts and Learning: An Integrated Approach to Teaching and Learning in Multicultural and Multilingual Settings*. New York: Longman.

Greene, M. (1997). Art and Imagination: Reclaiming a Sense of the Possible. In Clinchy, E. (Ed.) *Transforming Public Education: A New Course for America's Future*. New York: Teachers College Press, pp. 56-65.

Greene, M. (1992). Texts and Margins. In Goldberg, M. and Phillips, A. (Eds.) *Arts as Education*. MA: Harvard Educational Review Reprint Series, pp. 1-17.

Grossberg, L. (1992). *We Gotta Get Out of This Place: Popular Conservatism and Postmodern Culture*. New York and London: Routledge.

Hall, S. (1997). *Representation: Cultural Representations and Signifying Practices*. London: Sage.

Hall, S. (1991). Ethnicity: Identity and Difference, *Radical America*, Vol. 13, No. 4, pp. 9-20.

Hall, S. (1986). On Postmodernism and Articulation: An Interview. *Journal of Communication Inquiry*. Vol. 10, No. 2, pp. 56-59.

Hall, S. and du Gay, P (Eds.) (1996). *Questions of Cultural Identity*. London: Sage.

Haraway, D. (1991). *Simians, Cyborgs, and women: The reinvention of nature*. New York: Routledge.

hooks, b. (1994). *Teaching to Transgress: Education as the Practice of Freedom*. New York: Routledge.

Ibrahim, A. (2003). Black-in-English: Black English as a Symbolic Site of Identification. In G. Smitherman, S. Makoni, and A. Ball (Eds). *Black Linguistics: Language, Society and Politics in Africa and the Americas*. London: Routledge, pp. 110-123.

Ibrahim, A. (2002). "Hey, ain't I Black too?": Rap and Hip-Hop as Sites of Learning and Investment. Paper presented at annual meeting of the American Educational Research Association, New Orleans, March 28-April 1st.

Ibrahim, A. (2000a). "Hey, ain't I Black too?" The Politics of Becoming Black. In R. Walcott (Ed.) *Rude: Contemporary Black Canadian Cultural Criticism*. Toronto: Insomniac Press, pp. 109-136.

Ibrahim, A. (2000b). Trans-re-framing identity: Race, language, culture, and the politics of translation. *trans/forms: Insurgent Voices in Education* Vol. 5, No. 2, pp. 120- 135.

Ibrahim, A. (1999). Becoming Black: Rap and Hip-hop, Race, Gender, Identity and the Politics of ESL Learning, *TESOL Quarterly*, Vol. 33, No. 3, pp. 349-369.

Ibrahim, A. (1998). *"Hey, Whassup Homeboy?"; Becoming Black: Race, Language, Culture, and the Politics of Identity; African Students in a Franco-Ontarian High School.* Unpublished Doctoral thesis, Department of Curriculum, Teaching and Learning, Ontario Institute for Studies in Education, University of Toronto.

Kelley, J. (1998). *Under the Gaze: Learning to be Black in White Society.* Halifax: Fernwood Publishing.

Kristeva, J. (1982). *Powers of Horror.* New York: Columbia University Press.

Lacan, J. (1977). *Écrits.* London: Tavistock.

Morgan-Fleming, B. (1999). Teaching as Performance: Connections between Folklore and Education, *Curriculum Inquiry*, Vol. 29, No. 3, pp. 273-291.

Nieto, S. (2000). *Affirming Diversity: The Sociopolitical Context of Multicultural Education.* USA: Longman Publishers.

Nietzsche, F. (1977). *A Nietzsche Reader.* New York: Penguin Classics.

Powell, C. (1991). Rap Music: An Education with a beat from the street, *Journal of Negro Education*, Vol. 60, No. 3, pp. 245-259.

Quinn, T. and Kahne, J. (2001). Wide Awake to the World: The Arts and Urban Schools—Conflicts and Contributions of an After-School Program. *Curriculum Inquiry*, Vol. 31, No. 1, pp. 11-32.

Rose, T. (1991). Fear of a Black Planet: Rap Music and Black Cultural Politics in the 1990. *Journal of Negro Education*, Vol. 60, No. 3, pp. 276-290.

Simon, R. I. (1992). *Teaching Against the Grain: Texts for a Pedagogy of Possibility.* New York: Bergin & Garvey.

Simon, R. and Dippo, D. (1986). On Critical Ethnography Work, *Anthropology and Education Quarterly*, Vol. 17, No. 3, pp. 195-202.

Smedley, A. (1999). *Race in North America: Origin and Evolution of a Worldview.* Oxford: Westview Press.

Smitherman, G. (2000). *Black Talk: Words and Phrases from the Hood to the Amen Corner.* Boston: Houghton Mifflin.

Spady, J. (1993). 'I ma put my thing down': Afro-American Expressive Culture and the Hip-Hop Community. *TYANABA Revue de la Société d'Anthropologie.* Vol. 20, No. 2, pp. 93-98.

Walcott, R. (2000). By way of a Brief Introduction – Insubordination: A Demand for a Different Canada. In Walcott, R. (Ed.) *Rude: Contemporary Black Canadian Cultural Criticism.* Toronto: Insomniac Press, pp. 7-10.

West, C. (1993). *Race Matters.* Boston: Beacon Press.

Williams, R. (1979). *Politics and Letters: Interviews with New Left Review*. London: New Left Books.

Yon, D. (2000). *Elusive Culture: Schooling, Race, and Identity in Global Times*. New York: State University of New York Press.

Awad Ibrahim is Assistant Professor at the Department of Educational Foundations and Inquiry, Faculty of Education, Bowling Green State Univesity, Ohio. He teaches and publishes in the areas of antiracism and critical multiculturalism, applied socio-linguistics, cultural studies, critical pedagogy and educational foundation. He is interested both in exploring the connections between race, language and culture and the politics of identity, and in film and popular music studies, especially Hip-Hop and rap. E-mail: ibraham@bgnet.bgsu.edu.

Notes

1 For Bourdieu (1993), a *champ* "is a separate social universe having its own laws of functioning independent of those of politics and the economy" (p. 162). It is a space where art works, for example, "are produced in a particular social universe endowed with particular institutions and obeying specific laws" (163). It is a "veritable social universe where, in accordance with its particular laws, there accumulates a particular form of capital and where relations of force of a particular type are exerted" (p. 164). Put otherwise, according to Bourdieu, any social formation is structured by and configured through a series of fields (the educational field, the economic field, the political field, the cultural field, etc.). Each field is relatively autonomous but structurally homologous with the others and defined as a structured space with its own laws of functioning and its own relations of force independent of those of politics and the economy, except in the cases of the economic and political fields (p. 6). Within this space, agents occupy the diverse available positions and in some cases, create new ones, always competing for control and interests. In the cultural field, for example, the authority inherent in recognition (*reconnaissance*), economic rewards, celebrity, consecration, and prestige become the parameters of competition. To propose popular culture as a *champ*, then, is to recognize it as a space of cultural production that relates to other social fields and as a structuring structure with its own rules and regulations that permit certain practices and exclude others. Using particular forms of disposition, it is a *milieu artistique* that deploys an economy of *symbolic capitals* and rewards certain *habitus*.

2 But Black popular culture is not alone, critical discourses such as Critical Theory, cultural studies, poststructuralism, Marxism, and postcolonialism are also part of the excess in the academy, the left aside or left over.

3 Eloquently, she put it as such "In truth, I do not see how we can educate young persons if we do not enable them on some level to open spaces for themselves – spaces for communicating across the boundaries, for choosing, for *becoming different* [my emphasis]... so that ... [they] will be less likely to confine themselves to the main text" (Greene, 1992, p. 2).

4 I am using 'discourse' in a Foucauldian (1977) sense where the symbolic is as central as the material, if not more. As a regulatory category, it includes institutions (the school, for example), their norms, regulations, and cultural practice.

5 Hip-Hop, Russel Simmons has recently explored in an interview with the *City Paper* of Toledo, is inherently political, from its inception. He argued, "Hip-hop has always been about politics. It was and is a means to an end. I wouldn't be here [at the University of Toledo] today if it wasn't. But, now it is time for hip-hop to assert itself. Politics has changed. It used to that the Democrats were there for the underdog, they supported civil rights and the poor. Now, that shit's out the window." Hip-Hop, he continues, is also an economic force, a way into the corporate capitals and decision making towers. He wonders, "So, why shouldn't we who are in hip-hop start making a difference with the influence we have? Again, hip-hop's purpose was to develop a way out. We now have the ability to give youth a way out of poverty" (City Paper, March 6-12, 2003, p. 14; can also be accessed through www.toledocitypaper.com).

6 A critical curriculum studies would recognize "everyday things" (Nietzsche, 1977: 270), including popular cultural forms, as central apparatus to the formation of identities. As a matter of fact, it is in the everyday that our students translate, negotiate, figure and reconfigure, form and reform their identities and it should therefore be taken very seriously. Succinctly and convincingly, Nietzsche sums up the centrality of the *little everyday things* in the learning process when he writes:

> I shall be asked why really I have narrated all these little and, according to traditional judgment, insignificant things [...]. Answer: these little things—food, place, climate, recreation [popular culture], the whole casuistry of egoism—are beyond all comparison more serious things than anything that has been taken seriously hitherto. It is precisely here that one must begin to *learn anew*. [...] Every question of politics, of the social order, of education has been falsified to the very bottom through taking the most pernicious men [sic] for great men [sic]—through teaching contempt for the 'little' things, which is to say for the fundamental affairs of life itself. (1977, p. 270; italics in original)

7 The psychic act of "choosing" here must be located at the borderline between the subconscious and the conscious (since one might wonder, do African youth really have a choice?).

8 Elsewhere (Ibrahim, 2000a), I narrated an incident with a White policeman who stopped me and almost arrested me for no reasons other than that "we", as he put (I still wonder who is included in this "we"?), "are looking for a dark man with a dark bag." After questioning him about the "dark man," he said "we are looking for a Black man with a dark bag." At this point, there was no need to mention that my bag was actually light blue. The significance of this incident stems from the fact that it graphically performs the nature of the social imaginary which is fed by the historical representation of blackness and which we—African students and I—encounter everyday.

9 By *cartography of Blackness*, I am referring to the maps, charts and borders created around Blackness, which are as much historical as they are contemporaneous. Even if they are symbolic and fictional in some cases, they are very real in their material effects (Ibrahim, 1998, 2000a).

10 All names are pseudonym.

11 Each student name is followed by age, gender (Male=Male, F=Female), and country of origin; and each extract is followed by the type of interview (individual or group) and the language in which it was conducted. The following transcription conventions are used: <u>underlined text</u> English spoken with French speech or French spoken within English speech.

12 Master T. is an MC of a local Canadian rap music TV program called *Rap City* which airs mostly American rap lyrics.

13 The names cited in the extracts are Sam (19, M, Djibouti), Juma (19, M, Senegal), Jamal (18, M, Djibouti), and Shapir (17, M, Somalia).

14 For an excellent discussion of how the Other can be hated and at the same time desired, see Hall, 1991.

15 Dewey (1916, p. 120) calls this "the traditional scheme, " which for him "is, in essence, one of imposition from above and from outside. It imposes adult standards, subject matters, and methods upon those who are only growing slowly toward maturity." He goes on to explain, "The gap is so great that the required subject matter, the methods of learning and of behaving are foreign to the existing capacities of the young. They are beyond the reach of the experience the young learners already possess."

16 Given their diasporic histories, Black cultures, Gilroy (1997, p. 341) asserts, are syncretic and work purposely beyond national borders, on an inter-national scale. This is how African American soul singers were able to send "a letter to their friends" in Africa and elsewhere. Heretofore, "A new structure of cultural exchange has been built up across the imperial networks which once played host to the triangular trade of sugar, slaves and capital." Their contribution and impact, however, is yet to be recognized by the "main text" and its history.

CHAPTER ELEVEN

Research as an Act of Love: Ethics, Émigrés, and the Praxis of Becoming Human

(REPRINTED WITH PERMISSION) Ibrahim, A. (2014). Research as an act of love: Ethics, émigrés and the praxis of becoming human. *Diaspora, Indigenous and Minority Education* 8(1), 7-20.

> Conceptual in nature, this paper revisits the debate on the nature and ethical implication of what it means to conduct research with/in immigrant communities. The view from "inside" is different from the view from "'outside," I am contending, and both are mediated by what I am calling I–Thou Research Ethics. This is an Ethics that places émigrés as our neighbors, engineers, doctors, etc. Mexico now lives next door, I am arguing, and Mexicans are now hyphenated: Mexican-Americans (for example). Gilles Deleuze (2005) refers to this as "post-identity phenomenon." To deal with it, I shall (a) discuss its ethics through The Stephen Tyler Affair (hooks, 1990); (b) build an "I–Thou Research Ethics" as a response to this Affair; and (c) conclude with a genuine dialogue in which research becomes an act of love, and "researcher–researched" becomes an "'I–Thou relationship." Only then can we hope for the transformative praxis of becoming human.

The view from the inside and the view from the outside when it comes to research, ethics and methodology is a central contention of this article. I am not approaching it from the classic, modernist sense of inside(r) and outside(r), but within a poststructural framework mediated by what I am calling *I-Thou Research Ethics*. Central to this Ethics is a required deep understanding that, thanks to the facilitation of migratory ideas, technologies and people, émigrés are no longer in India, China, Sénégal, Central Africa, Chili or Venezuela. They are next door; they are our neighbors, taxi drivers, shopkeepers, and if your imagination is not colonized, they are our doctors, engineers and university professors. Mexico now lives next door, and Mexicans are now hyphened: Mexican-Americans. "Welcome to post-identity!" as Gilles Deleuze (2005) would have put it. To deal with this post-identity, I shall discuss its ethics by (re)introducing bell hooks' (1990) discussion of Stephen Tyler's picture, which I am calling, modestly and maybe not unproblematically, "The Stephen Tyler Affair." This is the anthropologist who, despite his best intentions, ends up colonizing. To colonize, etymologically, is to make another place one's own without regard for settlement or original occupiers. The anthropologist does so, hooks argues, not by physical occupation but through the knowledge he produces, through writing his own imagination of what he sees. The I-Thou Research Ethics is built in relation to this and as a response to it. This Ethics is articulated at a philosophical and conceptual level but has broad methodological implications, especially when it comes to conducting research with immigrant communities—the category under investigation for this chapter. It requires a different language where "research" becomes "dialogue," a genuine conversation and an act of love; "researcher-research participant relationship" is turned into "I-Thou relationship"; and, finally, we conduct research *with* (not in) immigrant communities. Here, I am contending, the distinction between insider and outsider is both problematic and absolutely necessary. Insiders, it must be noted, have a nuanced understanding of immigrant communities that outsiders do not. To contend this is not universally true, that is to say not *all* insiders have the same nuanced understanding of their own communities, is tautological. Of course, no two people have the "same" understanding, whatever the issue might be, but their common linguistic, cultural, social, and historical background would allow for a deeper and maybe a different understanding than outsiders. It is this different understanding that *appoints* them as witness for their own lives, as *strong poets* who need to write vigilant, critical, and visionary verses that we have not yet heard. Only then, I conclude, can we hope for transformative and genuine dialogue.

An Economy of Partial Truths: Yet, Becoming a Shadow in It

In his introduction to *Writing Culture*, James Clifford (1985) writes that, "Ethnographic truths are ... inherently partial—committed and incomplete" (p. 7). This is clearly the case in all forms of research (Denzin, Lincoln & Smith, 2008). Yet, as bell hooks (1990) had shown, these partial truths are not so partial after all. Even in the space of partial truths, hooks (1990) argues, some truths are not only made more significant but they are presented and represented as worthy of writing and thinking thanks to power and privilege. They are thus universalized. S/he who writes, it seems, has always the possibility of slipping back into their own image, hence writing themselves in the process. Writing in this context is about "the making of texts" (Clifford, 1985, p. 2), the making of truths and eventually the making of people. Here, as Nietzsche (n. d.) would have put it, we are clearly not talking about interpretation, meaning or even truth itself. We are talking about the intervention of power in closing its multiple interpretations. Unfortunately, when it comes to research, writing is heretofore "reduced to method: keeping good field notes, making accurate maps, 'writing up' results" (Clifford, 1985, p. 2), and the 'researched' is reduced to object of study: a background shadow against which theory is made. The researched thus becomes a collective that is arranged, a tableau that is drawn, a "strange" that is made familiar and space where theory is tested. This is perfectly illustrated by bell hooks' (1990) discussion of what I am calling The Stephen Tyler Affair.

What I am calling The Stephen Tyler Affair was not the Sokal Affair nor something that shook the academy to its core, and it certainly did not overthrow the colonizing nature of classic anthropology and social science in general. The Sokal Affair is worthy of remembrance. Alan Sokal, a physics professor at New York University, sent an article to *Social Text*, a postmodern cultural studies journal, in 1996. The article was a "hoax" to test whether such a journal would publish an article "liberally salted with nonsense if it (a) sounded good and (b) flattered the editors' ideological preconceptions" (Sokal, 1996, n.p.). The article was published and the result was a historical debate on: scholarly merit, the relation between the humanity and (natural) sciences, the influence of postmodern philosophy, academic ethics, peer-reviewing, intellectual rigor and pseudoscienticism. At first glance, one may argue that it is immodest to call or compare the Sokal Affair with what I am calling The Stephan Tyler Affair. For it is precisely this obscure, insidious, and "banal" (Billing, 1995) nature of Stephen Tyler, as we shall see, that I am calling it an "affair" (see also Merelman, 1995).

The Stephen Tyler Affair is indeed about a picture on a cover of a book. The picture is of Stephen Tyler of the Anthropology Department of Rice University, and the book is *Writing Culture*, an edited anthology by James Clifford and George Marcus (1986). The picture is taken in 1963 while Tyler was doing fieldwork in India. As hooks (1990) describes it:

> One sees in this image a white male sitting at a distance from darker-skinned people, located behind him; he is writing. Initially fascinated by the entire picture, I begin to focus my attention on specific details. Ultimately I fix my attention on the piece of cloth that is attached to the writer's glasses, presumably to block out the sun; it also blocks out a particular field of vision. [For hooks,] this "blindspot," artificially created, is a powerful visual metaphor for the ethnographic enterprise as it has been in the past and as it is being rewritten... [Behind Tyler, who is sitting on a bed is an Indian man. H]e is visually separated from family, kin, community, his gaze turned away from them... [Behind this man is a shadow where faintly one sees a "brown" woman and a child.] The face of the brown/black woman is covered up, written over by the graphics which tell readers the title of the book and its authors. Anyone who glances at this cover notes that the most visible body and face, the one that does not have to be searched for, is the white male image. (pp. 127-128)

hooks (1990) concludes thus: "Perhaps to the observer trained in ethnography and anthropology this cover documents a very different history and vision from the one I see. I look at it and I see visual metaphors of colonialism, of domination, of racism" (p. 128).

What is troubling for hooks is not only the neutral ways in which the picture was dealt with and celebrated by the editors, but the symbolism invoked by it, especially when it is intersected with race, gender and ethnography (and I take ethnography here as a metaphor representing the question of 'methodology'). Described almost as a perfect illustration of how "authorial presence" might look like, James Clifford writes in his introduction that,

> Our frontispiece shows Stephen Tyler... at work in India in 1963. The ethnographer is absorbed in writing—taking dictation? Fleshing out an interpretation? recording an important observation? dashing off a poem? Hunched over in the heat, he has draped a wet cloth over his glasses. His expression is obscured. An interlocutor looks over his shoulder—with boredom? patience? amusement? In

this image the ethnographer hovers at the edge of the frame—faceless, almost extraterrestrial, a hand that writes. (Clifford, 1985, p. 1)

For Clifford, this is not "the usual portrait of anthropological fieldwork. We are more accustomed to pictures of Margaret Mead excuberantly playing with children in Manus or questioning villagers in Bali," he explains. Here, "Participant-observation, the classic formula for ethnographic work, leaves little room for texts" (p. 1). For bell hooks (1990), however, and as a visual and cultural reader who is conscious of the politics of race and imperialism, she is quite "conscious of the concrete whiteness and maleness" and the picture "is anything but extraterrestrial" (p. 127). Symbolically, the picture does three things. First, it obliterates any notion of subjectivity where brown and black bodies can speak. Similar to Gayatri Spivak (2008), hooks was asking "Can the subaltern speak?" Both for hooks and Spivak (among so many others), the subaltern is still "talked about" and "discovered." Here, "indigenous ethnographers" (read insiders) who enter "cultures where they resemble the people they are studying and writing about" (hooks, 1990, p. 126) are not given any (or enough) attention.

Second, hooks adds, there is something symbolically unsettling on how "the brown man" was represented. Being in the middle between "the ethnographer" and his family, he acted as a mediator who subtly may "desire" the "authorial power" of the White man. His gaze, hooks writes, is "visually separated from his family" and his gaze is "turned away from them" (p. 127). Finally, but very significantly, "the brown woman" is not only silent and silenced but she does not have a gaze. She and her gaze are doubly erased, doubly annihilated: "first by the choice of picture where the dark woman is in the shadows, and secondly by a demarcating line" (p. 127). In fact, her gaze is veiled by the graphics of the cover where a black line is drawn across her face.

My revisit of bell hooks' analytic reading, which is now more than 20 years old, is by no means meant to be a suggestion that there is a lack of contemporary scholarship problematizing and thinking through the role and ethics of the researcher in social sciences. Recently, Kathleen Kalligher (2008) has done us a great favor in comprehensively collecting essays on the ethics of research in, among others, education, anthropology, sociology, political science and international relations fields.

There are two primary reasons for revisiting bell hooks' reading in 1990. Firstly, because this reading triggered a whole field of research known in antiracism as "everyday racism"—that deictic, banal, unnoticeable, and naturalized racism (see especially Essed, 1991; C. Smith, 2010). Subsequently, secondly, I am referring back to hooks' reading precisely because it is not a wiz-bang kind of "affair" like Sokal. For this reason, however, some may question whether it deserves the term *affair*. bell hooks, for me, is one of the first scholars who, genealogically (Foucault, 2009), made us pause and think through this "deictic racism" (B. Smith, 2012). hooks' reading is invoked here, in sum, to demonstrate my argument that 'insiders,' as I hope to show below, have a 'third eye,' a nuanced and layered reading that outsiders do not have. Clifford, one of most critical anthropologists, thought nothing of Stephen Tyler's picture. In fact, he thought it represented a different, complicated and post-colonial type of anthropolog(ist)y. Some times, one many contend, it takes a post-colonial subject to do a post-colonial reading.

When it comes to research ethics, for me, the lessons learned from The Stephen Tyler Affair in sum are: first, as we attempt to rethink research ethics and politics, especially *with* immigrant communities, it is important to re-examine and remake research in ways that do not disadvantage, colonize or perpetuate what we already know about the plight of minoritized communities; second, researchers whose bodies are historically allied with (racial, class, and gender) privilege (among others) should be cautious, wary and vigilant about the kind of knowledge their bodies produce, that is, the impact of their historical and subject location on the conclusions they reach since they cannot talk about what they do not know; third, intentions do not matter in a context like The Stephen Tyler Affair since, whether he wants to or not, Tyler's picture is deeply historical and is read in a particular way; (one might thus conclude, intentions matter only in their final effects, in how they make people feel and in how they are read); fourth, and finally, we need a radical politics of representation, one where indigenous researchers are at the center of what it means to pose "questions at the boundaries of civilizations, cultures, classes, races, and genders" and to decode and recode and to tell "the grounds of collective order and diversity, inclusion and exclusion" (Clifford, cited in hooks, 1990, p. 126).

Researching (with) immigrant communities, one might argue therefore, has the extra ethical layer of history, colonization, and hegemony. That is to say, the care researchers need to display, especially outsiders, when working with immigrant communities comes from the long history of exclusion where immigrant communities are silenced (Lee, 2009), their stories are told by others—usually scholars who claim objectivity and so-called rigorous academic standard, and their internal complexity is reduced to typologies, models, or statistical numbers. Here, the subaltern will speak only when three conditions are met. First, when we move from the idea of researched to subjects. Modernistically framed, researched are meant to be known, discovered, risked being rendered without perspective, thus always vulnerable. On the other hand, inherent in subject is both subjectivity and agency: two central elements that enable speech act. Second, when the notion of the expert is de-centred to mean the research subject and not the expert in its traditional academic sense. Indigenous people know (in the sense of being experts of their own lives) and not simply *know about* (in the academic sense of being expert about something, an area of specialization). Three, and finally, when we move from fear to dialogue since dialogue, as I discuss below, invests research with potential to decolonize the future. Here, the very term research is hyphenated—re-search—to question and search *anew*; while fear works to perpetuate power relations where the so-called academic expert *write* and *name* the researched and, more importantly, *write* and *zone* society itself in the known, not-known and to-be-known. Here, empiricism (be it statistics, numbers, graphs – 'data') operates as a cover, behind which the researcher hides her/his history, subjectivity, power, interpretation, colonial gaze and hegemony. This is why, given certain forms of institutional power structure where researchers always have the potential of becoming 'big brothers,' *informed consent* does not mean carte blanche and therefore has to be approached with mindfulness of this history of colonialism and hegemony. These express my reasons for why I am calling for a radical research ethics, one where scholarship does not become another mechanism of marginalization, hegemony and colonization. Discussed later, I want to term this radical research ethics: "I-Thou Research Ethics."

Before doing so, however, the idea of the insider and the outsider should not be taken for granted nor unproblematically approached. Ever since Weber developed his idea of *verstehen* (or understanding), where the researcher "needs to empathize with the group under study, to try and put themselves in their shoes, in order to gain rich understanding of the motives and values of the study group" (MacRae, 2007, p. 52), the notion of the insider and the outsider has been a dilemma in qualitative research, especially ethnography. Thinking through this dilemma, Rhoda MacRae

(2007) proposes three approaches or ways of understanding and seeing it: *outsider-in*, *outsider-out* and *insider-in*. For outsider-in, the researcher does not "belong to" the group s/he is studying (p. 53). The researcher starts the research as "cultural stranger" who "learns" about the "groups' beliefs and practices through observation" and then leaves "the field to analyse the observational data" (p. 53).

Outsider-out is exemplified in the work of the University of Birmingham's Centre for Contemporary Cultural Studies (CCCS), where the researcher leaves "unexamined the impact of their social distance on the research process or its outcomes" (MacRae, 2007, p. 54). Except for Paul Willis, according to MacRae, CCCS was interested mostly in two things: 1) in combining Marxist theory and external textual analysis, on the one hand, and as "outsiders" to the group and site under study, 2) in keeping their distance. So, in the outsider-out approach, the researcher is an "outsider" and they keep their outsider position.

Closer to what I am proposing in this article, MacRae's third approach is called: insider-in. Heavily influenced by feminism, MacRae explains, insider-in approach pays particular attention to questions of status and power between the researcher and the so-called researched and recognizes the multifaceted nature of identity, context and local. The insider-in is one whose proximity is close enough that they assume certain commonalities with the group under study. In her classic study, Oakley (1981), "a woman with children, interviewing other women with children, ... assumed she had enough commonality to be an insider" (see MacRae, 2007, p. 54). On his part, as a Japanese-American studying Japanese, Hamabata (1991) created a research situation characterized by what MacRae (2007) calls "social proximity and familiarity" (p. 55).

For Atkinson & Hammersley (2007), Hamabata (1991), Hodkinson (2005), MacRae (2007), Roseneil (1993) and Schutz (1976), this insider-in approach, also known as "insider research," refers to the following five elements: 1) social, cultural and linguistic proximity and familiarity between 'researcher' and 'researched,' 2) for the researcher, it means fewer barriers to the research process (from research site, to participants, to data collection), 3) for the researcher, it also means fewer barriers especially when it comes to accessibility and to getting in-depth data (crucial points for ethnography), 4) insider-researchers "participate fully and competently, ... communicate more confidently, freely and informally without being preoccupied with the unfamiliar" (MacRae, 2007, pp. 55-56) and 5) insider-researchers are usually in tune with, especially, research participants' generalized, ideologically-leaning or simply inaccurate statements. Reflecting on this last point, MacRae argues that, it "may be that in some cases those working from the outside in are more likely to be misled if they do not critically reflect on the process of fieldwork, and that 'insider researchers' with their personal experience may be better placed to verify accounts and to achieve in-depth understanding" (p. 60). Put simply, while outsiders-in have the objective of learning about immigrant communities and in some cases these communities might open up to them, insiders-in take it to a deeper level of nuancing and talking about their lives and the lives around them. Therein lies the significant difference between the two communities of practice: the former learns about and have the luxury of stepping in and out of (immigrant) communities, while the latter is 'researching' herself and her community, hence bringing different kind of ethics – I-Thou Research Ethics.

But, as Hodkinson (2005) reminds us, if the insider is not vigilant, sincere and approaching the position of the insider in a multi-dimensional and complex way, one may do more harm in perpetuating common sense, in accepting habitual modes of thinking and in not challenging the taken-for-granted. Highly cautiously, therefore, insider-researchers need to be "methodologically reflexive" and strangers-in-their-own-land/within-their-own-communities. They need to be let-in, and not to assume, arrogantly, that their cultural, linguistic, and social background is an automatic guarantee to high, special or sophisticated knowledge, on the one hand, and that they should be given full and authorized access, on the other. If one assumes thus, then one is committing violence (more than conducting research), perpetuating a uni-dimensional definition of identity (more than recognizing the multifaceted nature of it) and deploying exploitation and insincerity (not love, as I will discuss next). In this case, one may argue, "outsiders" might be better than "insiders." These are difficult lessons learned the hard way by Oakley and Hamabata, and it is why I am proposing to think about "love" more than "research," "dialogue" more than "methodology."

Research as an Act of Love: Becoming Human in Research

In his classic book, *Between Man and Man*, Martin Buber (2002) proposes two ideas that are central to this article: 'dialogue' and 'relationship.' Concerning dialogue, Buber argues that there is no humanity without dialogue: I, the Self is an empty signifier without the Other or Thou. For Buber, even though dialogue can take place in silence, language and communication are central to any form of dialogue. To be able to communicate in silence is a human capacity which Buber terms "communicating intersubjectively," that is, outside language and speech act. By way of explaining, Buber offers this example: Two men sitting beside one another, the first is disposed to receive and hear whatever comes along, and the second "holds himself in reserve, withholds himself" (p. 4). Something within the rigid man cannot communicate itself—"until he releases in himself a reserve over which only he himself has power" (p. 4). In this moment, "communication streams from him" (p. 20), although in silence, and in silence it directs itself to the other man. Only in moments like these can we deploy the term 'love.' The communication, or is it love?, was indeed intended for the other, who receives it. In this story, the "word of dialogue has happened sacramentally" (p. 5). When it is sacramental, dialogue is holistic, it is beyond language; we can almost name it or touch it, but then it slips away. This is the space of awe, an overwhelming moment of pure feelings. This is the difficulty of talking about love, but we must.

Put otherwise, even though dialogue can exist outside the boundary of language (i.e., through feelings and in gesture and in silence), nonetheless communication is an essential component of dialogue. As an event, dialogue is deeply embedded in time and space. In this sense, Buber argues, we need to distinguish between dialogue and monologue. If two strangers exchange glances, that reveals nothing but two people glancing at each other, there is not necessarily a dialogue. But for dialogue to take place, especially "genuine dialogue," it requires a quality of communion, a sense of time, place and above all 'love.' To explicate this, Buber cites the personal example of being at a conference where he engages in an emotional debate with a man who argues for the censorship of Jewish participation in a public initiative. A Jew himself, Buber engages the man through the story of Christ, using the story as an example of how Jews understand Christ in a way that is inaccessible to Christians. Despite their different perspectives, this dialogical moment ends in a kiss of brotherhood. For Buber, opinions are gone at that moment, because the factual has occurred, and in the factual, a bond of communion has occurred which is transformative. This is what Buber calls *genuine dialogue*; it happens in spite of intellectual, social and historical differences. It is a communion and transformative act of love. It requires intellectual rigor as it does humility.

For this article, there are four points to retain so far. First, Buber was not writing for research audiences but more for Philosophers, so I have the absolutely difficult task of bringing philosophy to research discourses and the latter to the former. Second, with this bridging comes the unenviable task of talking about love. How can one talk about that which is beyond language, the slippage, the left over and the purely emotional? I will attempt to do so later. Third, for dialogue to take place sacramentally, Buber contends, it requires, on the one hand, an established human relation between researcher and so-called research participants (in the case of this special issue, immigrant communities) and, on the other, a linguistic (language and speech act) and paralinguistic code (communication in silence). Here, Buber might have been talking about insider-researcher, because when communication happens in silence, a movement has happened from the mechanical to the genuine, from word to wordless, from language to the sacrament of love. Insider-researchers have, by and large, a deeper understanding of their community's nuanced and unspoken language, customs and ways of being and thinking. Fourth, and finally, there is a parallel line between Buber's distinction between how Christ is approached and read by Jews and Christians and the ethical and procedural contentions posed earlier in this article: Can outsiders do research in immigrant communities, and what are the ethical and procedural implications of/in doing so? If one is to refer back to The Stephen Tyler Affair, one may argue that, this is the wrong question to ask whether outsiders *can* do research in immigrant communities. "The right" question – to use the language of Socrates – is whether 'outsiders' are mindful of their historical and subject location, especially of privilege, and the knowledge produced out of that location (see especially Oakley and Hamabata). Using Buber's vignette, one thing can be immodestly reiterated: insiders have nuanced understanding and knowledge that outsiders do not have. Nonetheless, always according to Buber's vignette, both for outsiders and insiders, research has to be an act of love; it is not a simple intellectual and academic exercise. Indeed, it is about engaging in and creating moments of *genuine dialogue*, where a kiss of comradery and brotherhood is possible and should be the ultimate aim of conducting research.

For this to happen, Buber (2002) makes a distinction between three types of dialogue (note the similarities between dialogue and research here). 1) "genuine dialogue," one "where each of the participants *really* has in mind the other or others in their present and particular being and runs to them with the intention of establishing a living mutual relation between himself and them"; 2) "technical dialogue," one "which is prompted solely by the need of objective understanding"; and 3) "monologue disguised as dialogue," one where two or more people "meeting in space, *speak each with [her]himself* in strangely tortuous and circuitous ways and yet imagine they have escaped the torment of being thrown back on their own resources" (p. 22, emphasis added). Again, if we apply these contentions onto Stephen Tyler's picture, what is revealed is this: what is setup as a dialogue is in fact a monologue, one where one writes oneself. In the picture, the brown and black bodies are actually blocked by what appears as a towel or a handkerchief. They are—literally—lurking in the background shadow of the ethnographer. The ethnographer is writing: *the center of the research here is not the brown body but the ethnographer's notes.* This is why, for Buber, we need to distinguish between dialogue and monologue, especially for those of us who are working and doing research not in, but *with* immigrant communities.

Not to fall into the trap of monologue disguising as dialogue, Buber makes a distinction between three types of human perceptions (again, note the parallel between 'dialogue' and 'research'):

1. *The observer:* one who perceives another, takes notes, probes, writes up traits, and fixes the other intently in her mind as a mere set of physical features.

2. *The onlooker:* one who suspends judgment and lets herself go in an effort to perceive the other freely and undisturbed. In this sense, "All great artists have been onlookers," Buber concludes (p. 10). For both onlookers and observers, other individuals are 'objects' which address them only within the utility of the research (that is, their usefulness is bound by the contribution to research data and findings). Furthermore, given this distance they create between themselves and these 'objects,' these individuals are thus turned into 'objects of study' (data) whose relation ends when the research finishes.

3. *Becoming aware:* here "a word demanding an answer has happened to me" (p. 12). Perception, Buber contends, is thus altered in a way that demands a shift in subjectivity for the individual who becomes aware. I am no longer an observer or onlooker, I am fully integrated into what I am studying. *Becoming aware* is becoming *wide-awake* (Greene, 2007) not only of my own subject

location as a researcher (especially as a privileged outsider) but also of the powerful possibilities of my research findings and its social, historical and pedagogical implications.

Put otherwise, in *becoming aware*, one is addressed, one makes oneself fully present, one opens oneself to the concrete world reality—not one's imaginary notion of it—a world "which is constantly, in every moment, reached out to me.... [and to comprehend this reality as] inseparable, incomparable, irreducible, now, happening once only... gaz[ing] upon me with a horrifying look" (Buber, 2002, p. 15). Research is no longer about collecting data, organizing notes, testing theories, but an act of love.

To become an act of love, research has to live a tension between that which is linguistically communicable and that which is purely emotional and beyond language; that is to say, between being exceptionally conscious, systematic, organized and thoroughly ethical, on the one hand, and emotionally satisfying and gratifying, on the other, where one is fully present and deeply connected to the history, culture and language of the people one is researching. Here, the notion of love deserves special attention. I am deploying the term *love* throughout this paper as a complex, multilayered, multifaceted, all encompassing category that is referring to passion as much as it is referring to caring, intimacy (that is, the sharing of deep thoughts and private feeling with an Other/Thou), compassion, mutual relation, understanding, respect, trust, fulfillment, security, Eros, selfless, consummation, and commitment. Given the academic nature of this article, a definition is required. But, I request of you, my gentle reader, to leave the concept open! Bring yourself, your reading and your history to it. But if I am asked to define what I mean by "love," it is all of the terms above that I cited three sentences ago. They are not feathery, flimsy and fluffy notions; and they encompass a psychoanalytic, anthropological, indigenous and sociological approach.

To propose 'research as an act of love' does not take away from the rigor of conducting research, as I already alluded to. Indeed, the total opposite is true. To move from research to love and from methodology to dialogue, a deep, extensive and exceptional level of knowledge of the research techniques (field notes, interviews, coding/decoding, surveys and statistical analysis, if required, among so many others) is not only and absolutely required but without it, one is prone to fall back into a traditional notion of research. Simply put, to practice research as an act of love one has to be fully immersed into the traditional notion and techniques of research. To push the boundary, in other words, one has to know *what* one is pushing, *why* as well as *how* to push it. Only then, for me, can we talk about the possibility of an I-Thou Research Ethics.

Hanging Out in Love: I-Thou Research Ethics

Two examples might illustrate what I am proposing thus far. Dwayne Donald (2010), a Canadian First Nation scholar, tells us about conducting research – "having conversations and genuine dialogue," as he put it – with the elders of the Papaschase Cree Nation in Alberta, Canada, where he grew up and breathed the air of the place. He was seeking a deeper understanding of his own culture, language and tradition; not simply to share it with others (First Nations and non-First Nations; as his Ph.D. thesis research) but for his own "sanity" and for himself first. The paper I am referring to here, interestingly enough, is titled, *On what terms can we speak?* Without any essentialism, it is this collective insider-in 'we' that makes research an act of love and turns methodology into dialogue. My second example, on the other hand, shows how the I-Thou Research Ethics is turned into its head, thus harming research participants. A friend of mine (Ms. R), an African American spoken word poet and a teacher, invited a White woman academic to attend and witness some of the workshops Ms. R was conducting in northeast New York schools. The academic ended up, on the one hand, creating rapports with the schools that Ms. R introduced her to without letting her know and, on the other, writing a book on these schools without any credit to Ms. R. Beside being unethical, this episode is one of the reasons why I am calling for I-Thou Research Ethics, but also why we need to research our own communities. Should it surprise us that less and less sites, especially schools, are giving us-researchers access to conduct research (Gallagher, 2008)?

To gain their trust, for me, we need to rethink research as act of love and approach our research participants with an I-Thou Research Ethics. This Ethics presupposes that one has to love the community *with* which one is conducting research; even more, one has to love humanity itself to study it. Only then, in Buber's language, can we talk about I-Thou relationship, which he distinguishes it from I-It relationship. Buber argues that frequently we view both objects and people by their functions. When a doctor examines us for specific illness, they most likely examine organisms; when a scientist observes, measures and examines the world, they learn a great deal. For Buber, all such processes are I-It relationships. In them, the world becomes disjointed and fragmented parts, a series of "things" and "objects" to be researched and, similar to a chemical lab experiment, elements to be investigated and in some cases manipulated.

The Stephen Tyler Affair is an unfortunate illustration of this type of relationship. Without suggesting that Tyler did not love the community where he conducted research (after all some anthropologists went 'native' to express their love), but Tyler's figure and final product, at least according to bell hooks, are both problematic and colonizing. Welcome to I-It Research Ethics! Intentions matter only in their final effect. In this Ethics, rather than truly making ourselves available to the communities we are conducting research with; rather than understanding them, sharing totally with them, really talking *with* them, we observe them or keep part of ourselves outside the moment of relationship. We presumably do this either in search for the so-called objectivity or to get them respond to preconceived conclusions, hence turning findings into monologue.

For Buber, there is another way of conceiving 'researcher-researched' relationship: I-Thou. This is a g(G)od-like relationship that is respectful of être en soi, the being in its own term. It finds itself mesmerized by the beauty of creation and the awesome responsibility of having to care for it and respond to it. Here, there is no 'research' per se, there is instead genuine dialogue *with* Thou. Very significant to note, Thou for Buber does not refer only to God, but it refers also, and probably more importantly, to every creature, every plant, every insect, every stone and every human that crosses its path. This I-Thou relationship paves the ground for the radical ethics I am proposing here: I-Thou Research Ethics.

In it, it is possible to place ourselves as humans and in this case as researchers completely into a relationship, to truly understand and "be there" with another person, without masks, pretenses, even without words. Significantly, each participant comes to such a relationship without preconditions. The bond thus created enlarges each person, and each person responds by trying to enhance the other person. The result is true dialogue, true sharing. The categories of 'researcher' and 'research participants' are here reconfigured as 'I' and 'Thou,' where the latter is no longer a thing to be researched and where conclusions and theories are to be tested, but a being whose very existence is baffling and any research should therefore aim at expressing the power that binds us as researchers with it.

In the I-Thou Research Ethics, moreover, the researcher is also a research participant, she is an integral part of the research and the questions posed. Dwayne Donald (2010) shows us how this might look like in his 'dialogue' with the elders in the Cree Nation of Alberta. He is not an observer or onlooker since both "are similarly oriented, in that they have a position, namely, the very desire to perceive the man who is living before [their] eyes" (Buber, 2002, p. 11). Because of this desire, Buber contends, observers and onlookers may very well end up writing their perceptions (read what they think) of "the man who is living before [their] eyes." With them, the possibility is always present that their perception of the being does not necessarily mean a faithful translation of 'reality.' In the I-Thou Research Ethics, on the other hand, the so-called researcher is aware, *wide-awake* not only of the power bestowed on him/her by virtue of his/her subjectivity (falling under the privileged category of researcher or Whiteness) or professional location (being a university professor), but also of the limits of knowing. The term research is thus substituted by dialogue and as Buber (2002) put it, the "limits of the possibility of dialogue are the limits of awareness" (p. 12).

Fully conscious of her power and subject position, with humility, the researcher enters this dialogue with an incredible sense of responsibility. The aim of this dialogue (otherwise called research) is to create a genuine dialogue not a technical dialogue or even a monologue where one sees one's self and hears one's own voice. In genuine dialogue, beings are experienced and discovered in their own terms; they speak and reveal themselves to us in ways that have never been spoken or revealed since nothing can be repeated twice. Notions of research reproducibility and generalization are therefore put into serious questioning. As significant, Buber (2002) explains, "it is no experience that can be remembered independently of the situation, it remains the address of that moment and cannot be isolated, it remains the question of a questioner and will have its answer" (p. 14). In other words, nothing can be interpreted, translated or explained outside the context of its happening or those who are making sense of it.

There is no contradiction, here, between the Buberian notion of dialogue and my contention that nothing can be interpreted outside its context. For Buber, there is no universal dialogue. Dialogue can only happen in context and with Thou. The challenge for the I-Thou Research Ethics, therefore, is that I-Thou is not a constant or even static relationship. As humans (and for this paper, as researchers) we go back and forth between I-Thou and I-It. Ironically, Buber explains, any attempt to achieve an I-Thou moment will fail because the process of trying to create an I-Thou relationship objectifies it and thus makes it I-It. So, as researchers, the most we could do to achieve genuine dialogue is simply *be available* to the possibility of I-Thou moment. Given its ephemeral nature, however, an I-Thou moment is beyond language, as already explained, it is a moment of being. To reach it, one has to be absolutely and fully conscious of one's role as researcher; so much so that one finds oneself in a radical space of genuine dialogue. Being a continental African myself, and working primarily with continental African communities in North America, elsewhere (Ibrahim, 2010a), I called this *hanging out methodology*. Framing my study squarely within an I-Thou Research Ethics, I spent more than two years dialoguing (i.e., researching) *with* a group of African youth who find themselves in a high school in a metropolitan city in southwestern Ontario, Canada. Because of my involvement in the weekly and for a long time, daily school activities—eventually becoming their academic advisor, Big Brother and basketball team coach—my status as a researcher had different names. Inside and outside school, I was called by first name, I was invited to attend their classes, I was invited to their houses, I was invited to picnics and I came to know their families. Immodestly, and maybe arrogantly, in one occasion (Ibrahim, 2007), I argued that my position as a researcher "was forgotten." My intent there was neither to erase the students' side and how they saw me as a university professor and researcher nor to unproblematically obscure my power, subject position or privilege. I was too conscious of that power and location. Instead, my argument was that we were engaged in creating a complex space of research, power, and dialogue. If one is ever allowed a position of judgment, I would say there was a genuine dialogue, a conversation that did not merely involve speaking at one, but existed in silence. It happened when we became unreserved, a total being in time and space. Similar to Donald (2010), research was thus turned into dialogue and heretofore an act of love. As one student put it after dinner in one of the students' house: "that was a great conversation" (for detailed description of my research, see Ibrahim, 2006a, 2006b, 2007, 2008a, 2008b, 2009, in press).

This Is Not A Conclusion: Toward A Strong Poetry

Dialogue—if I may so term research—is unapologetically subjective when it comes to I-Thou Research Ethics. It requires human relationships that are beyond the confines of imposed categories of 'researcher' and 'research subjects.'

Furthermore, one has to take his/her ethical responsibility very seriously since, when it comes to immigrant communities, one is called-on to be a witness and with witnessing comes the ethical responsibility of telling. Very significantly, this telling may involve the telling/writing of stories that the community might not want to hear (Ibrahim, 2001b). This is the *ethics of the appointment*, which is an integral part of the I-Thou Research Ethics, where one is called-on, appointed to tell others either what they do not know or know but do not have the language to articulate.

For dialogue (i.e., research) to be transformative, especially when immigrant communities are involved, the researcher has to become a *strong poet*. Strong poets, Richard Rorty (1989) explains, do not simply write verses or tell us what we already know. Strong poets are so eloquent in their language, so visionary in their conviction, that the familiar, the immediate, and the known become unfamiliar and unknown. The strong poets, Rorty adds, are horrified of simply being "a copy or a replica"; they have the courage and audacity to engage, look for, and think through the "blind impresses," the gaps and the blind spots of thoughts, ideas and practices. The blind impresses are the difficult knowledges—problems, if you like—that society prefers not to face, be it aggression, war, xenophobia, ethno-supremacy, racism, sexism, or homophobia. In the face of formidable pressure, the strong poets will choose to walk through these "problems," so to speak, and deal with them at the individual, national, and global level. When it comes to I-Thou Research Ethics, this requires not only humility but wide-awakeness to what is here-and-now and what is there-and-possible. It requires a vigilant and keen observer who is mindful of the limits of love, that it should not blind us, and not to reinscribe the Tyler handkerchief. It requires a new language, a radical I-Thou Research Ethics where research does not become another tool of/for colonization. Above all, it requires a new politics, conceptualization and relationship between the so-called researcher and his/her research participants. Here, if one is left to imagine, Buber would have told Stephen Tyler to move away his handkerchief, turn his face toward his host and humbly have a genuine I-Thou dialogue (for similar arguments based on 'relational-cultural theory,' see Walker & Rosen, 2004). So, one might ask in conclusion, the people we are dialoguing with (i.e., researching) offer us their lives, especially immigrant communities, what are we-researchers bringing to the table? I certainly hope our contribution will be a new verse, a symphonic poem or a sonata that we have not heard before. Dare we become strong poets who are wide-awake of the possibility and responsibility of the I-Thou Research Ethics?

Reference:

Atkinson, P. and Hammersley, M. (2007). *Ethnography: Principles in practice* (3rd Ed.). London: Routledge.
Billing, M. (1995). *Banal nationalism*. London: Sage.
Buber, M. (2002). *Between man and man*. London & New York: Routledge.
Clifford, J. and Marcus, G. (1986). *Writing culture: The poetics and politics of ethnography*. Berkeley: University of California Press.
Deleuze, G. (2005). *The time-image*. London: Continuum.
Denzin, N., Lincoln, Y. and Smith, L. (2008). *Handbook of critical and indigenous methodologies*. Los Angles: Sage.
Donald, D. (2010). *On what terms can we speak? Aboriginal-Canadian relations as a curricular and pedagogical imperative.* Invited Lecture, Faculty of Education Graduate Studies, University of Lethbridge. Lethbridge, AL.
Essed, P. (1991). *Understanding everyday racism: An interdisciplinary theory*. Newbury Park, Calif: Sage.
Foucault, M. (2009). *Naissance de la Clinique*. Paris Quadrige /Presses universitaires de France.
Hamabata, M. (1986). Ethnographic boundaries: Culture, class and sexuality in Tokyo. *Qualitative Sociology* 9(4): 354-371.
Hodkinson, P. (2005). Insider research in the study of youth cultures. *Journal of Youth Studies* 18(2): 131-149.
hooks, b. (1990). *Yearning: Race, gender and cultural politics*. Boston, MA: South End Press.
Ibrahim, A. (2006a). Rethinking displacement, language, and culture shock: Towards a pedagogy of cultural translation and negotiation. In Amin, N. and Dei, G. (Eds.), *The poetics of anti-racism* (pp. 33-45). Halifax: Fernwood Books.
Ibrahim, A. (2006b). Becoming Black: Rap and Hip Hop, race, gender, identity, and the politics of ESL learning. In Matsuda, P., Cox, M., Jordan, J., and Ortmeier-Hooper, C. (Eds), *Second-language writing in the composition classroom: A critical sourcebook* (pp. 131-148). New York: St. Martin's.
Ibrahim, A. (2008a). Operating under erasure: Race/Language/Identity. *Canadian and International Education Journal* 37(2), 56-76.
Ibrahim, A. (2008b). The new *flâneur*: Subaltern cultural studies, African youth in Canada, and the semiology of in-betweenness. *Cultural Studies* 22(2), 234-253.
Ibrahim, A. (2009). Operating under erasure: Race/language/identity. In Ryuko, A & Lin, A. (Eds.), *Race, language and identity* (pp. 176-194). London & New York: Routledge.
Ibrahim, A. (2010a). "Hey, whadap homeboy?" Identification, desire & consumption: Hip-Hop, performativity, and the politics of Becoming Black. In Steinberg, S. & Cornish, L. (Eds.), *Taboo: Essays on culture and education* (pp. 117-137). New York: Peter Lang.

Ibrahim, A. (2010b). "Yes, my name is Ibrahim and I am an atheist!" Confessing *asrar*: Atheism, arts, answerability, imagination and the Muslim you have never known. In Stonebanks, C. & Steinberg, S. (Eds.), *Teaching against Islamophobia*. New York: Peter Lang.

Ibrahim, A. (in press). *"Hey, whassup homeoby?" Becoming Black: Hip-Hop language and culture, race performativity, and the politics of identity in high school*. Toronto: University of Toronto Press.

Kalligher, K. (2008). *Methodological dilemma: Creative, critical and collaborative approaches to qualitative research*. New York: Francis & Taylor.

Lee, S. (2009). *Unraveling the Model- Minority Stereotype: Listening to Asian American Youth* (2nd Edition). New York: Teachers College Press.

MacRae, R. (2007). 'Insider' and 'outsider' issues in youth research. In Hodkinson, P. & Deicke, W. (Eds.) *Youth cultures: Scenes, subcultures and tribes* (pp 51-61). New York: Routldge.

Merelman. R. (1995). *Representing Black culture: Racial conflict and cultural politics in the United States*. New York: Routledge.

Nietzsche, F. (n.d.). BrainyQuote.com. Retrieved September 11, 2010, from BrainyQuote.com Web site: http://www.brainyquote.com/quotes/quotes/f/friedrichn109379.html

Oakely, A. (1981). Interviewing women: A contradiction in terms. In Roberts, H. (Ed.) *Doing feminist research* (pp. 15-23). London: Routledge.

Rorty, R. 1989. *Contingency, irony, and solidarity*. Cambridge: Cambridge University Press.

Roseneil, S. (1993). Greenham revisited: Researching myself and my sisters. In Hobbs, D. & May, T. (Eds.) *Interpreting the field: Accounts of ethnography* (pp. 15-25). Oxford: Claredon Press.

Schutz, A. (1976). *Collected papers II: Studies in social theory* (4th Ed.). The Hague: Martinus Nijhoff.

Smith, B. (2012). *Racializing the nation through pronouns: A study of how banal language articulates identity and the national community in grade eight Ontario textbooks*. Unpublished Ph.D. thesis proposal. Ottawa: University of Ottawa.

Smith, C. (2010). *Anti-racism in education: Missing in action*. Ottawa: Canadian Centre for Policy Alternative.

Spivak, G. (2008). *Les subalternes peuvent-elles parler?* Paris: Éditions Amsterdam.

Sokal, A. (1996). A Physicist experiments with cultural studies. *Lingua Franca*. Retrieved June 4, 2012, from web site:
http://www.physics.nyu.edu/sokal/#debate_linguafranca

Walker, M & Rosen, W. (2004). *How connections heal: Stories from relational-cultural therapy*. New York: Guilford Press.

CHAPTER TWELVE

Wide-Awakeness: Toward a Critical Pedagogy of Imagination, Humanism, Agency, and Becoming

Cara Rautins & Awad Ibrahim

(REPRINTED WITH PERMISSION) Rautins, C. & Ibrahim, A. (2011). Wide-awakeness: Toward a critical pedagogy of imagination, humanism and becoming. *International Journal of Critical Pedagogy* 3(2), 24-36.

> Poetically framed around Maxine Greene's notion of *wide-awakeness* and Paulo Freire's *conscientization*, this paper elucidates a critical pedagogy that seeks enlightenment towards a democratic classroom community of creative imaginings, pluralism, and hope. By delving into the praxis of these two "strong poets," among others, a critical pedagogy of imagination, humanism, agency, and becoming is organically discussed and considered to 'dialogue' with new spaces of teaching and learning ("outside the box"), thus moving students from a mechanized (oppressive) curriculum to a more humanized curriculum of *wide-awakeness*. As the paper concludes, it is proposed that a democratic pedagogy which seeks to harmonize the tension between freedom and authority is necessary to foster *wide-awakeness* and move students toward creative possibilities for a promising future.

Introduction:
Becoming "Strong Poet," Or Daring to Teach in "Times like These"

In his wonderful discussion with Sophie, the protagonist Alberto in *Sophie's World* reminds the fourteen-year old Sophie about the meaning of life and our roles in it. As humans, argues Alberto, "We are condemned to improvise. We are like actors dragged onto the stage without having learned our lines, with no script and no prompter to whisper stage directions to us. We must decide for ourselves how to live" (Gaarder, 1996, p. 457). Thus, as philosophers, educators and humans, we are left with this question: In this improvised theatre that we call life (or education), which direction and/or destination should we take and *how* do we get there? We propose that once in awhile, someone comes in with strong conviction, clear mind and convincing articulation to show us the way. Their articulation, ideas and the totality of their scripts are so freshly new that one finds oneself mesmerized by the texts as much as by the ideas. This is (the power of) the "strong poet."

The "strong poet," according to Richard Rorty (1989)—does not simply write verses. The "poet" is a broad, generic term used to refer to someone who not only has the language but also the vision to tell us something new, or invent the known in an unknown language. The strong poet, Rorty (1989) explains, is horrified at simply being "a copy or a replica"; s/he has the courage and audacity to engage, look for and think through the "blind impresses," the gaps and the blind spots of thoughts, ideas and practices (p. 43). The blind impresses are the difficult knowledges—problems, if you like—that society prefers not to face, be it racism, sexism, xenophobia, ethno-supremacy or homophobia. In the face of formidable pressure, the strong poet will choose to walk through these "problems," so to speak, and deal with them at the individual, national and global level.

We believe that both Maxine Greene and Paulo Freire fall under this umbrella of strong poets, and that their ideas are exceptionally visionary, and thus helpful as we chart what we call a *critical pedagogy* of *imagination, humanism, and becoming*. This is a pragmatist pedagogy that begins by acknowledging the historical moment in which we live: a startling world of uncertainty, a world saturated by unknown complexities of future sustainability, interdependence, and human possibility (Greene, 1995; see also O'Hara, 2006). A world where the educational landscape is shifting as it attempts to grapple with global issues, and where we, as critical pedagogues, provoke global citizenship and wakefulness in our students (O'Hara, 2006).[1] Clearly, perturbing social conditions (terrorism, poverty, violence, and economic and environmental crises) and educational challenges (standardized testing, discipline/punishment, and oppressive pedagogy) are now especially profound. Yet, Greene (2008) dares to ask: "How can we commit ourselves to [teaching and] learning in times like these?" (p. 18).

---

1 Here, the work of Westheimer & Kane (2003) is noteworthy as they call attention to the process of how educational discourse surrounding democracy and civics is expanding away from narrow conceptions (e.g. charity, community service, patriotism) to underscore the importance of dialogue, critical inquiry, and social analysis.

For precisely these challenges, the concept of *wide-awakeness*—"awareness of what it is to be in the world" (Greene, 1995, p. 35)—remains fundamental to a critical pedagogy of possibility, imagination, and social change. According to Leistyna & Woodrum (1999), critical pedagogy (a term first coined by Giroux in 1983) "challenges us to recognize, engage, and critique (so as to transform) any existing undemocratic social practices and institutional structures that produce and sustain inequalities and oppressive social identities and relations" (p. 2). Therefore, as we conceive it, a critical pedagogy of *wide-awakeness* empowers learners to be mindful of oneself and others, opening up space for conscious deliberation of how the world is constructed in terms of knowledge, power, and inequality (Greene, 1995; 2000; 2005). As Greene (2005) articulates, educators are entrusted with a consequential task:

> The... educator must be awake, critical, open to the world. It is an honor and a responsibility to be a teacher in such dark times—and to imagine, and to act on what we imagine, what we believe ought to at last be (p. 80).

If not, we will fall into the trap of silencing our students and impeding the positive processes of critical pedagogy of *wide-awakeness*. This silencing, Greene (2005) writes, "may be like that of being in a closed room with the windows shut against the "world" others are seeing and accepting" (p. 78). Therefore, it is imperative for teachers to unbar the "doors" and "windows" of their classrooms and accompany students on the road to consciousness, imagination, pluralism, and the meaningful pursuit of knowledge and discovery.

Historically preceding Greene's (1995) discourse of *wide-awakeness* is Freire's (1998) critical consciousness or *conscientization*, related to raising consciousness in students to unmask oppression and liberate the capacity to learn, imagine, act, and openly dialogue with the world. Freire (1998) defined *conscientization* as an unfinished "requirement of the human condition...as a road we have to follow to deepen our awareness of the world, of facts, of events, of the demands of human consciousness to develop our capacity for epistemological curiosity" (p. 55). Freire's critical pedagogy is also premised on reflecting on one's place, and a transformative praxis centered on literacy to engage students to be capable of "reading the world" through relevant textual encounters (see also Greene, 1995, p. 190). In the subsequent sections, we will carefully consider a pedagogy of imagination, humanism, praxis, agency, and becoming to expand the notion of *wide-awakeness* and *consciousness* into purposeful discourse for students, learners, and pedagogues.

Before proceeding, however, it is worth noting that this paper itself is an exemplary demonstration of what we call for. It is a labour of engagement, commitment, and dialogue; and of how one can accompany one's students into the journey of wide-awakeness. The paper was first conceived in a graduate course offered by the second author. In the course, we read the work of Greene, Freire, Giroux and Ayers, among many others. For the first author, reading these strong poets and discussing their work in class instigated poetic moments of *wide-awakeness* and *conscientization*. We, as authors, then had intense discussion about the pedagogical implication of *why* we teach *what* we teach and *how* we teach it (at least differently). The result of this discussion is this conceptual paper, which we offer to the reader—with humility—as a dialogic moment of hope, imagination, and becoming. In this sense, the most 'practical' thing the second author offered in the course was not a lesson plan, a unit or a classroom 'practice,' but the very philosophical, theoretical, and conceptual ground upon which *any* lesson plan or unit would stand. Thus, the paper in its final analysis is a refutation--a 'talking back' to the critics of critical pedagogy that it is not practical enough. Oddly enough, one of the strongest notions in critical pedagogy is 'praxis,' that is, the link between theory and practice. This is why, one may venture to argue, (some) critics are not objecting to critical pedagogy but to its radical politics, especially when it comes to imaging ourselves and others otherwise.

Critical Pedagogy of Imagination

Imagination is the capacity to invent new realities, perhaps new worlds.
(Greene, 2007, p. 1)

Imagination embodies voice, consciousness, community, pluralism, and the human condition. A critical pedagogy opens up spaces for imaginative possibilities and a caring, unconditional dialogue, within the bureaucracy of schooling. The invigorating spaces of imagination also provide learners with the capacity to reach beyond conventional ideology to engage in free, unpredictable and internalized thought, while also building on lived experience (Egan, 2005; Eisner, 2005).

Nevertheless, a pedagogy of imagination may appear arduous within the boundaries of a standardized and seemingly mechanized curriculum, and becomes even further detached by the market economy, social injustice, high-stakes testing, and disciplinary management. Therefore, what conditions are necessary to revive a pedagogy of imagination which will foster new beginnings and *wide-awakeness* in students?

A curriculum of imagination is exemplified by innovative and creative renderings of arts-based pedagogy and exploration (Greene, 1995). Decades ago, Maslow (1971) fervently proposed that intrinsic learning and arts in education could provide meaningful discovery into oneself and foster growth of consciousness and "becoming fully human" (p. 150). Furthermore, as Hanna (2008) conveys:

> Curriculum theorists have provided a knowledge base concerning aesthetics, agency, creativity, lived experience, transcendence, learning through the body, and the power of the arts to engender visions of alternative possibilities in culture, politics, and the environment. (p. 491)

Through various mediums of arts-based pedagogy, such as poetry, story-telling, illustration, imagery, music, film, and dance, students engage in imaginative learning which serves to release creativity and convey originality and free expression (Greene, 1995). Moreover, Irwin (2005) features how learning *in, through,* and *from* art by means of holistic encounters can offer students rich learning opportunities to construct meaning, and imagine and open up possibilities for new interpretations and understandings. Kind (2005) further adds to the discussion of arts-based pedagogy by signifying how art is predominantly "an engaging, embodied, sensory, sensual, tactile, kinaesthetic, communicative, critically reflective, culturally negotiated, private and social endeavour" (p. 13). This is powerfully conveyed in the following example, depicting a humanistic and imaginative interchange between a child and his father while riding a subway:

> The train was very crowded and there was only enough room for the boy to sit down, so the father stood in front of him. He put the child in the seat and gave him some paper and a pen to draw. The child look around and then finally began drawing. The father

asked the child what he was drawing and he said he was drawing the father riding the subway. The father replied, "But I'm standing, not sitting down. The child then said, "Not on this train, the train in my drawing has seats for everyone to sit down." This child has used some very important critical literacy through his imagination and his art. (Quintero, 2007, p. 207)

Thus, the role of provoking imagination through a rich environment of artistic expression and dialogue may be critical in preparing students for an unforeseeable future (Quintero, 2009).

To follow with another example, a Toronto based theatre/play titled *Danny, King of the Basement*, provides a concrete representation of how imagination through arts can foster critical thinking, empathy, and social responsibility. As Giles (2008) describes, "a great deal of research shows that live theatre touches the children's imagination with an immediacy that is real and emotional and that it's complexities engage students' critical thinking" (p. 36). Perhaps this is why imagination engrossed the works of Greene (1995), and brought forth her assertion that "imagination is what, above all, makes empathy possible" (p. 3). In the award-winning play, *Danny, King of the Basement*, children become engaged in the story of an eleven-year-old boy whose imagination cultivates resiliency and community in the face of poverty, hunger, and homelessness. The play also provoked awareness and empathy about important social issues, allowing students to creatively and critically think about how their actions can contribute to a more hopeful and just future (Giles, 2008).

With these developments in mind, we must question: Does the arts developed curriculum provide enough space for students' imaginative possibilities? And do teachers prioritize classroom time in consideration of arts-based learning? We focus on the arts not because it is the only space to develop imagination, but because a) it is a particular area of interest to us, b) it is the first area of curriculum to be cut in a budget crisis (the result of which is a technocratic notion of curriculum), and c) it is a proven research area for developing imaginative consciousness (Greene, 2007). Finally, we think the arts are a kernel space in what we call a *critical pedagogy of imagination*. To further develop our point, we examine the Ontario curriculum. Ontario is the largest province in Canada with the most diverse population compared to other provinces and territories.

The revised Ontario curriculum Arts document (Grades 1-8) exemplifies how the "arts nourish and stimulate the imagination, and provide students with an expanded range of tools, techniques, and skills to help them gain insights into the world around them and to represent their understandings in various ways" (Ministry of Education, 2009, p. 5). Through a critical lens, arts-based pedagogy is thus vital to supporting how students come to know, perceive, and act on their surroundings. This organic practice of curriculum integration with respect to the arts is demonstrated by Wiebe and coauthors (2007):

> Supporting and extending the research that integrative arts practices lead to imaginative, flexible, and embodied pedagogical praxis, a rhizomatic integration of the arts values complicated and disruptive possibilities that enliven the imagination toward more socially just ways of living and learning (p. 263).

Through integrated and enriching practice, teachers can enable students to embrace diversity, transform, and broaden ways of knowing and coming to understand the unfolding global issues around them (Wiebe et al., 2007). Moreover, to further problematize arts-based pedagogy, Egan (2003) questions whether one should "start with what the student knows or with what the student can imagine" (p. 443). Egan (2003) suggests how reducing artistic exploration to content and knowledge within a prescribed curriculum can suppress the imaginative lives of students and disengage meaningful expression.

As educators, to restore imaginative possibilities in learners, it is critical to unleash our own repression and delve into forgotten realms of creativity and imaginings. As Freire (1995) purposefully reveals—we cannot teach what we do not know (p. 89). For some, this may stir the opening of Pandora's box, to "break through the crusts of the conventional and the routine, to light the slow fuse of possibility" (Greene, 2007, p. 1). Reviving the pedagogy of imagination demands imaginative action shared by teachers and students, to reach beyond what is and what should be in a fragile world. Greene (1995) puts it best: "Imagination may be a new way of decentering ourselves, of breaking out of the confinements of privatism and self-regard into a space where we can come face to face with others and call out, "Here we are"" (p. 31). Then, as teachers, we must be willing to awaken new perspectives and balance the tension between a curriculum of imagination and *consciousness* and one of banking knowledge (e.g. Freire, 1998) and the strain of efficiency, accountability, and bureaucracy. If educators are to release the social imaginations of students, a pedagogy of unconditional and open dialogue, attuned to the social realities of the class and/or community is necessary to initiate meaning-making, humanism, and *consciousness* (Freire, 1998; Greene, 1995). Thus, at the heart of imagination, is the work of building an open, endless, and unfinished bridge between the possible and impossible, to restore our capacity to dream, reach, and fully *be* in a challenging world (Freire, 2007).

Critical Pedagogy of Humanism

On becoming *wide-awake*, a deep-seated precondition entails critical consciousness of the human condition and understanding of oneself as a coexisting entity in the world. To be conscious of one's existence as an intertwined "body in the body of world" (McIntosh, 2005, p. 24), affirms integrity in human solidarity and voice (Freire, 1995). Noteworthy to education is teaching as "a human act" (Freire, 1998, p. 85), a concept which positions teachers as a driving force of "care, concern, and connection" with humanity (McIntosh, 2005, p. 34). Thus, a critical pedagogy of humanism provokes *wide-awakeness* as a possible response to the question: How might one inspire a fuller humanity (Ayers, 2004)? What is our collective purpose in the world? What is our unfulfilled human potential? And what role does education serve in cultivating student capabilities of acting in and changing the world? In an endeavour to address these meaningful questions, a critical pedagogy of humanism, focused on pluralistic dialogue, the "living" curriculum, and a humane climate of learning is considered below.

According to Greene (1995): ""Plurality" is "the condition of human action because we are all the same, that is, human, in such a way that nobody is ever the same as anyone else who ever lived, lives, or will live" (pp. 155-156). As well, Noddings (2005) describes pluralism as a binding component of human survival, valuing social, cultural, and religious diversity and seeking to promote inclusion, peace, voice, and community. Thus, the notion of *wide-awakeness* actualizes the pluralistic reality encircling students to uncover the unconditional nature of accepting oneself and others in the world. For teachers, this translates into fostering a nurturing classroom climate of pluralistic dialogue and meaningful curricular experience. This was the explicit philosophy of/in the course offered by the second author. The course was Socratic in nature, where the most banal was the most difficult and where our questions as a class determined our answers. The instructor was there to ask questions as much as anyone else in class without imposing his answers. This is because *wide-awakeness* and consciousness-raising are described in the course as "unfinishedness" and "the open-minded teacher," and therefore, "cannot afford to ignore anything that concerns the human person" (Freire, 1998, p. 127). Although teachers are entrusted to "develop the plural capacities and the wide-ranging awareness" (McIntosh, 2005, p. 39) of students, we argued in class that this humane objective often gets overlooked, resulting in a spectator approach or the reduction of social and global problems to distant concern (see especially Freire, 1998; Giroux; 2005).

Greene (1995) depicts the ideals of a pluralistic classroom: "We want our classrooms to be just and caring, full of conceptions of the good. We want them to be articulate, with the dialogue involving as many persons as possible, opening to one another, opening to the world" (p. 167). To consider the role of caring, Noddings (2005) identifies how teachers need to be mindful of the overwhelming needs of students, and how a curriculum of intentional caring can offer rich possibilities for meeting these needs. Through this "caring relation," teachers may become conscious of the inferred and expressed needs of students, and find a delicate balance in negotiating, uncovering, and attending to such needs (Noddings, 2005, p. 148). Thus, to bring pluralism to fruition in education, teachers must themselves be *wide-awake* and conscious of *knowing*, so that students are entitled to multiple voices and perspectives. This also translates to providing students with an active and liberating space to voice their human rights and responsibilities. Open classroom dialogue is a precondition to pluralism, and Freire (1998) underscores the necessity for teachers to learn to "speak by listening" (p. 104), and to be "open to the word of the other" (p. 107), so as not to induce silence or devalue the voices of our students. Providing an inclusive space for open and accepting dialogue is central to democratic education, fortifying belongingness and voice among students (Stanley, 2003). Hence, pluralism calls attention toward a multifaceted and perhaps "living" curriculum of social issues, multiculturalism, global citizenship, and diverse forms of knowing and being—to render *wide-awakeness* in students for a more hopeful future (Carlsson-Paige & Lantieri, 2005).

Awakening Praxis and Agency

In an increasingly complex and problematic world, education faces the heavy burden of reclaiming hope and the possibilities, for change. Encumbered with political, ethical, economic, and social problems, the educational system is seemingly clouded, which obstrucs possibilities for a meaningful curriculum of imagination and learning. It is vital to step away from an orderly, predictable, and mechanized curriculum into one premised upon critical content, a dialogic and student-centered process, a democratic climate of shared participation and critical self-reflection (Martin, 2008). By confronting praxis and agency, educators can seek to collectively transform and act on existing educational conditions to restore purpose and democracy in education (Giroux, 2009). To what extent does awakening praxis and agency contribute to *wide-awakeness* and social transformation?

'Praxis' is an ongoing process enabling the intersection of theory and practice. In education, praxis acts as a site of social transformation—through informed *conscientization* and committed action toward humanity and the world (Freire, 2000). Antecedent to praxis, according to Alexander (2005), is agency: the embodiment of human self-entitlement to values, beliefs, actions, and choices. For Alexander (2005), fulfillment of human agency in the curriculum must be premised upon three conditions: free will, moral intelligence, and fallibility. Thoughtful consideration of each condition of human agency delivers a meaningful curriculum to students by enabling self-determined choices, moral understanding, and freedom of expression. However, as powerful social agents, it is teachers who make the choice of what to teach our students and ultimately dictate the visibility of the implicit, explicit, or null curriculum (Alexander, 2005).

A pedagogy of praxis and agency requires working between the messy spaces of conservative and radical educational theory and practice. The possibilities for enabling *wide-awakeness* require a progressive and critical pedagogy which seeks to prepare students for an "unknowable future" and reform educational efforts to enhance the future capacity of our students (Eisner, 2004, p. 6). Moreover, the progressive teacher does not necessarily need to be radical to transform education, but needs to question, challenge and work *with* the system, in an endeavour to restore democracy. In the wise words of the late pedagogue Frank McCourt (2005), teachers must persistently engage in a tug-of-war with tension, in an effort to move students from fear to freedom. Moreover, Freire (1998) contended that "practice and theory, authority, and freedom, ignorance and knowledge, respect for the teacher and respect for the students, and teaching and learning" work powerfully in concert with one another and cannot be separated (p. 88). Therefore, by deconstructing the tensions between authority and freedom, teachers can encourage a reciprocal student-teacher interchange of fearlessness and authentic learning experiences (Freire, 2000). Thus, the making and re/making of oneself as a teacher seeks to open up new spaces for a critical pedagogy of democratic ideology and purpose.

Again, we turn to the metaphor of opening Pandora's box, whereby chaos, oppressive regimes, and fear may need to be encountered in order to truly become *wide-awake* and liberate oneself and others within the context of education. It is only then, that we can find our voice and place, alongside our students, and strive to find middle ground between administrative/governmental control and our own creativity and free will.

For us, this paper is a humble demonstration of how to work through the messy spaces of conservative and radical praxis, of how true dialogue and reflection can come about. Critical reflection of pedagogic praxis, we thus argue, is imperative to social transformation. Teachers need to perpetually question: To what extent is the content I am teaching meaningful to students? To what regard am I valuing certain perspectives and ways of *knowing* over others? How am I am learning *from* and *with* my students to engage and transform? As Freire (1998) aptly phrased: "Whoever teaches learns in the act of teaching, and whoever learns teaches in the act of learning" (p. 31). Thus, if we consider our agency as educators, we must also carefully consider how our decisions and actions will affect how our students think and perceive the world (Thayer-Bacon & Bacon, 1997). Thus, through thoughtful interrogation of our pedagogy and praxis, we have the capacity to transform education and seize further awareness of what it means to be and act in a shared world (Greene, 1995).

Toward a Critical Pedagogy of Becoming

> It is *dreaming* and *existing* that "allows" us to keep making ourselves into beings who fight for liberation, *Being More* (Freire, 2007, p. XI).

The capacity for *wide-awakeness* challenges the psyche to dream, reflect, and encounter the possibilities of becoming in the world (Freire, 1998; 2007; Giroux,

2009; Greene, 1995). As Freire (2007) avowed, it is "impossible to live without dreams" (p. 3) and we must embrace the "unfinishedness of our human condition" (Freire, 1998, p. 66). Thus, a critical consciousness of hope and becoming can transform pedagogy and awaken new beginnings for students (Freire, 2007; Giroux, 2005; Greene, 1995). At the heart of becoming is confronting what is possible by our capacity to teach and open ourselves and our students to imagination, curiosity, and dialogue (Greene, 1995; 2000; 2007). As eloquently expressed by Greene (2000)—"if we keep our own questions open and take intentional action against what stands in the way of learner's becoming, of our becoming, the spaces for freedom do enlarge" (p. 13). Also critical, is the underlying objective of social transformation—through conscious deliberation of freedom, community, and pluralism (Freire, 2007; Greene, 1995). Through this process—of dreaming and becoming—we engage in a critical pedagogy of the now and of tomorrow (Freire, 2007).

In reworking some of Freire's (2007) ponderings into pedagogical discourse, one might question: How do I see myself as a teacher in the world; at *whose* service; and at what capacity (p. 62)? And how might pursuit of educational change render imaginative possibilities for learners? As teachers, we must be *wide-awake* to the complexities facing our students, moving beyond the systematic transmission of knowledge, to reinvent and expand the space for a becoming discourse (Freire, 2007). As progressive "provocateurs," one can liberate dreams and possibilities of a better education for our students (Giroux, 2009, p. 17). We must discard conventional notions of the "*training* and *taming*" of learners (Freire, 2007, p. 26), and comprehend our intrinsic responsibility to respect, captivate, and inspire all students within a democratic and caring classroom community. To Carlsson-Paige & Lantieri (2005), the nurturing of a classroom community, modelling of social responsibility, fostering of perspective-taking skills and confrontation of social injustice is analogous to the planting of seeds to nourish student consciousness of global belonging. Thus, as the seeds in the garden cultivate, so too, are *wide-awake* teachers—who not only grow with students, but reflect on their "gardening" while desperately trying to unearth weeds of oppression in the process.

A critical pedagogy of becoming confronts tension, transforms, and critically reflects on doing and what has been done (Freire, 1998; Greene, 1995; 2007). It questions, reinterprets, renews, reinvents, and informs critical pedagogy and centers on making students visibly engaged in the process. Ayers (2001) further illustrates how teaching demands reflection:

> Thoughtfulness requires time and focus and wide-awakeness—a willingness to look at the conditions of our teaching lives, to consider alternatives and different possibilities, to challenge received wisdom and what is taken for granted, and to link our conduct with our consciousness—to think about what we are doing. (p. 6)

As teachers, we must strive toward what is humanly possible, while recognizing our own shortcomings of reaching *wide-awakeness* within a classroom community of authentic learning. Thus, a critical pedagogy of becoming "involves a dynamic and dialectical movement between "doing" and "reflecting on doing" (Freire, 1998, p. 43) to open oneself and allow more spaces for change, and transformation. Freire (1998) accentuated the need for reflective practice: "Thinking critically about practice, of today or yesterday, makes possible the improvement of tomorrow's practice" (p. 44). Thus, our capacity to teach demands openness and transformation to restore space for invigorated imaginings and a deepening discourse. Moreover, we need to look for enigmatic openings in our teaching, as new beginnings and freedom can only be restored in the process. In the compelling words of Greene (2005): "The... educator can be initiator of new beginnings; and to act at a beginning is to move towards possibilities, to live and teach in a world of incompleteness, of what we all are but are not yet" (p. 80). Finally, we need to critically ask ourselves: What is the purpose of education? What is my place in it? And how do my intentions influence my capacity to *become*?

Conclusion: Our Becoming, Daring to Teach

In this paper, a critical pedagogy of imagination, humanism, agency, and praxis and becoming was considered to dialogue with new spaces of teaching and learning. In awakening a critical pedagogy, a curriculum of *wide-awakeness*, and *conscientization* provokes the necessity of a democratic classroom community of imaginings, pluralism, and hope (Freire, 1998; Greene, 1995). Thus, to address Greene's (2008) aforementioned question, "How can we commit ourselves to [teaching and] learning in times like these?" (p. 18), we can respond in the promising words of Giroux (2005): "Everything is possible...but it can only happen if you imagine the unimaginable, think differently in order to act differently," and "give imaginative shape to humanity's hope for a better and more inclusive future" (p. 217). As teachers, we need to believe that we can commit ourselves to learning in times like these and inspire our students to make a difference in the world. We are also fully aware that hopeful reality has to be imagined first before it becomes real, but it needs—desperately—a pedagogy of *conscientization* and *wide-awakeness*. Only then can we both motivate and empower our students—as the second author hoped to have done in his course—and enable them to locate themselves in time and history, *and* at the same time, critically interrogate the adequacy of that location. Only then will we hear the trumpet of joy, smell the clean scent of mint, and be able to mouthfully say:

> For she who hopes,
> Tell her the journey has begun
> For she who loves,
> Tell her love is around the corner.

References

Alexander, H. A. (2005). Human agency and the curriculum. *Theory and Research in Education, 3,* 343-369.

Ayers, W. (2009). The hope and practice of teaching. *Journal of Teacher Education, 57,* 269-277.

Ayers, W. (2006). Toward a fuller humanity: The author responds. *Phi Delta Kappan, 88,* 237-240.

Ayers, W. (2001). To teach: The journey of a teacher: A study guide for the college classroom. Retrieved June 10, 2009 online from http://www.teacherscollegepress.com/pdfs/ayersguide.pdf

Carlsson-Paige, N., & Lantieri, L. (2005). A changing vision of education. In Noddings, N. (Ed.), *Educating citizens for global awareness* (pp. 107-121). New York: Teachers College Press.

Egan, K. (2005). *An imaginative approach to teaching.* San Francisco: Jossey-Bass.

Egan, K. (2003). Start with what the student knows or with what the student can imagine? *Phi Delta Kappan, 84,* 443-445.

Eisner, E. W. (2005). *Reimagining schools: The selected works of Elliot. W. Eisner.* New York: Routledge.

Eisner, E. W. (2003/2004). Preparing for today and tomorrow. *Educational Leadership* (Dec/Jan Issue).
Freire, A. M. A (Ed). (2007). *Daring to dream: Toward a pedagogy of the unfinished.* Boulder: Paradigm Publishers.
Freire, P. (2000). *Pedagogy of the oppressed* (30th anniversary ed.). New York: The Continuum International Publishing Group Inc.
Freire, P. (1998). *Pedagogy of freedom: Ethics, democracy, and civic courage.* Oxford: Rowman & Littlefield Publishers, Inc.
Gaarder, Jostein. (1996). *Sophie's world: A novel about the history of philosophy.* New York: Berkley Books.
Giles, J. (2008). The play's the thing: Danny starts a conversation. *Voice (Poverty and Learning), 10,* 36-37.
Giroux, H. A. (2009). Education and the crisis of youth: Schooling and the promise of democracy. *The Educational Forum, 73,* 8-18.
Giroux, H. A. (2005). Translating the future. *The Review of Education, Pedagogy, and Cultural Studies, 27,* 213-218.
Greene, M. (2008). Commentary: Education and the arts: The windows of imagination. *Learning Landscapes, 1,* 17-21.
Greene, M. (2007). Imagination and becoming (Bronx charter school of the arts). Retrieved June 4, 2009 from http://www.maxinegreene.org/articles.php
Greene, M. (2005). Teaching in a moment of crisis: The spaces of imagination. *The New Educator, 1,* 77-80.
Greene, M. (2000). The ambiguities of freedom. *English Education, 33,* 8-14.
Greene, M. (1995). *Releasing the imagination: Essays on education, the arts, and social change.* San Francisco: Jossey-Bass.
Gruenewald, D. A. (2003). The best of both worlds: A critical pedagogy of place. *Educational Researcher, 32,* 3-12.
Hanna, J. H. (2008). A nonverbal language for imagining and learning: Dance education in a K-12 curriculum. *Educational Researcher, 37,* 491-506.
Irwin, R. L. (2005). Learning in, through, and from art. In Grauer, K., & Irwin, R. L (Eds.), *Starting with...*(2nd ed) (pp. 1-8). Toronto: Canadian Society for Education through Art.
Kind, S. W. (2005). Windows to a child's world: Perspectives on children's art making. In Grauer, K., & Irwin, R. L (Eds.), *Starting with...*(2nd ed) (pp. 9-18). Toronto: Canadian Society for Education through Art.
Leistyna, P. & Woodrum, A. (1999). Context and culture: What is critical pedagogy? In Leistyna, P., Woodrum, A., and Sherblom, S. A. (Eds.), *Breaking free: The transformative power of critical pedagogy.* Cambridge, MA: Harvard Educational Review (pp. 1-11).
Maslow, A. H. (1971). Peak experiences in education and art. *Theory into Practice, 10,* 149-153.

McCourt, F. (2005). *Teacher man*. New York: Scribner.

Ministry of Education (2009). The arts: the Ontario curriculum grades 1-8. Retrieved July 11, 2009 from http://www.edu.gov.on.ca/eng/curriculum/elementary/arts18b09curr.pdf

Noddings, N. (2005). Identifying and responding to needs in education. *Cambridge Journal of Education, 35*, 147-159.

O'Hara, M. (2006). In search of the next enlightenment? The challenge for education in uncertain times. *Journal of Transformative Education, 4*, 105-117.

Quintero, E. (2007). Critical pedagogy and young children's worlds. In McLaren, P., & Kincheloe, J. L. (Eds.), *Critical pedagogy: Where are we now?* (pp. 201-208). New York: Peter Lang Publishing.

Rorty, R. (1989). *Contingency, irony, and solidarity*. Cambridge: Cambridge University Press.

Stanley, T. J. (2003). Creating the 'space' for civic dialogue. *Phi Delta Kappan, 85*, 38.

Thayer-Bacon, B., & Bacon, C. (1997). "Individual selves and communities" in *Philosophy applied to education: Nurturing a democratic community in the classroom* (pp. 1-35). Columbus: Merrill-Prentice Hall.

Westheimer, J., & Kahne, J. (2003). Reconnecting education to democracy: Democratic dialogues. *Phi Delta Kappan, 85*, 9-14.

Acknowledgment

I would like to thank the publishers for their generous offer to reprint book chapters and articles in this book.

1. Ibrahim, A. (2004). One is not born Black: Becoming and the phenomenon(ology) of race. *Philosophical Studies in Education, 35,* 89-97.
2. Ibrahim, A. (in press). The (un)naturalization of Blackness: A rhizomatic analysis of Blackness. This chapter was originally written under a different title for The Nuances of Blackness Collective (Eds.), *Nuances of Blackness in the Canadian Academy.*
3. Ibrahim, A. (2014). Body without organs: Notes on Deleuze & Guattari, critical race theory and the socius of anti-racism. *Journal of Multilingual and Multicultural Development 35*(3), 1-14.
4. Ibrahim, A. (2005). The question of the question is the foreigner: Towards an economy of hospitality. *Journal of Curriculum Theorizing, 21*(2), 149-162.
5. Ibrahim, A. (1999). Becoming Black: Rap and Hip-Hop, race, gender, identity, and the politics of ESL learning. *TESOL Quarterly 33*(3), 349-369.
6. Ibrahim, A. (original, not published). Intersecting language, immigration and the politics of becoming Black: Journaling a Black immigrant displacement
7. Ibrahim, A. (2008). The new *flâneur*: Subaltern cultural studies, African youth in Canada, and the semiology of in-betweenness. *Cultural Studies 22*(2), 234-253.
8. Ibrahim, A. (2017). Don't call me Black! Rhizomatic analysis of Blackness, immigration, and the politics of race without guarantees. *Educational Studies 53*(4), 511-521.
9. Ibrahim, A. (original, not published). When neoliberalism meets race, post-colonial displacement and immigration, it creates *Americanah*: A teacher education complicated conversation.
10. Ibrahim, A. (2004). Operating under erasure: ~~Hip-Hop~~ and the pedagogy of affect. *Journal of Curriculum Theorizing, 20*(1), 113-133.
11. Ibrahim, A. (2014). Research as an act of love: Ethics, émigrés and the praxis of becoming human. *Diaspora, Indigenous and Minority Education 8*(1), 7-20.
12. Rautins, C. & Ibrahim, A. (2011). Wide-awakeness: Toward a critical pedagogy of imagination, humanism and becoming. *International Journal of Critical Pedagogy 3*(2), 24-36.

Biography

AWAD IBRAHIM IS an award-winning author and a Professor on the Faculty of Education, University of Ottawa, Canada. He is a curriculum theorist with a special interest in diasporic and continental African identities; cultural studies; applied linguistics; Hip-Hop; youth, and Black popular culture; philosophy and sociology of education; social justice; and ethnography. He was born in Sudan and arrived in Canada, through the United States, as a refugee. He has published more than 100 books and journal articles.